SEP 12

Appetite for Life

appetite
for life

The Thumbs-Up, No-Yucks Guide
to Getting Your Kid to Be a Great Eater

Including Over 100 Kid-Approved Recipes

Stacey Antine, MS, RD
Founder and CEO of HealthBarn® USA

HarperOne
An Imprint of HarperCollinsPublishers

HarperOne

APPETITE FOR LIFE: *The Thumbs-Up, No-Yucks Guide to Getting Your Kid to Be a Great Eater—Including Over 100 Kid-Approved Recipes.* Copyright © 2012 by Stacey Antine.
All rights reserved. Printed in China. No part of this book
may be used or reproduced in any manner whatsoever without written permission
except in the case of brief quotations embodied in critical articles and reviews.
For information address HarperCollins Publishers,
10 East 53rd Street, New York, NY 10022.

HarperCollins books may be purchased for educational, business,
or sales promotional use. For information please write:
Special Markets Department, HarperCollins Publishers,
10 East 53rd Street, New York, NY 10022.

HarperCollins website: http://www.harpercollins.com

HarperCollins®, 📖®, and HarperOne™ are trademarks of HarperCollins Publishers.

FIRST EDITION

Designed by Terry McGrath
Photography by Ted Axelrod Photography

Library of Congress Cataloging-in-Publication Data is available upon request.

ISBN 978–0–06–210370–3

12 13 14 15 16   RRD(CHINA)   10 9 8 7 6 5 4 3 2 1

To the HealthBarn USA kids, who have
proven that kids will eat healthy foods;
and to their parents, who have
braved the healthy lifestyle frontier.
May you continue to inspire me and
motivate others to live the healthy way.

contents

welcome to HealthBarn USA

Come Eat at Our Table

"She won't eat it," Kim said to me as we walked through the organic garden. The garden was at its summer peak and bursting with a bounty of ripe tomatoes, crisp bell peppers, several varieties of beans, tender salad greens, herbs, berries, and other edible delights. The "it" in question was just-picked Swiss chard, which Kim was sure that her daughter would reject. She described her daughter and son as picky eaters who would not eat green food.

"She's not going to touch it," Kim said with conviction as we harvested the produce and moved into the barn to make pizzas, rolling out whole-grain crusts and topping them with natural tomato sauce, herbs, cheese, and lots of veggies—including Swiss chard. We had instructed the kids to make their individual pizzas as colorful as possible with the fresh vegetable toppings, but Kim was so focused on her finicky daughter that she allowed her to make a "plain" pizza with just sauce and cheese, but no green herbs or veggies. Meanwhile her son, who Kim had left alone during the class, had dutifully followed the instructions and like all the other kids was busily piling his creation high with toppings, including Swiss chard.

"She's going to hate it," Kim said, shaking her head and hovering over her daughter as the delicious-smelling, kid-created pizzas began to come off the grill and the kids gathered hungrily at the table to sample their savory creations.

As Kim predicted, her daughter ate a plain slice and wouldn't try a bite with the dreaded "green." Meanwhile her son sat down at his place and, like his classmates, quietly began devouring every bite of his pizza, Swiss chard and all. When she finally left her daughter and went to check on her son, Kim was totally amazed. Swiss chard—he ate Swiss chard!

Real Food, Good Food—It's Not Just for Grown-Ups!

Kim was astonished that her child ate healthy food—green food, at that. I, however, am anything but surprised when I see kids thoroughly enjoy delicious, fresh, whole foods—vegetables, fruits, whole grains, lean protein, and more. This is just one of many turnarounds I've witnessed at HealthBarn USA.

I founded HealthBarn USA in 2005 on the grounds of Abma's Farm in Bergen County, New Jersey, just outside New York City. We sprouted another location in 2011 at Hilltop Hanover Farm and Environmental Center in Westchester, New York. Part working farm, part classroom, HealthBarn USA has shown thousands of kids and parents how to live and eat healthfully from nature through our on-site programs and outreach into schools and communities. In fact, I've seen countless kids do an about-face on things like "icky" vegetables and "weird" foods, often to the utter disbelief of grown-ups and parents like Kim.

Why wouldn't kids like to eat pure food from nature? Children aren't born hating green vegetables and loathing fresh fruit. Babies don't toddle into the grocery store on their own and exit with salty chips, greasy donuts, and sugary soda any more than they crawl into the kitchen and microwave a frozen burrito. We strive to teach our children the best life lessons, but based on what I've observed as a longtime proponent of healthy-lifestyle education for families, even the best parents are often passing along a bias against healthy foods via an assumption that kids just won't "like" them.

As adults, we may be concerned that children's palates can't handle the "grown-up" flavors of vegetables like brussels sprouts and kale (which seem to put off a lot of adults too), whole grains like quinoa, fish like salmon, or even dark chocolate. Or, perhaps as babies they start out eating everything put in front of them (including the Swiss chard) but when they hit toddlerhood and preschool they begin rejecting what they once enjoyed and adamantly refuse new foods. (Some evolutionary biologists say this narrowing of tastes among children is not uncommon, as it reflects an instinctively cautious approach to food. To survive, humans had to learn what was safe to eat and what would kill them. When babies learn to walk and eventually explore their world—no longer protected by their mothers—they naturally become more careful.)

The littlest eaters, searching for some control over their world, quickly learn the word "no!" and the art of flinging unwanted food, even if you lovingly made it from scratch. Then they learn to speak in complete sentences, including, "Yuck, what is that?" and "I'll only eat white food." What parent doesn't get tired of playing enforcer

Nourishment from Nature

Throughout this book, you'll see the phrase "foods from nature"—and that is exactly what I mean. I'm not talking about processed, packaged, boxed foods that say "all-natural" on the front of the box. That's merely marketing, not fact. The label "all-natural," unlike "organic," is not strictly regulated by the FDA, and it can be applied to many processed foods. (Manufacturers of foods with dyes and additives will argue that their foods are "all-natural" because ingredients like high-fructose corn syrup, for example, come from corn.) Instead, I'm talking about pure food, made from unadulterated ingredients direct from nature—food straight from the ground, from the farm, from the garden, but not from the factory. Foods from nature are what we eat at HealthBarn USA, and they're what your family can begin to eat, starting now.

("Eat your peas!") or detective ("Why aren't you eating that chicken? Does it need salt? Is it too spicy?") or martyr ("I made this just for you and you won't eat it!") at the dinner table. The angry scraping of leftovers into the trash typically follows.

Worn-down parents, even those with healthy, varied diets, begin to wonder why they should bother serving their children "the good stuff"—real food, good food—if it always gets rejected. We're surrounded by heavily advertised convenience foods that we're led to believe all children love and are a snap for busy parents to put on a plate: frozen chicken nuggets shaped like dinosaurs, microwavable mac and cheese, yogurt in neon colors not found in nature, "juice drinks" that come in boxes and pouches, fast-food kiddie meals served with a toy, and so much more. Why not take the path of least resistance and bring peace (forget the peas) to the table? Why not just give up and give in to what he or she will eat?

We Can Make It Better—Here's How

Beyond the fact that as the parent you're in charge of the food (for now), by feeding your kids the healthy way you are giving them the gift of good health—helping them to make wise choices while they are young.

A child's diet and lifestyle will impact the quality of her life in adulthood, for better or for worse. When I was studying nutrition, the words of a well-known public health advocate shocked and saddened me. "We may be raising the first generation born after World War II whose lifespan may decrease," says Joanne Ikeda, "because of a lifestyle that puts its members at high risk of chronic disease."*

I vividly remember sitting in class, reading those words, and being stunned. Kids today might not live as long as their parents or grandparents? How could this be? We have made amazing strides in preventive medicine, haven't we? Living conditions around the globe are certainly better than they were fifty years ago. Today's children have so many advantages—but they also have a less active lifestyle and regularly consume foods that are more artificial than natural. Therefore, lifestyle diseases like obesity, heart disease, and diabetes are laying claim to younger and younger children. The list of weight- and diet-related problems that adults and increasing numbers of young children are facing today is endless and sobering, not to mention the low self-esteem and depression that accompany these physical ailments.

While Ikeda's words stunned me, they also marked the beginning of my career-changing wake-up call. I started HealthBarn USA to help reverse that chronic disease trend among children and to make families stronger. Not long ago, I wore corporate suits and Prada shoes to work, not jeans and boots. For many years I worked in public relations, eventually becoming a senior vice president for Ogilvy Public Relations Worldwide. Instead of spending my days with kids outdoors on a working farm, I was inside a conference room with all the other grown-ups in back-to-back meetings, eating trays of bagels and cookies and lunching on takeout as we—ironically—worked on national nutrition awareness campaigns for big-time food companies, specifically those aimed at educating families about making healthy choices.

As I learned more about the state of children's health in the United States—especially the alarming levels of diet- and weight-related illness—I realized that our corporate efforts weren't making much of an impact on the everyday lives of families. This only deepened my interest in nutrition, and I began night classes at New York University in pursuit of a master's of science in food, nutrition, and dietetics. Eventually I quit my "day job" to do a full-time dietetic internship at Beth Israel Medical Center in New York City, where I worked with families as part of my training.

Until then, I'd been sitting in a classroom, a very different experience than working directly with kids. Joanne Ikeda's words had haunted me, but now I saw in real life precisely what she meant. The children I counseled were in danger of not living as long a life as their own parents. Even more troubling to me was the fact

* Joanne Ikeda, "Using Candy as a Reward Leaves a Very Bad Taste," *Los Angeles Times*, September 27, 2003.

that the very people we were trying to reach considered nutrition education "boring"—because just talking about nutrition labels, carbohydrates, cholesterol, and trans fats *is* boring. The facts are often presented in a dry and condescending fashion ("we're the experts and we know what's good for you"), and with no nutritious food in sight the numbers can seem meaningless or confusing. Eventually no one looks beyond the calorie count.

One day I had an idea about how to be more effective in my work: if I wanted to improve the physical health of families, I would find greater success by *showing* them and not just telling them about good food. HealthBarn USA was born, an organization that now runs summer camps, after-school programs, weekend workshops, and school assemblies encouraging kids to participate in making their own meals and snacks with healthy, all-natural food.

I realize that it's easier for me to get kids to try new foods than it is for a parent, in the same way that it's easier for a math teacher to motivate a child to do his algebra than it is for Mom or Dad. I'm not a parent myself. At HealthBarn USA, the kids think of me as "Aunt Stace," the fun grown-up who wants to hang out and play games with the kids. My young friend Jamie, who has been coming to HealthBarn USA for years, tells me that children like me because I don't nag them to eat healthfully—I simply encourage them to do so by taking the mystery out of where food comes from, showing them how it grows, and getting them into the kitchen to prepare it themselves.

Bringing HealthBarn USA Home: One Day, One Meal, One Bite at a Time

Our ultimate success at HealthBarn USA is based on your success at implementing our principles at home. The recipes, activities, and nutritional information I'm about to share with you aren't effective if they're limited to a HealthBarn USA classroom or workshop. These tools can only be life changing if kids and parents *bring them home,* and thousands of families have done just that. With this book, you will be able to do the same.

After you finish our breakfast chapter, for instance, you can "leave the barn" to go into your own kitchen and create an energizing breakfast. Once you read our tips on choosing natural foods over artificial, you'll go shopping with your kids at a grocery store or farmers' market with eyes (and taste buds) open to fantastic new possibilities—all of them healthy and delicious. When you finish our snack chapters, your children will host playdates and offer our fun-to-make snacks, or when they're the guests, they will be more likely to choose the fruit instead of the candy. By the end of this book, your family will be able to visit a restaurant knowing how to order smartly and have a truly enjoyable experience. And, most important, you will be teaching, not preaching, and you'll see how quickly all eyes and ears will be on you!

Every day is a new opportunity to help your children choose a healthier lifestyle, starting with really good food. This book is designed to make that lifestyle a reality, whether your goal is to end the daily "food fights;" to get ideas for nutritious and great-tasting breakfasts, lunches, dinners, and snacks that everyone in your family

Healthy Recipes You Can Trust

Recently a parent asked me if I had a "healthy recipe" for mozzarella sticks. That's a tricky one—because whether they are homemade with farm-fresh mozzarella coated in Panko bread crumbs, purchased frozen at the grocery store, or ordered as an appetizer, they contain mozzarella cheese, which is high in saturated fat, the "bad" fat linked to heart disease. Coming up with a genuinely "healthy" recipe for a high-fat food is all but impossible . . . but I also know that mozzarella is a favorite with kids (and adults, of course).

So, we have found a way to use this great-tasting cheese in healthy recipes like our BBQ Turkey Pizza, Cheesy Lasagna Rolls, and Spinach and Artichoke Dip, just to name a few. As you'll see, we use mozzarella in a way that still offers the satisfying taste of a much-loved cheese, but without overdoing it for your heart! We don't hide the fact that a recipe made with an ingredient like mozzarella will have saturated fat, but our recipes still meet the highest nutritional standards. Every recipe here is healthy.

The nutritional analysis you'll find at the end of each recipe contains per-serving information on fat, cholesterol, carbohydrates, protein, and sodium content; daily values of certain vitamins and minerals; and calories per serving. Every HealthBarn USA recipe has been taste tested by the toughest critics out there (kids), but each is also thoroughly analyzed for its nutritional value and is designed to meet the nutrition standards set by the Food and Drug Administration and leading health organizations, such as the American Heart Association.

will love; to turn your children into smart eaters (and budding chefs); or to explore with your family the connection between the food we eat and the earth it comes from.

At HealthBarn USA, where our motto is "strong bodies, healthy minds," our goal is simple: to teach children (and the parents who love them) about great-tasting, nutritious food, with hands-on activities in the kitchen and in the garden, and to put some much-needed fun into preparing and eating meals and snacks. With this book's breakfast-to-bedtime approach, in addition to more than 100 kid-approved recipes, you'll find lots of useful nutritional information about the food we put

In addition, we put each of our recipes through vigorous testing using ESHA Research's Food Processor nutrition analysis system. We are especially committed to being vigilant when it comes to meeting healthy guidelines for saturated fat, cholesterol, and sodium—all major contributors to heart disease.

Even when eating healthy foods we need to be mindful of serving sizes (you'll learn more about serving sizes and healthy portions in chapter 6). We include serving sizes for each recipe and they are based on standard servings set by the USDA (not by the amount of food on your plate). The amount of servings in a recipe will vary because they are based on real-time cooking with kids in the way we serve them at HealthBarn USA for our programs and camps. For example the Yum! Yum! Dumplings recipe yields fifteen servings (five dumplings per serving) because we use the entire package of egg roll wrappers and freeze the extras (if there are any), rather than make four servings and refrigerate the remaining wrappers. We are very careful not to waste any food at the barn, and the recipes reflect this point.

The phrase "healthy recipe" has been misused a lot these days, but not in these pages. The nutritional information is here if you want to use it to educate yourself and your family. The recipes—each and every one of them truly healthy—are here for you to enjoy without worry.

into our bodies as well as fun activities for kids and grown-ups alike, such as our Supermarket Spy Kids game, which turns an ordinary trip to the grocery store into a family adventure. Each chapter will also have a Get Your Hands Dirty garden-related activity you can do no matter where you live that focuses on connecting our food to its source—mother earth. At HealthBarn USA, we teach basic conservation, from recycling to organic gardening, and emphasize the powerful connection between nature and nutrition. Look for lots of "earthy" fun at the barn.

The recipes at the end of each chapter, from breakfast favorites like our Chocolate Zucchini Cupcakes to main dishes like our Chicken Fiesta Fajitas and treats like The Perfect Pop, have all been created with young eaters in mind and taste tested and approved by thousands of kids at HealthBarn USA. You'll find simple dishes that older kids can make for themselves, like our Grilled Cheese Stackers or Pizza Potato Skins, and plenty that will satisfy adults as well. (Just try to resist seconds of our Rainbow Quinoa Salad and our Raspberry Crumble for dessert). All of it is healthy, everyday food that families can enjoy together. And because families should celebrate together too, we've also included ideas for special occasions, like birthdays, holidays, and relaxed weekends. At the end of the book, you'll find Sample Weekly Menu Planners featuring seven days of breakfasts, snacks, lunches, and dinners (including vegetarian and gluten-free options).

I've seen the activities and recipes that you're about to experience transform and improve the lives of thousands of kids and parents. After our students visit our pick-your-own organic garden or attend a HealthBarn USA "Try It You'll Like It" assembly at their school, they develop a preference for "the good stuff" and express a sentiment that I hear over and over again: "I didn't know healthy food could taste good!"

Most kids don't know—and that's what we're about to change.

Thumbs Up for HealthBarn USA (Where "Yuck" Is a Four-Letter Word!)

When I first started working with kids, I realized I was going to have to do something to quiet the chorus of "yuck!" and "gross!" and "ick!" every time I reached for a green veggie or served a meal that the kids helped to make.

Of course, not all kids have that reaction, but the reality is that children can be very stubborn or cautious about trying new foods, and they can fall into a kind of group-think that equates "healthy" with "yuck." So, I made a rule, and it's one that I strongly encourage you to put into practice at home. It will be the key to your success, and it will ultimately empower your child to make good decisions about food. It's a simple rule: No yucks allowed! Ever. "Yuck" and its many cousins— "gross," "blech," "eww," and "no way am I eating that, ever"—are banned from the table.

Now, of course kids have every right to express their opinions, and if you don't let them do so, they'll get stubborn and won't have any interest in meeting you halfway and trying a bite of bell pepper. So, I found a way to get around this by making it fun for kids to tell us what they think when they taste a new food. All they need is an opinion and a thumb.

Here's what you do. Whenever you serve a new food (and I encourage you to include kids in the kitchen to help you prepare new foods, whenever possible), whether it's a plain vegetable or fruit or a full-on recipe, tell your child that his opinion is very important. He isn't just trying a new food—he is an official taste tester for the family!

In order to be a taste tester, he has to chew and swallow what he tastes (no licking or smelling only!), and only then—using his all-important thumb—can he share his official taste tester opinion, which must be expressed the following way in order for it to count.

Take a bite, chew and swallow, and then:

 Give it a **THUMBS UP** to indicate: "It tastes really good. I like it!"

 Give it a **THUMB TO THE SIDE** to say: "Hmm, not so sure about this. Don't love it, don't hate it, just not sure."

 Give it a **THUMBS DOWN** to show: "No thanks, I didn't like it."

This may sound simple, but it gets big results. For one thing, it will open up a discussion between you and your child about what she likes, tastewise, and what she really doesn't like. If your child rejects a food, ask why (don't judge, just ask for information). You will probably get helpful answers. You may find out that the food wasn't what he expected, or that he wants more salt or cheese, or likes crunchy foods instead of soft. (For instance, kids often prefer raw veggies to cooked because of taste and texture.)

I can't guarantee that you'll immediately turn your pasta-and-butter-loving child into a miniature foodie, who demands seconds of poached salmon and grilled vegetables, by living the HealthBarn USA way. But I can promise that if you give the HealthBarn USA approach a try, and if you just stick with it for a bit, you'll be amazed at the little changes you can achieve very quickly—starting with breakfast tomorrow morning. Every meal, every bite of healthy food that your child takes, is a small step that will lead to a big lifestyle improvement that every family member will benefit from.

If you're ready for great food and happy, healthy kids, join us at the HealthBarn USA table. Your healthy day starts now.

CHAPTER 1

Making Every Day a Healthy Day: Getting Started

Before we share our first meal, I'm going to give you the most important piece of professional and personal advice I can share, one that will help your children develop a lifelong, satisfying, adventurous, and healthy relationship with food.

It's not about calcium or fiber; it's not about limiting sugar and salt intake; it isn't about deciding between fresh or frozen, or why to serve your child whole wheat bread instead of processed white varieties, or how to turn picky eaters into kids who will try new foods. In the pages to come, I will touch on these issues and many more, but first, I'm going to share with you the guiding principal that informs everything we do at HealthBarn USA—the key to living a healthy day through healthy, delicious food. Here it is:

Connect your kids to their food.

Getting children of all ages into the kitchen, or out to the farmers' market, grocery store, garden, or any place where good food from nature can be found, is the first step to getting them to eat healthily. When children are involved with what goes onto their plates—because they know where it comes from and perhaps because they picked it out and helped to prepare it—that food is more likely to wind up in their tummies.

Many kids (and many adults) are unaware of where their food comes from; at the very least, they don't think too much about it because food (both the good and bad) is always so available. At HealthBarn USA, we start by teaching children to make the connection between nature, good food, and good health. We educate kids on the difference between foods that come from natural sources—starting with the earth—and therefore offer numerous nutritional benefits for our bodies, and the artificial (processed) foods that come from factories and provide no benefits.

But we don't just tell them—we show the connection. For example, I don't lecture kids on why spinach is a healthy food and then serve it to them already cooked into a dish like a vegetable lasagna or stir-fry. Instead, I take the kids into the garden where they plant spinach, and we talk and play games about all the vitamins and minerals packed into this amazing leafy green. The children eventually harvest their own spinach, which they bring into our kitchen and turn into Spinach Pesto Pasta that they make themselves. Even our Seedling students, children between the ages of three and five, get involved. When kids are this invested in their food, they're much more likely to try it. Disbelieving parents have seen a forkful of our Spinach Salad with Raspberry Vinaigrette turn into a whole bowl and then a second helping! (Remember the Swiss chard mom?)

You may be thinking, "Wait a minute—I don't have a farm! I don't even have a garden! And are you telling me I have to start *growing my own food*?" I'm not suggesting you grab a hoe and dig up your patio. But I am urging you to concentrate on the connection that you and your family have with your food and its source, because the strength of that connection *will* make a difference in how you eat.

Right now, do you prepare family meals by yourself, set the food in front of your kids, and expect them to eat it without complaint? And if so, are you as successful in getting them to try new, healthy foods as you'd like to be? Do they ever enter the kitchen to help make meals or snacks, or do they just come in to open the fridge when they're hungry, or to find the pretzels in the pantry? Do they go with you to the grocery store to help choose the foods you bring into your home? Do they ever have a chance to visit a farmers' market or get "close to the land" with a trip to a working farm?

All of these questions should get you thinking about how closely your child is connected to the food that shows up on her plate. Parents always ask me a variation of this question: "Stacey, how do I get my child to eat more vegetables / yogurt / low-fat foods?" But you cannot easily get from point A (the way your child eats now) to point B (the healthy way you want your child to eat) without helping them connect the dots between eating good food from nature and feeling great every day.

Don't Veg Out!

Introducing HealthBarn USA's Seven Healthy Habits

Parents, in my experience, are **obsessed** with getting kids to eat their vegetables—as if veggies were the only thing figuring into a child's health. Yes, they are extremely important, but **vegetables alone aren't going to improve a child's health,** especially if she's still eating Frosted Flakes for breakfast (or not eating breakfast at all). That's why we developed HealthBarn USA's Seven Healthy Habits that, when taken together, make up our definition of a healthy lifestyle 24/7:

1. **Eat breakfast.**
2. **Exercise.**
3. **Eat fruits and vegetables.**
4. **Share a family meal.**
5. **Recycle.**
6. **Brush and floss teeth.**
7. **Get a good night's sleep.**

You'll hear about each of these habits as we go, chapter by chapter, through our healthy day. You'll begin to see that when you work on one habit, like breakfast, good health starts to take hold in other areas. For example, your daughter may loathe brussels sprouts, but if she's traded her Trix for a breakfast of Creamy Berry Crepes, I predict the veggie-eating will eventually follow. If she has more energy as a result of a better diet, she'll be more active. If she begins to get more exercise, she'll sleep better at night. It's all connected!

Being healthy means more than eating broccoli, so don't sweat the green stuff.

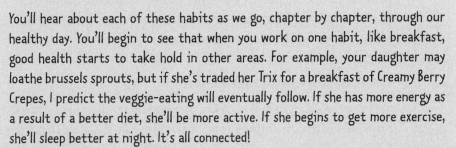

At HealthBarn USA, we simultaneously teach kids where our food comes from and why it's good for them, but you don't have to have a farm in your backyard or a classroom in your kitchen to do the same thing at home. You can re-create the learning experience of HealthBarn USA, as you'll see in the chapters to come, but first you have to re-create your mind-set and embrace it for yourself—not just farm-to-fork, but farm-to-*health*.

So, to all the parents who want to know the answer to this burning question, "How do I get my kid to eat more vegetables?"—sure, I can (and will) give you some basic tips (for instance, most kids like "crunch," so consider serving veggies raw or flash-blanched*), but good health is not just about getting your child to eat vegetables. It's about getting your child to *enjoy* eating the vegetables, so that they will choose to eat them for life, not just at dinner on Thursday. It's about savoring good food from nature and valuing the environment it comes from, as well as taking pleasure in its preparation and enjoying it together as a family.

And if you can help your child connect those vegetables to their source—or the fresh fruit, milk, cheese, fish, honey, almonds, whole grains, or whatever delicious and healthy food you'd like to add to your table—you'll be successful.

Getting Kids Involved

When you as a parent are the only person "controlling" your family's food—choosing foods, planning menus, cooking meals, organizing snacks, deciding what food comes into the house—you will have a very difficult time getting them to change the way they eat. At HealthBarn USA, we've created an environment in which kids feel empowered to make decisions about how they eat because they are involved. Our only rule is "No yucks allowed!" (see the introduction), and part of that rule is that each child try every new food we introduce. It works because we make it fun, and you can too. Here's how.

Let Your Kids into the Kitchen

Yep, they're going to make a mess. Depending on their ages, they may make a big mess. But when they start eating differently, you'll realize that it's oh-so-worth-it.

---

* To flash-blanch veggies, place them in bowl and cover with boiling water for a minute or two, then drain and serve. The longer you let them soak, the less crunchy they become and the more nutrients they lose.

At HealthBarn USA, we divide the kids by age into three groups—Seedlings (ages three to five), Sprouts (ages five to seven), and Young Harvesters (ages eight to fifteen). You know your own Seedling, Sprout, or Young Harvester better than anyone, and you understand what he or she is capable of; below are some examples of tasks your kids may be able to do, depending on their ages and abilities. If you have more than one child helping, break the recipe down into tasks for each young cook so that everyone has something to do. The more active they are, the more fun it will be. Kids can help:

✦ Plan the menu for the day using our recipes, and create a shopping list.

✦ Gather and organize ingredients and utensils for a meal or snack.

✦ Read the steps of the recipe out loud.

✦ Measure, pour, sift, stir, whisk, mash, and grate ingredients.

✦ Wash and dry fruits, vegetables, herbs, and greens. (I recommend using a salad spinner, a favorite tool with kids at the barn.)

✦ Slice berries and other soft items with a plastic knife. Older kids who can use sharper utensils safely can peel and chop veggies like carrots and cucumbers.

✦ Use blenders, mixers, food processors, or other small appliances.

✦ Preheat the oven.

✦ Monitor cooking or baking times; reduce or raise heat; keep food from burning; use a kitchen thermometer.

✦ Assemble sandwiches; toss salads; serve and garnish foods; pour smoothies or other drinks.

✦ Set the table, decorate for special meals, and call the family to the table for a meal; older siblings can make sure young ones have clean hands.

One important note: everyone, no matter how young or how old, needs to have clean hands before they handle the food. The first step in any recipe is *washing your hands.*

Supervise the little ones, of course, and use common sense when it comes to tasks like chopping, running small appliances, handling hot ingredients, and using the stove and oven. Some older kids and teens are capable of preparing entire meals, including cooking and baking on their own, and they should have no trouble following the directions in the recipes (all of which are designed to be clear for first-time cooks). Each recipe includes suggestions for specific tasks that kids can do.

Shop and Cook the Natural Way

Here are some tips to help turn your kitchen into a HealthBarn USA kitchen.

- ◆ Buy seasonal fresh produce. Visit www.sustainabletable.org/shop/seasonal where you can enter your zip code and see what's being harvested and sold fresh where you live. Shop at farmers' markets or consider joining a Community Supported Agriculture (CSA) organization to get a regular delivery of farm-fresh produce and other items, straight from local sources (for information on CSAs visit www.localharvest.org/csa).

- ◆ If you can't find fresh berries in season, use frozen, but be sure to get berries only, no added sugars or syrups.

- ◆ If you can't find fresh veggies, use frozen (with no added sauces or flavorings). Avoid canned vegetables. Frozen are usually picked at their peak; canned won't taste as fresh and may have added salt. The exceptions are beans and tomato products.

- ◆ Experiment with a variety of whole grains for fiber. Most commercially available sandwich bread is not a reliable source of whole grains (as we'll discuss in detail in chapter 4), but you can get loads of fiber from whole grains like brown rice, oatmeal, and of course whole wheat. Once-exotic grains like spelt, kamut, quinoa, and farro are now widely available in most major markets due to increased consumer demand, or you can find them online (for a wide selection of fiber-rich grains, seeds, and flours, check out Bob's Red Mill products, www.bobsredmill.com).

- ◆ Use a variety of fresh herbs to flavor recipes naturally. See our growing tips in the Get Your Hands Dirty feature "Growing Herbs" in chapter 7.

- ◆ Use sea salt for cooking and eating because it's loaded with minerals and contains less sodium than regular table or kosher salt since the sea salt crystals are larger than other salts.

- ◆ Incorporate healthy fats, such as walnut, almond, sesame, avocado, flaxseed, and olive oils. (You'll hear more about healthy fats throughout this book.)

- ✦ Choose low-fat dairy products, not full-fat or nonfat (with the exception of Greek yogurt).

- ✦ Purchase raw nuts, not roasted or salted ones, which have more added fat because they are usually fried in peanut oil.

- ✦ Include nontreated (also labeled "unsulfured"*) dried fruits a part of your family's diet.

- ✦ Add sweetness from nature, not from refined sugar, by using honey, agave nectar, maple syrup, and stevia.

For a more complete list of pantry essentials, including brand names, see "Stacey's Pantry List" at the end of this book.

Using Our Recipes

I'm not a trained chef, but I love to cook food that leaves kids clamoring for seconds. That will happen for you often with this book because all of the recipes that you find here are thoroughly taste tested by kids. We've served thousands of plates of food to children not only at HealthBarn USA but at our "Try It You'll Like It" school assemblies. If kids don't like it, I find out why—and I fix it. Rest assured that all these foods have gotten a thumbs up!

Each recipe contains complete nutritional information per serving, and the recipe headnotes point out why a dish or snack is particularly rich in a certain nutrient, so before you start cooking, read through them so you can share the benefits with your children!

Over the years as I've prepared and shared foods with HealthBarn USA families, I've come to favor certain brands over others for taste, nutrition, quality, and overall performance in a recipe. Below are my suggested brands. If you can find these brands in your store or online, they are worth seeking out.

- ✦ *Flaxseed oil.* Barlean's is high in quality because it's made on demand, so there is less time for the omega-3 fatty acids to break down. Unlike other brands,

---

* Dried fruit is often treated with sulfur to prolong shelf life, but I recommend avoiding this unnecessary preservative. Look for pure dried fruit. At HealthBarn USA, we make our own dried fruits and veggies with our food dehydrator, which the kids love to operate (they can turn old grapes into golden raisins, for example). Dehydrators also dry herbs and other foods. You might consider adding one to your kitchen.

Barlean's doesn't sit around in a warehouse before it hits supermarket shelves. But more important, Barlean's proves to be the kids' favorite flaxseed oil brand for the Popcorn with Brain Butter recipe, as well as other recipes that call for it.

✦ *Cheddar cheese.* Cabot's 50% reduced-fat cheddar has half the fat of regular cheddar, but the flavor is outstanding—easily equal to regular cheddar. Other low-fat cheddars I have tried have a disappointing taste and texture, but Cabot's works well in our recipes and tastes great on its own.

✦ *Pita bread.* Toufayan pita bread tastes good, is lower in sodium than other pita bread brands, and is made with minimal ingredients.

✦ *Yogurt.* Stonyfield yogurts are organic, delicious, and widely available. They also make a Greek-style yogurt (higher in protein than traditional yogurts and a great substitute for recipes that call for sour cream or cream cheese).

✦ *Mayonnaise.* Spectrum olive oil mayonnaise has a pleasing taste and has no hydrogenated fats or preservatives.

✦ *Turkey Bacon.* Applegate Farms makes a delicious organic or natural variety of turkey bacon that contains no added fillers and industrial sodium nitrites.

✦ *Chips.* Stacy's pita chips, Lundberg rice chips, Beanitos (a delicious gluten-free option), Food Should Taste Good chips, and Plocky's The Original Three Grain tortilla chips are favorites at the barn to accompany our dip recipes.

If you'd like a good resource for rating the healthfulness of specific foods and brands, visit the website for the Center for Science in the Public Interest (CSPI), at www.cspinet.org.

A few final recipe tips:

✦ If you require a milk alternative, we recommend rice milk because it doesn't alter the flavor of a recipe as much as soy or almond (especially in pancakes and baked goods).

✦ If your child has a peanut or tree nut allergy, just eliminate those ingredients from the recipe; it will not make a difference in the overall quality of the meal or snack. And, for sandwiches, try SunButter, made from sunflower seeds, as a suitable substitute.

✦ For vegetarians, check out page 109 for a list of our top picks, but most of our recipes can be made meatless and are still delicious.

◆ For gluten-free options, flip to page 113 for our favorite kid-tested recipes from the barn.

◆ For leftovers, we recommend no more than four days of refrigeration for most foods.

Don't Hide What's Healthy

I know some parents swear by being "sneaky chefs," adding pureed veggies and other nutritious ingredients to their children's meals, with their children being none the wiser—and therein lies the problem. How can a child learn to love good food from nature if he doesn't even know what he's eating? Children deserve to be educated not just about where their food comes from but *what their food is*.

Why demonize vegetables? Hiding the spinach doesn't make a spinach lover. Instead, once your child finds out what he's been eating (and they do find out), it reinforces a message from an adult that spinach is healthy but boring and yucky, and the only way to tolerate it is to hide it in the meatballs as if it were a despised medicine. Kids don't like surprises when it comes to food—and once they uncover your deception, well-meaning as it may be, they may not trust you when you say, "Really, it tastes great!" even if it does.

You're Part of the Team

As a parent, you already know that you lead by example—and that includes your eating habits. You can't tell your kids to eat healthy foods if you're not eating them too. If you want them to eat breakfast, *you* have to eat breakfast. If you want them to put down the soda and have milk or water instead, then *you* need to put down your soda too. If you want your kids to fix themselves healthy snacks (or eat the healthy snacks you provide for them), then you have to fix them and eat them too.

It goes beyond food, of course. If you want your kids to be active and healthy, don't just send them outside to play. Lace up your sneakers and go to the park with them. Jump on your bike and ride with them. Pull on your old baseball glove and go play catch. You'll be *showing* them, not just *telling* them—and that's exactly how we teach kids about healthy living at HealthBarn USA.

Finally, living well does not mean living expensively. As for exercise, you don't need to join a gym or a club to get exercise—just open the front door and go for a walk with your kids. Although they may have their critics, "big box" stores and price clubs like Walmart and Costco have responded to consumer demand for more natural foods, including organic produce, meat, and dairy items—and they are priced competitively. If you can afford to support smaller independents or buy direct from a local source (like an organic farm or farmers' market), then do so. But it's not the only way to eat healthfully, and shopping for foods from nature shouldn't break the bank.

There is a misconception that it's cheaper to eat fast food than it is to cook a wholesome meal—but it costs about thirty dollars to feed a family of four at McDonald's. For less than half that price you can feed a family of four a home-cooked meal of roast chicken and vegetables, plus low-fat dairy and whole grains.* Fast food, and processed convenience foods in general, doesn't just cost you your health—it's stealing your wallet too!

When you buy in to a healthy lifestyle, you don't need to buy anything expensive—you just need to make the commitment and bring your family with you.

Think Like a Kid

We adults think things through. When faced with a new challenge, we ask questions, anticipate problems, and make assumptions, and the result is that

sometimes we overthink it. In other words, we take the fun out of it. Over and over again, I see parents doing this—putting up roadblocks—when it comes to offering kids new and healthy food options.

For example, when I talk to kids about why it's important to choose a wholesome snack over chips and soda, and then show them how make a better option, like our kid-created, kid-approved Rainbow Swirly Smoothie (made with yogurt, fruit, and 100% fruit juice, honey, and ground flaxseeds that make you super smart), the kids don't balk and wonder, "Hmm, flaxseeds,

---

* Mark Bittman, "Is Junk Food Really Cheaper?," *New York Times,* September 24, 2011. The cost of two Big Macs, one cheeseburger, one six-piece order of Chicken McNuggets, two medium fries, two small fries, two medium Cokes, and two small Cokes (for a family of four people) is $27.89. The cost of ingredients for a dinner for four of roasted chicken with vegetables, a simple salad, bread, and milk is $13.78.

that sounds weird," or "I don't usually buy berries." Instead, the kids just mix up the ingredients, have fun running the blender, and drink this nutritious and vitamin-packed refresher—*which they made themselves*—with gusto. In other words, they approach this new taste the way many kids approach new experiences: with curiosity and enthusiasm.

By contrast, adults make assumptions: "I know he won't like it!" They worry: "What if I buy fresh berries and they don't get eaten?" They fret about feeding their families until they are paralyzed with inaction: "Why bother trying?" And then they give up.

There is, however, another approach: *think like a kid*. I'm asking you to do what your kids do, and approach the HealthBarn USA way of eating and living with curiosity and enthusiasm. Don't assume anything about what they will like and dislike—your kids, as you know, always surprise you. Don't worry about details like finding fresh berries—frozen berries will work beautifully; and I'm not asking you to find hard-to-get ingredients like fresh truffles. Forget about the mess kids may make in the kitchen (or perhaps take this opportunity to teach them about cleaning up). Instead, do what kids do and have fun—in this case, have fun with food. Don't think too hard about calories and grams of fat and sugar. Simply focus on healthy food that tastes delicious, and rest assured that all the recipes in this book have been tried out, tested, tweaked, and given a HealthBarn USA thumbs up from thousands of kids.

The best change is gradual change, because gradual change has the best chance of becoming lasting change. Learning to eat well and live a healthy lifestyle is not learned overnight. It is bite by bite, meal by meal, day by day—each one healthier than the last. It's about changing what goes into the grocery cart, adjusting cooking practices, and rethinking daily habits so that it becomes easier for you and your family to make healthier choices, like getting more exercise (even better, exercising together) and a good night's sleep. Learning to make each day a healthy day is a marathon, not a sprint—because it's not just for one day. It's for life.

CHAPTER 2

Rise and Shine! It's Breakfast Time

RECIPES

Mom was right, and she still is. Eat your breakfast, kids (and grown-ups too) because it really is the most important meal of the day.

Eating a nutritious breakfast is one of our Seven Healthy Habits at HealthBarn USA, but we're not just telling you to do it because Mom says so. Researchers have long noted the links between a good breakfast and improved health and well-being, including increased cognitive function and a lower risk of being overweight. Higher test scores, improved school attendance, and good behavior have all been connected to eating breakfast. Share the information below with your kids before your family starts their next healthy day!

Wondering what you get when you have a good breakfast?

✦ Lots of energy to start the day—and you'll be in a good mood too!

✦ A better grade on a test because you're paying attention in class (and not thinking about lunch at 10:00 A.M.)

✦ Faster runs, higher jumps, more points scored in the game— because you feel strong!

✦ Parents and teachers who are pleased with how you behave.

More Reasons to Join the Breakfast Club

Many people erroneously think that eating a tiny breakfast or skipping it altogether is an effective way to cut calories to lose or maintain one's weight. But just the opposite is true: adults and children who do not eat breakfast are at a higher risk for weight gain and being overweight, and breakfast eaters tend to have a healthy weight.[*] By the time lunch rolls around, it's been more than twelve hours since the body's systems have been properly fueled. When we skip breakfast entirely we're starving ourselves, and our instinct will be to make up for it by eating extra at the next opportunity.

As an adult, if you've skipped breakfast you no doubt have experienced that feeling of being so hungry at lunchtime that you could eat anything. As your blood

---

[*] Gail C. Rampersaud, Mark A. Pereira, Beverly L. Girard, Judi Adams, and Jordan D. Metzl, "Breakfast Habits, Nutritional Status, Body Weight, and Academic Performance in Children and Adolescents," *Journal of the American Dietetic Association* 105, no. 5 (May 2005): 743–60.

sugar level dips, your energy is so depleted that you are willing to settle for whatever you can get on a plate quickly.

Now, think about a child who skips breakfast or eats a poor one. If she is in school her lunch period is scheduled for a particular time. This child who ate no breakfast is absolutely starving by the time she gets to the cafeteria, and as her blood sugar level drops so does her energy. (We'll talk more about blood sugar in the next chapter, when we discuss the importance of a morning snack.) If she

brings her lunch, she eats it hastily and it may not fill her up, or she eats so fast that she feels queasy. If she buys "hot lunch," she's so hungry that her eyes will be bigger than her stomach and she'll likely fill her cafeteria tray with not-so-healthy choices, making more empty-calorie and high-fat choices than her breakfast-eating peers. This cycle—skipping a meal and making up for it at the next one by overeating—repeats itself daily, and the result is weight gain. Furthermore, this pattern of skipping meals and overeating later is imprinting itself on her young brain, growing body, and fluctuating metabolism; she's establishing a poor eating habit that will follow her into adulthood. Breakfast eaters avoid the starvation/overeating cycle altogether, which is why they are generally thinner than breakfast skippers.

Another important thing to consider is that as adults, when we're desperately hungry for lunch, we can tough it out more easily than kids can, physically and psychologically (even if it's not healthy for us to do so). But it's much harder for a young child, particularly when faced with the demands of a typical school day. The benefits of breakfast eating include higher cognitive function—the ability to focus and concentrate—and more stable energy levels.

Let's say today is the day that the math teacher is introducing decimals. Can your child follow the discussion and grasp new concepts if all he can think about is lunch? Can he concentrate and focus if his energy is flagging or his stomach is growling? Maybe today is the mile run in gym class, scheduled before lunch. Will he have the get-up-and-go to perform as well as he'd like? Or perhaps at recess it's his turn to be "it" in a friendly game of tag. Will he play good-naturedly or will a poor mood brought on by low energy cause him to explode in frustration, fight with others, and find himself explaining his actions to a disapproving teacher?

It's important for parents to recognize the consequences and long-term health risks that come with not eating breakfast; skipping this meal has a negative impact on adults, and it's even worse for children.

What to Do with Breakfast Boycotters

If you have a breakfast boycotter in your house, these excuses may sound familiar to you.

✦ "I don't have time! I'll miss the bus!"

✦ "I'm not hungry when I wake up. I like to watch TV instead."

✦ "I only like cereal with lots of sugar."

✦ "I don't like breakfast so I'll just have a cup of milk."

✦ "You don't eat breakfast—you just have coffee—so why should I?"

I've never met an excuse for not eating breakfast that I couldn't tackle, and I'm ready to bet that most of the time, it comes down to one thing: *routine*. More specifically, it's about a routine or a habit that needs some adjusting. Breakfast doesn't just happen; it needs to be planned for and integrated into your family's morning routine. Once that happens successfully, this healthy habit can stay with your family and your child for life. If your family's routine needs some fine-tuning, perhaps these ideas will help:

For Those Who Are Rushed ●

Fix the routine—reset your clocks. If your family is constantly rushing in the morning with little or no time for a good breakfast, get yourselves out of bed fifteen minutes earlier. (Try fifteen minutes earlier to start, and if necessary, increase this to a half hour or to whatever amount of time you think is right for your household. The key to success is to do it in manageable increments. Don't try setting the alarm clock an hour earlier tonight and expecting everyone to hop to tomorrow!) Still rushing, even with extra time? That happens—but solve the problem with the fast-and-easy breakfast solutions provided later in this chapter, including HealthBarn USA's grab-and-go Carrot Cake Muffins or Whole-Grain Breakfast Cookies.

For Would-Be Eaters Who Prefer TV to Food ● ● ● ● ● ● ● ● ● ● ● ● ●

Fix the routine—turn off the TV (at least until breakfast has been eaten). He needs food more than cartoons (and advertising). Your child hasn't eaten since dinner the night before—almost half a day has gone by! His body is hungry for fuel, though his mind may be elsewhere, so refocus his routine by downplaying the TV and playing up a delicious breakfast. Eating in front of the TV is never a great idea (see more on this subject in chapter 6), but if he's making the leap from not eating at all to eating breakfast in front of the television, be patient.

For Kids Who Only Want Sugary Cereal

Fix the routine—the grocery shopping routine, that is. Stop buying the heavily sweetened "candy" and "cookie" cereal and look for better, more wholesome alternatives that your child will accept. See page 35 for a list of kid-friendly breakfast cereals that have lots of crunch and a touch of sweetness. I'm not anti-sugar; I just want cereal that offers nutrition, and many children's breakfast cereals are loaded with artificial ingredients and added sugars and provide minimal nutritional benefits. Unfortunately, many kids have been trained by advertisers to think that the only "good" cereal is a super-sweet cereal. *Involve your child* in making the switch from sugary to satisfying—and you'll soon see that kids are pleasantly surprised when they discover that healthy tastes good!

To help explain your reasons for avoiding Cap'n Crunch, Reese's Puffs, and Froot Loops, and for some hands-on fun with your family, play the sugar-revealing Cereal Detective Game described later in this chapter.

For the Milk Drinker

Fix the routine—and turn milk into part of a complete breakfast, not the main course. Milk is a great source of calcium, vitamin D, and protein, but it's not enough. If your child is filling up on milk at breakfast or at other meals, and not leaving room for other nutritious foods, start by reducing the amount of milk she's drinking and offering fruit and oatmeal (or another food) to create a balanced meal.

For the Child Whose Parents Don't Eat Breakfast

Fix the routine—yours, that is! Don't expect your kids to eat breakfast if you're sitting next to them with a cup of coffee and nothing else. You've heard it a million times, but you're setting the example—eat breakfast and your kids will too. Even if your child is old enough to fix his own breakfast, he's unlikely to do so if you don't make it a morning priority yourself. I've presented you with many reasons for eating a healthy breakfast, but here's one more: do it for your child.

Putting Together a Healthy Breakfast

Breakfast can fuel our bodies efficiently and keep us going for hours—if we fill up on the right stuff! But what constitutes a "good" breakfast? I get this question frequently. Do you have to make whole-grain muffins and waffles from scratch? What is a good granola bar for breakfast? Are cereal, milk, and OJ enough to keep a body going? Speaking of juice, which some kids drink like water, how much is too much? Is whole fruit better? How many eggs should a child eat in a week? Aren't they high in cholesterol, and why are there so many varieties? What kind of milk or yogurt is the best choice—and what if dairy isn't an option due to allergies or other issues?

I'll get to all this shortly, but keep in mind that your family's first meal of the day does not need to be complicated or time-consuming, especially during the busy weekday mornings when school and work may cause us to watch the clock more closely. Below are some breakfast ideas from HealthBarn USA, simple solutions for what to put on the table. (At the end of this chapter you'll find detailed breakfast recipes.)

I like to include each of the following when I make a balanced breakfast:

◆ Lean protein to build muscles and fight hunger

◆ A little "healthy fat"—omega-3s—for brain power

◆ Calcium for growing bones and strong teeth

◆ Fresh fruit high in vitamins and minerals to boost the immune system

◆ Whole grains for fiber to fill you up and keep your tummy healthy

Breakfast Idea 1

Yogurt Sundaes with Crunchy Granola with Walnuts. This recipe includes a serving of fruit. (I always include a serving of fresh fruit—especially kid-pleasing and vitamin-packed berries—at breakfast.)

Breakfast Idea 2

Low-fat Greek yogurt sweetened with honey, with raspberries and ground flaxseed or hempseed (for protein, fiber, and some essential fatty acids we'll discuss later) sprinkled on top. Greek yogurt is higher in protein than regular yogurt.

Breakfast Idea 3

Scrambled or soft-boiled eggs (preferably DHA-fortified eggs) with reduced-fat cheddar cheese and chopped spinach (or any fresh veggie of your choice), with whole-grain toast, and 100% orange juice (*not* an orange drink). Try our Farm-Fresh Omelet.

Breakfast Idea 4

Warm farina cereal (iron- and calcium-fortified), made with water, low-fat milk, or nondairy alternative and topped with berries and a little drizzle of flaxseed oil. Or, substitute a high-quality cold breakfast cereal for the farina—see the list on page 35 for some ideas.*

Breakfast Idea 5

Whole-grain toasted bread with pure almond or peanut butter sprinkled with ground flaxseed, served with a banana and low-fat milk or nondairy alternative.

    With the exception of the eggs and farina (our granola recipe can be made in advance), there is minimal cooking involved, and older kids can prepare most of these quick and easy breakfasts on their own—as long as the kitchen is stocked with good food for them to choose from.

Breakfast Basics: What to Have in Your Kitchen

Take a look in your refrigerator or pantry and make sure you have these kinds of foods on hand. You'll find lots of ideas for what to put on your shopping list, as well as tips on what *not* to put in your grocery cart!

Lean Protein Sources

Eggs

Eggs are a complete protein, which means they contain all nine essential amino acids, the building blocks of protein, and in the correct order so the body can use them easily. I like cage-free eggs because the chickens they come from are free to

---

* If you consume the vitamin C found in citrus fruits and juices with iron-fortified foods like farina and other breakfast cereals, you increase the body's absorption of iron, which many kids (and adults) lack in their diets!

REAL-LIFE RESULTS:

Family Finally Eats Breakfast!

I worked with a family of picky eaters (not just the kids) who routinely ate little or no breakfast, and who seemed to embody nearly every excuse I've ever heard. One child wasn't hungry and her idea of breakfast was sipping at a flavored milk box while lying in bed. The younger brother ate a bowl of sugary cereal in front of the TV each morning. Time-challenged Mom ate nothing as she was rushing around trying to get lunches packed and kids dressed. Dad was nowhere to be found in the mornings because he headed for the gym and then went straight to his job. Then one day, the TV-watcher was diagnosed with a kidney ailment and his doctor prescribed something seemingly impossible: a healthy diet, starting with a balanced breakfast.

This mom didn't know where to begin, but I quickly realized it wasn't the food itself that was a problem. (She was sold on the idea of great-tasting, wholesome foods, especially if it meant helping her son get better.) The real obstacle was their lack of a working routine and the fact that they **never** sat at the kitchen table together for breakfast.

I suggested the recipe for HealthBarn USA's vitamin-packed Sweet Potato Pancakes, but that meant some advance preparation. The night before, Mom got the ingredients together and assigned the kids the task of setting the breakfast table before bedtime. Dad agreed to come home after the gym and join the family for pancakes before heading to work. The good food was a huge hit, the son isn't the only one who is healthier, and now this family regularly starts their morning together with breakfast.

"I never imagined how much sitting down for breakfast as a family could change and enhance our lives," the mother told me later. "It took some added effort and preparation on my part but we gained so much more in return."

You don't need to prepare homemade pancakes to get your family to the table (though once you taste them, you'll agree they are worth the effort!). You just need to commit to the idea of breakfast, get your family involved, and take some small steps to make it happen.

An Egg-cellent Choice, and Not Just for Breakfast!

To reduce the risk of heart disease, many experts, including those at the American Heart Association, recommend that healthy adults consume no more than 300 milligrams of cholesterol per day—and one large egg has about 186 milligrams.[*] (Eggs that are part of baked goods or other foods also count.) But what about our kids? Should we let them eat eggs without considering their cholesterol levels too? (Currently, there are no general recommendations on daily cholesterol limits for children, though some nutrition experts believe that the 300 milligram recommendation for adults should also apply to children.)

 The short answer is that we should always be aware of what our children are eating and how that can affect their health long term—including cholesterol levels, which you can discuss with your pediatrician. Unless your child has specific health issues (and assuming she is not allergic to eggs), the average large egg remains a very good source of lean protein. Also, if you are concerned about cholesterol, remember that the cholesterol-free egg white offers slightly more protein than the yolk (though some nutrients like DHA and folate are concentrated in the yolk).[**]

Eggs can be part of a satisfying and balanced breakfast. As a low-calorie, nutrient-dense food, they are also a smart choice at lunch (see our recipe for Crustless Veggie Quiche), and dinner (see our recipe for Moo Shu Chicken).

[*] For more information on cholesterol and heart disease, including children's cholesterol issues, visit the American Heart Association's website at www.heart.org.

[**] If you are cooking from our recipes, you'll notice we often call for egg whites only. If you are bothered by throwing away yolks, purchase pasteurized liquid egg whites, widely available in most supermarkets.

roam and are more humanely treated than "factory-farm" chickens. DHA-fortified eggs are also a good choice because the chickens get the DHA naturally through their feed.

DHA is an omega-3 fatty acid, an important substance that cannot be made by our bodies and therefore must be obtained through food sources. For children, DHA is a major factor in brain development; some researchers even believe that DHA-deficiency has a direct link to behavioral issues like ADHD. DHA is also a component of heart tissue as well as nerve cells in the eyes. (There are other good food sources for DHA, like fish, which I'll discuss later.)

Turkey Bacon

If your family eats pork bacon, switch to turkey bacon for less total fat, saturated fat, and sodium. Avoid fillers and added industrial sodium nitrites (the fewer ingredients the better), and try organic turkey bacon if you can find it. (Applegate Farms brand is our choice at HealthBarn USA; if you have a Trader Joe's store in your community, their brand is also good.) Test out your taste buds with our TLT Wrap.

Nut Butters

Peanut and almond butters, as a spread on whole-grain breads or crackers, are a nutrition-packed alternative to butter or margarine. Choose pure nut butters with no additives or fillers (look for nuts and salt only). In some markets, you can even "grind your own" peanut butter. Kids love watching the nuts transform into spreadable peanut butter!

Healthy Fats

We have been conditioned to be wary of fat in our diets, but "healthy" fats—like monounsaturated fats (olive oil), polyunsaturated fats (sunflower oil and seeds), and omega-3 fatty acids offer important benefits, including protection from heart disease. That may sound like a concern for an adult and not a child, but for kids a lifetime of good health through a good diet starts *now,* not decades from now. Fish (particularly salmon) and fish oils are a top source of omega-3s, but they are not usually featured during a typical weekday breakfast. (But make time on a more relaxed morning for our fantastic Salmon and Swiss Cheese Crepes.)

Butter Up!

A small amount of unsalted butter is better than a lot—and for kids a dab of pure butter may also be better than no fat at all. Children need some fat for brain and nervous system development. If you're concerned about saturated fat, consider a product with less saturated fat than butter such as dairy-free Earth Balance Natural Buttery Spread, made with a blend of palm fruit, soy, and olive oils, and free of artery-clogging trans fats.

When choosing butter, pick one of the unsalted varieties to avoid extra sodium. Unsalted butter is generally a better choice in cooking and baking as it allows you to control how your food is flavored.

In the morning, you can include healthy fats in your family's breakfast by adding walnuts and ground flaxseed and hempseed to yogurts and cereals. Ground flaxseed and hempseed, which are also high in fiber and have a nutty taste that kids like, can also give breakfast smoothies a nutritional boost.

The nut butters—peanut and almond—mentioned above are also good sources of healthy fats.

Calcium

Milk

For children who don't have allergies or sensitivities to dairy products, one of the best sources of calcium is cow's milk, which contains 300 milligrams of calcium per eight ounces.* By drinking just one cup of milk, a school-age child is getting about a third of her daily recommended calcium intake (see the calcium chart opposite).

Two to three eight-ounce servings of milk is plenty for most children, assuming they're getting calcium from other sources besides milk. Milk is healthy, but if a child fills up on milk, he won't have an appetite for other nutritious foods to balance out his diet. Milk should not take the place of food.

But what kind of milk should your child be drinking? Pediatricians generally recommend whole milk for babies between the ages of twelve months and twenty-four months (that is, babies starting cow's milk who are partially or fully weaned, as well as formula-fed babies); growing babies need the higher saturated fat content and calories found in whole milk. At age two, most babies can be switched to 2% or even 1% milk.

For school-age kids, I recommend 1% milk, which contains lower amounts of fat and calories than whole or 2% milk. (I have found that most kids don't really like the taste of skim milk; if your pediatrician recommends switching to skim, start by blending 1% or 2% with skim and gradually increasing the amount of skim.)

Chocolate, vanilla, and strawberry-flavored milk are packed with added sugars and artificial ingredients that kids don't need, and using them runs contrary to everything we embrace at HealthBarn USA. Sweetened milk does not come from nature, and it's made in a factory and contains artificial ingredients that are hard to pronounce! Unfortunately, some companies like Horizon—an otherwise reliable

---

* Though fat and calorie content will vary depending on whether it is skim, low-fat (1%), reduced-fat (2%), or full-fat milk, the calcium content stays the same, at about 300 milligrams per eight ounces. Some products, like Skim Plus, are fortified skim milks with added vitamins A and D, and have higher levels of calcium than regular skim milk.

producer of quality organic dairy products—have created organic milk marketed as kid-friendly: strawberry, chocolate, and vanilla-flavored milks available in single-serve boxes. These boxes appeal to parents who may assume that if it's organic, it's high quality and healthy.

But look closely at the nutrition labels on flavored milks. An eight-ounce box of Horizon organic low-fat chocolate milk has 150 calories and 22 grams of sugar.* An eight-ounce serving of Nesquik Double Chocolate low-fat chocolate milk has 180 calories and 29 grams of sugar. An eight-ounce glass of regular low-fat milk has 100 calories and 12 grams of sugar (naturally occurring milk sugar, or lactose, not added sugar). If a child chooses chocolate milk three or four times a day over low-fat white milk, he's getting about an extra 200–300 calories per day—most of it from sugar, which offers no nutritional benefit. I regularly ask kids, "What color is the milk when it comes out of the cow? That's the stuff you want—the white stuff!"

> ### Daily Calcium Needs
>
> How much calcium does your child need? For strong bones and healthy teeth, aim for these daily amounts.**
>
> | | |
> |---|---|
> | 1 to 3 years old | 700 milligrams |
> | 4 to 8 years old | 1,000 milligrams |
> | 9 to 18 years old | 1,300 milligrams |

Alternatives to Cow's Milk—Kids Give These the Thumbs Up!

Some children are milk drinkers from day one, while others may not like the taste (or perhaps they don't consume dairy). I like to present kids—including the ones who drink cow's milk—with other alternatives that are healthy, calcium-filled, and palate-pleasing. Let your kids do a taste test with rice, soy, and almond milks, which we regularly use at HealthBarn USA (and which you'll find in some of our recipes, such as Homemade Chocolate Milk). We usually use rice milk as an alternative for kids with milk allergies in the Blueberry Buckwheat Pancakes and Simply Crepes. They often get a kick out of drinking something that looks like milk (and acts like milk)—but that comes from a plant and not a cow!

How do these milk alternatives stack up to cow's milk for calcium? As mentioned, a one-cup serving of low-fat milk has about 300 milligrams of calcium. Enriched rice

---

* Horizon's old formula contained 180 calories and 27 grams of sugar, and 50 percent more fat (5 grams of fat instead of 2.5 grams); they reduced these levels by switching from 2% to 1% milk and by lowering added sugar.

** Calcium guidelines are based on information from the National Institutes of Health. For more information on calcium and children's health from the NIH, see their free publication, "Kids and Their Bones: A Guide for Parents," available online at www.niams.nih.gov/Health_Info/Bone/Bone_Health/Juvenile/default.asp.

milk also has 300 milligrams of calcium, while calcium-fortified soy milk has about 370 milligrams. Almond milk contains 200 milligrams of calcium. (If you are seeking calcium, choose *enriched* or *fortified* versions of rice and soy milks. Regular soy milk has less than 100 milligrams of calcium; regular rice milk has less than 20 milligrams. Almond milk is naturally high in calcium so you don't need to seek out enriched or fortified.) Almond and soy milks are also a terrific protein source.

Other Sources for Calcium

Low-fat yogurt and cheese can help your child meet her daily calcium needs. For a discussion on yogurt, see the Pantry Pick tip in chapter 3. In later chapters, you'll find recipes featuring foods like salmon, tofu, and leafy greens, all of which are also good sources for calcium.

Fresh Fruits and Juices

Keep a bowl of seasonal fresh fruit in your kitchen and keep it filled!

At every meal, I recommend a cup of cut-up fruit, a piece of whole fruit, or a cup of berries. At breakfast, fruit is a natural choice. In fact, my favorite breakfast fruits are berries—all varieties, but especially blueberries and strawberries. Berries are packed with antioxidants that have been shown to boost the immune system and improve health. Berries can be added to cereal and yogurt, or to batters for muffins, waffles, and pancakes. They can also be eaten on the side. Kids like berries because they're naturally sweet—and they are fun to eat, without utensils!

Berries can be purchased fresh when in season, or you can buy them frozen year-round. Because berries are eaten with their skin, I prefer organic—especially strawberries, which can have high levels of pesticides. Organic frozen berries are usually less expensive than fresh, and we like them at HealthBarn USA because they are easy to stock up on and have on hand. If you really want to get around the pesticide issue (and save money), grow your own! See our tips on berry growing in the Get Your Hands Dirty feature later in this chapter.

If you and your family are juice drinkers, look for 100% juice only—no added sugars or water. (See the "Stacey's Tips" section on juice in chapter 3.) Calcium-fortified OJ may appeal to you if you're looking for more nondairy calcium sources. At HealthBarn USA, kids enjoy using appliances like juicers and blenders because they can watch food transform from solid to liquid—and it's a great way for them to get involved in making their own healthy drinks. If you have a blender that's been gathering dust, let your children put it back to good use making the Rainbow Swirly Smoothie or the Banana Cream Smoothie!

Whole Grains for Fiber

Cereals

Cereal companies spend millions of dollars marketing their products straight to your kids, and not just on television, where, according to the Rudd Center for Food Policy and Obesity at Yale University, the average preschooler sees more than 642 commercials per year for sugary cereal. Cereals have their own websites where kids can play games, and toys and merchandise keep the brands front and center. Children aren't the only ones being lured by Lucky Charms and Cocoa Pebbles. Parents, too, are drawn to boxes with health claims on the packaging, including phrases such as "smart choice," "now made with whole grains," or "better for you." According to a report from the Rudd Center, the cereals with the worst nutrition ratings are the ones that most often carry these claims!*

Homemade oatmeal and granola, and recipes like our Sweet Berry Polenta, provide hearty, whole-grain alternatives to boxed cereal, but when your family is in a hurry—and when kids are serving themselves—cold cereal makes a lot of sense. Think of fortified cereal as a vitamin and mineral delivery system for your child, and choose quality, whole-grain cereals without a lot of added sugar. Here are my favorites:

✦ Cheerios—original

✦ Barbara's Puffins—original or cinnamon

✦ Kashi Cinnamon Harvest

✦ Mother's Toasted Oat Bran or Cinnamon Oat Crunch

✦ Erewhon crispy brown rice cereal (with a gluten-free option)—this always gets a thumbs up from kids at our HealthBarn USA school assemblies

All of these cereals have three or more grams of dietary fiber (except for Erewhon, which is wheat-free and therefore has only one gram of fiber) and are low in sugar, especially when compared to cereals like Trix and Corn Pops. Serve them with regular low-fat milk or try rice or soy milks.

A lot of kids I've worked with, especially those who are making the switch from sugary cereal to less sweet, like to "blend" cereals and mix up different varieties in a

---

* According to "Cereal f.a.c.t.s." [Food Advertising to Children and Teens Score], a report published by the Rudd Center for Food Policy and Obesity, major cereal companies spent a combined total of more than $156 million in 2008 advertising their products to kids. For more information and to read their full report, go to www.cerealfacts.org.

single bowl or add natural ingredients to the cereal such as raisins and sunflower seeds. They tell me that they love the added "crunch" they get from doing this, plus, kids just like playing around with their food—and if the end result is healthy, let them. Similarly, some kids don't like pouring milk on their cereal and prefer to drink it on the side. At some point, they'll do it the "grown-up way," but for now, if the good stuff is all getting mixed together in their tummies, don't sweat it.

Even if it's not the way *you'd* eat breakfast, allowing a child to have some control over what they eat—and how they eat it—is all part of encouraging kids to make healthy choices.

Breads

Whether you're about to make toast for breakfast or prepare a sandwich for your child's lunchbox, here are some things to keep in mind when choosing store-bought breads.

In general, with bread and with so many other foods we buy, the fewer ingredients the better! Whole-grain bread should contain 100 percent whole-grain flour (such as

The Problem with Our Daily Bread

It's difficult to find a "simple" loaf of bread in most supermarkets, which is why I do not rely upon it as a major source of whole-grain fiber and nutrition for breakfast (or at any other meal). Have you looked at the ingredients closely? You may feel that you need an advanced degree in chemistry just to decipher some of those words—and that's why a freshly baked white baguette with five ingredients is generally a healthier choice than a whole wheat loaf with twenty! Of course, if you are a home baker, you can sidestep the ingredients maze of mass-produced breads and create your own healthy, whole-grain loaves, but most of us still rely on the bread rack at our local store. (In the "Supermarket Spy Kids" game in chapter 3 we'll teach you and your family all about reading labels and navigating ingredients lists.)

Many parents ask me questions like, "How much fiber should our bread have? What about sugar or sodium content? How about calories per slice?" Don't get hung up on those questions because **it's all about the ingredients.** You may find whole-grain bread that is high in fiber, but if it's loaded with preservatives, trans fats, and high-fructose corn syrup, it's not a healthy choice. As you'll see from the recipes and tips in this book, there are other ways to get whole grains into your family's diet besides a slice of whole wheat bread. For more information on whole grains, see pages 109–14 in chapter 4.

pantry pick

Agave Nectar Besides the breakfast basics we've just discussed, another ingredient I'd like to highlight is agave nectar, made from the blue agave cactus found in Mexico (yes, the same cactus that tequila is made from). Agave nectar or syrup is actually an ancient sweetener that the Aztecs prized (not only as a food but as a home remedy for many ills), but its growing popularity in the U.S. as a healthy alternative to refined sugars is fairly recent.

At HealthBarn USA, we use this natural sweetener, which tastes a little bit like honey, instead of refined sugar in many of our recipes such as Berrilicious Risotto, which makes a delicious warm breakfast. Many HealthBarn USA families have used it successfully to wean kids off of artificially flavored pancake syrups, particularly for children who don't like the taste of pure maple syrup.

Though it has more calories than table sugar, it is a far more concentrated sweetener, so you'll use a lot less of this than you will refined sugar. To use it in a recipe that calls for regular sugar, try using a half cup of agave nectar for every full cup of sugar; because the nectar is a liquid, decrease the liquid that's called for in the recipe by one-fourth of a cup. (You can adjust this formula to taste; it's better to start with less agave than you think you may need because you can always add more.)

Agave nectar also has a low glycemic level—meaning that its sugars release more slowly in the bloodstream—so kids won't get the blood sugar spike they get from refined sugar. It's also a good choice for diabetics. You'll find agave nectar in most large supermarkets in the honey section.

whole wheat flour),* a liquid such as water or milk, perhaps a bit of oil, yeast, salt, and sugar (which the yeast needs to do its job), and not a whole lot more than that, though by necessity, manufacturers sometimes add other ingredients to increase shelf life.

One of my favorite breakfast breads is Ezekiel 4:9 cinnamon raisin bread, a flourless bread made from organic sprouted whole grains including wheat, barley, and millet. Nutty and delicious, it's also a good source of protein. Kids like it toasted and spread with almond or peanut butter; add a serving of whole fruit and a glass of low-fat milk or nondairy alternative, and breakfast is served!

---

* A whole grain, like whole wheat, or mix of whole grains should be the first ingredient listed. If a product is made with "enriched white flour" it is not a whole-grain product. For more on whole grains, see chapter 4.

Stacey's Tips

Breakfast on the Go

Here's a question I get from children who are always in a hurry, especially older kids—tweens and teens—who get themselves out of bed (and even out the door), but who are still learning how to manage their morning time.

I just can't help it—I'm always rushing in the morning and don't have time to sit down and eat, even though I'm hungry. What can I have for breakfast?

You don't have to sit at the table to get a good morning meal, though it's often a pleasant way to start your healthy day. However, if you've tried to adjust your routine and you're nevertheless pressed for time, you can still fit breakfast in, even if you eat it on the go. Here are some ideas for when you're really rushing. Unless you have three hands I don't recommend eating and riding a bike to school at the same time, but you can enjoy all of these while you're walking or riding in the car. Don't forget the napkins.

Sweet Potato Pancakes. Our Sweet Potato Pancakes can be made ahead and frozen (best if wrapped individually), then popped in the toaster to reheat—ready to eat in minutes. (They also work as an energizing pregame/sports practice meal.) You can freeze and reheat waffles this way too (using the same batter)!

Breakfast Cookie. Cookies for breakfast? Yes! Our Whole-Grain Breakfast Cookie is full of energizing protein, the mineral iron, and good-for-you fiber, and it tastes terrific, even if you eat it on the way to school. (It's a much better alternative than most commercially produced and overly sugared granola bars, which are *not* granola cereal without the milk. We'll talk more about granola bars in chapter 3.) Our cookies are super moist, so keep them in the refrigerator and put them in the toaster in the morning to reheat quickly.

Grab-and-Go Smoothie. This smoothie takes some advance planning but it's worth it. Make up a batch of healthy smoothies after dinner and refrigerate. Before you go to bed, set out a reusable cup with a lid (a "to-go cup" for coffee will work) and a straw. Take a few minutes the next morning to stir your smoothie, then pour into your cup and head out. (Of course, smoothies taste best right after they're blended, but if you don't have time in the morning, you can make them about twelve hours in advance and have breakfast ready right when you wake up.)

Muffins. At HealthBarn USA, we love the convenience (and taste) of muffins for breakfast, including our famous PB&J Muffins and the deliciously moist Carrot Cake and Zucchini Muffins. Make, wrap individually in foil, freeze, and take one out the night before to defrost on the kitchen counter. When morning comes, you've got a healthy breakfast you can hold in one hand.

WHEN IT'S TIME TO CELEBRATE

Our Favorite Weekend Breakfasts

Monday through Friday, particularly during the school year, breakfast is a get-up-and-go kind of affair. When kids need to be at school and parents need to head to work, time is limited. But when the weekend rolls around, the pace slows for most families. Weekend mornings can be an ideal time for turning breakfast into a more relaxed family meal, and best of all, everyone can stay in their pajamas! Here are some of my favorite weekend breakfast foods. Older kids can handle some of these recipes on their own, and younger kids can get involved in preparing ingredients, setting the table, and waking up any sleepyheads who are still in bed! And don't forget to send your budding farmer outside to harvest some fresh berries for the table.

You'll find all of these breakfast recipes, and many others, on the pages that follow. All of these foods are wonderful choices year-round, but if you want to think seasonally:

On cold winter mornings. Take the chill off with a bowl of Berrilicious Risotto or a warm batch of pancakes—like our Blueberry Buckwheat or Sweet Potato Pancake varieties. Keep frozen berries on hand to jazz up your pancakes, waffles, and muffins even in the coldest winter.

Our Salmon and Swiss Cheese Crepes will also warm up your insides!

When spring has sprung. How about our Mini Potato Leek Frittata or our Creamy Berry Crepes? Both hearty enough to ward off spring's chill, but with fresh herbs, veggies, and fruits that hint at the season to come!

For a lazy summer morning. Have breakfast outside! Who says picnics are just for lunch or dinner? Serve up a chilled seasonal fruit salad and pick up some raspberries or spinach greens at the local farmers' market to make our yummy Raspberry Muffins or Farm-Fresh Omelets. Too hot to cook? Our Crunchy Granola with Walnuts (yes, you have to toast it in the oven but it can be made in advance) is perfect in our Yogurt Sundaes.

To toast the fall harvest. Bring the flavors of autumn to your family table with Maple Walnut Oatmeal and buckwheat pancakes made with pumpkin, a variation on our Blueberry Buckwheat Pancakes. And don't forget to visit the farm stand one last time to stock up on last-of-the-season produce to freeze and feast on in the months to come.

Let's Play Cereal Detective!

At HealthBarn USA, we love to play a game called "Cereal Detective," in which kids get to see how much sugar goes into their food—particularly their breakfast cereal. If you are trying to help your children make the switch from sugary cold cereals to more healthy alternatives, or if you're just trying to explain why some cereals are better than others, this hands-on activity speaks louder than words!

WHAT YOU NEED: White table sugar, a measuring teaspoon, a cereal bowl, and a variety of breakfast cereals with varying sugar content.

hands-on family fun

This activity works best if you use about five different cereals from your pantry. At HealthBarn USA, we like to use Apple Jacks, Froot Loops, Special K, Barbara's Puffins (original), and Cheerios (original). Just pull out whatever cereals you have on hand, but make sure you have at least one low-sugar pick like original Cheerios (see my "favorites" list on page 35).

WHAT YOU'LL DO: Ask your child to guess the order of most to least sugars just by looking at the front of the cereal box. (Parents, be aware that some cereal companies have started to put sugar content on the front

of the box, so make sure that info is covered up.) Next, have them line up the boxes based on their guesses, from most to least sugar. Now let them do some hands-on detective work to find out if they were right!

Ask your child to look at the nutrition facts label for each cereal and point out the sugar content, which will be in grams. Also, ask your child to look at the ingredients list and note where sugar is listed. Tell them they now have all the evidence they need to solve the mystery!

Given that 1 teaspoon equals 4 grams of sugar, your child can show off his math skills and calculate the number of teaspoons of sugar in one serving of cereal. (For instance, a one-cup serving of Froot Loops has 12 grams of sugar, which is the equivalent of 3 teaspoons of sugar.) Have them scoop the correct number of teaspoons per serving into the empty cereal bowl. Let them try it with a few different cereals to see how sugar content varies and how good their guesses were. When they're done analyzing all five cereals, have them reorder the boxes to reflect their detective work.

WHAT KIDS LEARN: When they get to see how much sugar is added into some of their favorite cereals per serving, and when they understand that too much sugar (especially for breakfast) makes them feel crummy after it wears off and can affect their bodies in negative ways (mention cavities!), they get the message more powerfully than if they are just told. When we do this activity at HealthBarn USA, the kids can hardly believe their eyes as they scoop teaspoon after teaspoon of sugar—and many parents are just as surprised!

You can do this activity with table sugar and a measuring spoon with other sugary foods—especially sodas and other sweetened beverages.

Grow Your Own Breakfast Berries!

Berries are a great addition to the breakfast table—or any meal or snack. Many varieties are very easy to grow, even for nongardeners and dirt rookies. Kids will enjoy watching their berry plants grow and savoring the fruits of their labors! At HealthBarn USA, children regularly fall in love with fruits and veggies that they've never tried before—because they grow them. You can reproduce this same farm-to-table experience for your children in your backyard or even in a pot on your patio.

get your hands dirty

Start with a healthy seedling—we suggest strawberries or raspberries, as children seem to enjoy them the most—and put the plant in the ground in early spring (if you choose to plant in a container, you'll have to keep it well watered; strawberry jars are popular, but if a plant dries out it will not thrive and may die). Make sure the plant gets plenty of sun—about eight hours a day—and use an organic fertilizer, controlling weeds by hand. Berry plants are perennials but need protection in colder climates to survive through winter. If you mulch them well against plant-killing frost, you'll be rewarded with green leaves and a lot of buds (a good indication of an abundant harvest) come spring.

Most kids love to garden and work with plants—it's one of the few times when they are encouraged to get dirty! Whether you plant berries or other edibles, let kids play an age-appropriate role in planting and caring for their "crop." Put them in charge of digging the hole where the plant will go; watering (they go a little crazy with this if they like to play with water, so make sure they don't drown their new plants!); and weeding. Encourage them to document the growth of the plants, perhaps by snapping digital photos every other day, or measuring with a yardstick once a week, and recording their findings.

In the chapters to come, I'll share more gardening ideas with you—including composting tips and ways to grow food organically, as we do at HealthBarn USA.

Chocolate Zucchini Cupcakes

Cupcakes for breakfast? Yes, if they are made with zucchini! We grow so much of this veggie in our HealthBarn USA garden that we've found dozens of delicious ways to use it in our recipes. This low-fat breakfast treat is a good source of fiber and will be sure to get the whole family up and energized to start their healthy day!

ingredients

1 cup unsweetened applesauce

¼ cup packed brown sugar

2 tablespoons agave nectar

1 teaspoon vanilla extract

1 cup whole wheat flour

½ cup unbleached all-purpose flour

½ cup unsweetened cocoa powder

¼ cup ground flaxseeds

1 teaspoon ground cinnamon

1 teaspoon baking soda

½ teaspoon baking powder

½ teaspoon ground ginger

¼ teaspoon ground cloves

¼ teaspoon grated nutmeg

¼ cup semisweet, mini chocolate chips

1 large zucchini (12–14 ounces), shredded

Icing (optional)

¼ cup agave nectar

½ teaspoon ground cinnamon

directions

1. Preheat oven to 350°F. Line 12 muffin cups with paper liners.

2. In a large bowl, stir together applesauce, brown sugar, agave nectar, and vanilla until well mixed.

3. Add flours, cocoa, flaxseeds, cinnamon, baking soda, baking powder, ginger, cloves, and nutmeg; mix well.

4. Add chocolate chips and zucchini and stir until well blended. Spoon batter evenly into prepared muffin cups. Bake for 18–20 minutes or until a toothpick inserted in center of cupcakes comes out clean. Allow cupcakes to cool.

5. For the optional icing: In a small bowl, mix agave nectar with cinnamon. Before serving, drizzle icing over cooled cupcakes.

Makes 12 servings (1 cupcake per serving)

Nutrition Facts per serving: 140 calories; 3g fat (1g sat fat, 1g mono, 1g poly, 0g trans fat); 0mg cholesterol; 27g carbohydrate (3g fiber, 12g sugar); 4g protein; 110mg sodium; 6% Daily Value (DV) vitamin C; 2% DV calcium; 8% DV iron

---

Kids can shred zucchini and spoon mixture into muffin cups.

Sweet Potato Pancakes

These sweet potato pancakes are delicious *and* nutritious! Sweet potatoes are an excellent source of beta-carotene (vitamin A), which keeps your eyesight laser sharp. Made with whole wheat flour and milk, these pancakes are a good source of fiber and bone-building calcium. They're a top "game day" pick for athletes because they provide a perfect balance of protein, healthy fat, and whole grains. Go team!

ingredients

1 medium sweet potato
(10–12 ounces)

1 cup whole wheat flour

¼ cup walnuts or whatever nut you like, chopped (optional)

3 tablespoons cornmeal

3 tablespoons packed brown sugar

1 tablespoon baking powder

1 teaspoon ground cinnamon

¼ teaspoon sea salt

1⅓ cups low-fat (1%) milk

1 tablespoon canola oil

½ teaspoon vanilla extract

2 large eggs, separated

Maple syrup or agave nectar

Nutrition Facts per serving (pancakes only): 170 calories; 6g fat (1g sat fat, 2g mono, 2g poly, 0g trans fat); 45mg cholesterol; 25g carbohydrate (3g fiber, 7g sugar); 6g protein; 240mg sodium; 50% Daily Value (DV) vitamin A; 4% DV vitamin C; 10% DV calcium; 8% DV iron

---

directions

1. Pierce the sweet potato with a fork in several places. Place potato on a paper towel in a microwave oven. Cook on high for 3–4 minutes or until fork-tender, turning the potato over once halfway through cooking. (Or, preheat oven to 450°F. Pierce potato with fork; place on oven rack and bake for 45 minutes or until fork-tender.) Cool potato until easy to handle.

2. Scoop out cooled sweet potato from skin and place in a small bowl; set aside.

3. In a large bowl, stir together flour, walnuts (if using), cornmeal, brown sugar, baking powder, cinnamon, and salt. In a medium bowl, whisk together sweet potato, milk, oil, vanilla, and egg yolks. In a small bowl, whisk egg whites until foamy.

4. Add the sweet potato mixture to dry ingredients and stir until blended. Fold egg whites into the batter.

5. Heat a nonstick griddle or large nonstick skillet over medium heat until hot. Pour batter onto a hot griddle or skillet using a ¼-cup measure.

6. Cook pancakes until bubbles form on top, about 5 minutes. Turn over and cook a few minutes longer or until underside is golden. Transfer to a plate; keep warm. Repeat until all batter is used.

7. Serve hot with maple syrup or agave nectar.

Makes 9 servings (2 pancakes per serving)

Kids can crack and separate eggs, and can flip pancakes with adult supervision.

Whole-Grain Breakfast Cookies

We mixed whole grains and other yummy ingredients to make a natural, low-fat, high-fiber cookie that you can eat for breakfast and as a snack. This filling treat is a great way to begin your day, plus these cookies are a good source of iron, one mineral that most kids don't get enough of in their daily diets.

ingredients

1 cup whole wheat flour

¼ cup ground flaxseeds

1 tablespoon ground cinnamon

1 teaspoon baking soda

¼ teaspoon sea salt

2 large eggs

1 cup vanilla low-fat yogurt

¼ cup agave nectar

1 teaspoon vanilla extract

1 cup old-fashioned oats

1 cup whole-grain cereal
  (We used Cheerios for
  the nutrition analysis.)

¼ cup raisins

directions

1. Preheat oven to 350°F.

2. In a large bowl, stir together flour, flaxseeds, cinnamon, baking soda, and salt. Add eggs, yogurt, agave nectar, and vanilla. Stir until well blended. Stir in oats, cereal, and raisins. Mix until blended.

3. Drop dough by ¼ cup onto a nonstick or greased baking sheet, about 4 inches apart (they will spread out). Flatten slightly and form into 4-inch rounds.

4. Bake for 10–12 minutes or until browned. Cool on a wire rack. If not serving immediately, store in an airtight container for up to three days.

Makes 12 servings (1 cookie per serving)

Nutrition Facts per serving: 150 calories; 3g fat (0g sat fat, 1g mono, 1g poly, 0g trans fat); 30mg cholesterol; 25g carbohydrate (3g fiber, 9g sugar); 6g protein; 160mg sodium; 2% Daily Value (DV) vitamin A; 2% DV vitamin C; 6% DV calcium; 10% DV iron

Kids can crack eggs and spoon mixture onto baking sheet.

Sweet Berry Polenta

This creamy and colorful dish is a breakfast favorite at the barn. It will satisfy a sweet tooth and kick-start your morning with whole grains for fiber, a super boost of vitamin C to protect your immune system, calcium to keep your bones and teeth strong, and iron to keep your blood and muscles healthy.

ingredients

1½ cups low-fat (1%) milk

1½ cups water

½ teaspoon ground cinnamon

⅛ teaspoon sea salt

1 cup polenta or cornmeal

1½ tablespoons agave nectar

1 pint strawberries, cut into quarters

directions

1. In a medium saucepan, heat milk, water, cinnamon, and salt to boiling over medium heat. Reduce heat to low and slowly whisk in polenta until smooth. Cook on low heat 5 minutes or until very thick, stirring frequently.

2. Remove from heat and stir in agave nectar and strawberries. Serve warm, topped with more milk if you like.

Makes 5 servings (1 cup per serving)

Nutrition Facts per serving: 180 calories; 1.5g fat (0g sat fat, 1g mono, 0g trans fat); 5mg cholesterol; 36g carbohydrate (3g fiber, 12g sugar); 6g protein; 55mg sodium; 4% Daily Value (DV) vitamin A; 70% DV vitamin C; 10% DV calcium; 10% DV iron

Kids can whisk polenta and quarter strawberries using plastic knives with adult supervision.

Mini Potato Leek Frittata

Eggs aren't just for breakfast anymore. These little frittatas have a big taste and are more than a Sunday morning favorite; leftovers (if you have any) are great for lunch and dinner any day of the week. Savor our seasonal combination of veggies, herbs, and cheese and boost your immune system with vitamin C at the same time.

ingredients

½ pound baby Yukon Gold potatoes or whatever baby potato you like, unpeeled

¼ teaspoon sea salt, divided

2 medium leeks (1 pound), tough green tops trimmed

1 tablespoon olive oil

3 large eggs

10 large egg whites

½ cup low-fat (1%) milk

⅛ teaspoon freshly ground black pepper

⅓ cup shredded low-fat Swiss cheese (1.5 ounces)

1 tablespoon chopped fresh parsley leaves

1 tablespoon chopped fresh chives

Nutrition Facts per serving:
80 calories; 2.5g fat (0.5g sat fat, 1g mono, 0g trans fat); 50mg cholesterol; 6g carbohydrate (1g fiber, 2g sugar); 6g protein; 90mg sodium; 8% Daily Value (DV) vitamin A; 10% DV vitamin C; 6% DV calcium; 4% DV iron

directions

1. Preheat oven to 375°F. Grease 12 muffin cups.

2. Cut potatoes into ½-inch chunks. In a medium saucepan, place potatoes, ⅛ teaspoon salt, and enough water to cover; heat to boiling over high heat. Reduce heat to medium and cook for about 10 minutes to partially cook potatoes (a fork should be able to go through them). Drain potatoes in a colander and set aside to cool.

3. Cut leeks lengthwise in half and clean thoroughly under cold running water. Pat dry, then slice crosswise into ¼-inch slices. In a medium skillet, heat olive oil over medium-low heat; add leeks and cook until fragrant and wilted, about 10 minutes, stirring occasionally. Remove from heat; cool.

4. Into a large bowl, carefully crack eggs. Add egg whites, milk, pepper, and remaining ⅛ teaspoon salt, and whisk until mixed. Add cooled leeks, potatoes, cheese, and herbs and fold ingredients together until combined.

5. Ladle the frittata mixture evenly into prepared muffin cups (filling will come almost to the top). Set the pan in the middle of the oven. Bake for 14–16 minutes or until egg mixture puffs up and knife inserted in frittatas comes out clean. Cool for 1 minute then loosen edges of frittata with a sharp knife and scoop them out of the pan one by one. (They will deflate somewhat after cooling.)

6. Serve the frittatas warm or at room temperature.

Makes 12 servings (1 frittata per serving)

Kids can crack and separate eggs and can chop leeks and herbs using a plastic knife with adult supervision.

Carrot Cake Muffins

Who doesn't love a great-tasting carrot cake? This grab-and-go muffin captures that classic flavor in a perfect serving size, and it's low in fat. It's made with fiber-packed whole wheat flour; flaxseeds that are high in healthy omega-3 fatty acids; and carrots loaded with vitamin A to boost the immune system and fight illness and disease. It's also a good source of vitamin C.

ingredients

1 cup whole wheat flour

1 cup unbleached all-purpose flour

⅓ cup packed brown sugar

¼ cup ground flaxseeds

1 tablespoon ground cinnamon

¼ teaspoon grated nutmeg

1 teaspoon baking powder

½ teaspoon baking soda

¼ teaspoon sea salt

1 large egg

¾ cup calcium-fortified orange juice

½ cup unsweetened applesauce

½ teaspoon vanilla extract

1½ cups shredded carrots
  (about 3 carrots)

½ cup raisins

directions

1. Preheat oven to 350°F. Line 12 muffin cups with paper liners.

2. In a large bowl, combine flours, brown sugar, flaxseeds, cinnamon, nutmeg, baking powder, baking soda, and salt; stir to mix.

3. Add the egg, orange juice, applesauce, and vanilla and mix thoroughly. Fold in carrots and raisins until blended.

4. Spoon the batter evenly into prepared muffin cups. Bake for 18–20 minutes or until tops of muffins are browned.

5. When muffins are finished baking, cool on a wire rack before serving.

Makes 12 servings (1 muffin per serving)

Nutrition Facts per serving: 150 calories; 1.5g fat (0g sat fat, 1g poly, 0g trans fat); 15mg cholesterol; 30g carbohydrate (3g fiber, 12g sugar); 4g protein; 125mg sodium; 45% Daily Value (DV) vitamin A; 10% DV vitamin C; 6% DV calcium; 8% DV iron

---

Kids can shred carrots and spoon mixture into muffin cups.

Maple Walnut Oatmeal

Set the alarm clock fifteen minutes earlier because this breakfast is worth lingering over. Its great-tasting whole grains are an excellent source of soluble heart-healthy fiber and protein, and you'll love the natural energy boost delivered by the sugar in its apples and maple syrup. The walnuts are a bonus because they contain healthy omega-3 fatty acids, protein, and iron to help build muscles.

ingredients

3½ cups water

2 cups old-fashioned oats

1 medium green apple, cored and chopped

½ cup walnuts, coarsely chopped

3 tablespoons pure maple syrup

½ teaspoon ground cinnamon

directions

1. In a medium saucepan, heat water over medium heat to simmering.

2. Stir in oats; bring to a boil. Reduce heat to low and simmer for 8–10 minutes, stirring occasionally.

3. Remove from heat and stir in apple, walnuts, maple syrup, and cinnamon.

4. Cover and let stand 3 minutes to allow flavors to combine. Serve warm, topped with low-fat (1%) milk and extra maple syrup if you like.

Makes 5 servings (1 cup per serving)

Nutrition Facts per serving: 250 calories; 10g fat (0.5g sat fat, 2g mono, 6g poly, 0g trans fat); 0mg cholesterol; 35g carbohydrate (5g fiber, 11g sugar); 7g protein; 10mg sodium; 2% Daily Value (DV) vitamin C; 4% DV calcium; 10% DV iron

Kids can chop apples using a plastic knife with adult supervision.

Rainbow Swirly Smoothie

The Rainbow Swirly Smoothie was created at HealthBarn USA for kids by kids! It's so easy, refreshing, and vitamin-packed that parents love it too. Blend this yummy smoothie for breakfast or share it with friends for a high-energy after-school snack. It's loaded with vitamin C to help keep your body running strong, it's a good source of calcium, and it has fiber to keep your digestive system regular. Drink up!

ingredients

1½ cups frozen strawberries (can substitute frozen blueberries or raspberries)

1 banana, cut in half

1 cup vanilla low-fat yogurt

¾ cup calcium-fortified orange juice

2 tablespoons ground flaxseeds

1 teaspoon honey

directions

1. Place all ingredients in blender; blend until smooth.
2. Pour into glasses and serve.

Makes 4 servings (1 cup per serving)

Nutrition Facts per serving: 120 calories; 2.5g total fat (0.5g sat fat, 1g poly, 0g trans fat); 5mg cholesterol; 22g carbohydrate (3g fiber, 12g sugar); 4g protein; 40mg sodium; 4% Daily Value (DV) vitamin A; 70% DV vitamin C; 15% DV calcium; 2% DV iron

---

Kids can add ingredients into blender and blend.

Homemade Vs. Store-Bought: The Facts!

HealthBarn USA's Rainbow Swirly Smoothie	McDonald's McCafé Strawberry Banana Real Fruit Smoothie (12 oz) Reference: www.mcdonalds.com
Ingredients: Frozen strawberries, banana, vanilla low-fat yogurt, calcium-fortified orange juice, flaxseeds, honey	**Ingredients:** Strawberry puree, banana puree, water, grape juice concentrate, clarified demineralized pineapple juice concentrate, sugar, low-fat yogurt (cultured grade A reduced-fat milk, sugar, whey protein concentrate, fructose, cornstarch, gelatin, contains active yogurt cultures), ice, contains less than 1% of the following: cellulose powder, natural (botanical source) and artificial flavors, pear juice concentrate, peach juice concentrate, xanthan gum, citric acid, colored with fruit and vegetable juice, pectin, ascorbic acid (preservative)
Nutrition Facts (per serving): 120 calories; 2.5g total fat (0.5g sat fat, 1g poly, 0g trans fat); 5mg cholesterol; 22g carbohydrate (3g fiber, 12g sugar); 4g protein; 40mg sodium; 4% Daily Value (DV) vitamin A; 70% DV vitamin C; 15% DV calcium; 2% DV iron	**Nutrition Facts** (per serving): 210 calories; 0.5g fat (0g sat fat, 0g trans fat); 5mg cholesterol; 49g carbohydrate (2g fiber, 44g sugar); 2g protein; 35mg sodium; 2% Daily Value (DV) vitamin A; 70% DV vitamin C; 8% DV calcium; 6% DV iron
OURS: • 6 ingredients	**THEIRS:** • 24 ingredients • contains artificial flavors

Crunchy Granola with Walnuts

Why buy granola in a box when this homemade mixture tastes better and is so easy to make? We lowered the fat content of traditional granola and still kept the great taste. We chose oats, a whole-grain base, and added flaxseeds and walnuts for healthy polyunsaturated fats and omega-3 fatty acids. We gave it a naturally sweet taste by finishing it with agave nectar and raisins. We bake this versatile granola in large quantities because it stores easily, and because we use it in our Yogurt Sundaes (page 176), Apple Crisp (page 237), and Raspberry Crumble (page 236) recipes.

ingredients

3 cups old-fashioned oats

⅓ cup ground flaxseeds

⅓ cup hulled raw sunflower seeds

¼ cup walnuts, chopped (optional)

1 tablespoon ground cinnamon

½ cup agave nectar

¼ cup sunflower oil

1 tablespoon vanilla extract

½ cup raisins or dried cranberries

directions

1. Preheat oven to 350°F.

2. In a large bowl, combine oats, flaxseeds, sunflower seeds, walnuts (if using), and cinnamon.

3. Add agave nectar, oil, and vanilla, and stir to mix thoroughly.

4. Spread the mixture onto a rimmed baking sheet and bake for 25–35 minutes or until lightly browned, stirring about every 5–10 minutes to make sure it cooks evenly.

5. Cool completely in pan. When cool, stir in raisins or cranberries. Store in tightly sealed container for up to 2 weeks or freeze to last longer.

Makes 20 servings (½ cup per serving)

Nutrition Facts per serving: 140 calories; 6g fat (1g sat fat, 1g mono, 3g poly, 0g trans fat); 0mg cholesterol; 19g carbohydrate (2g fiber, 10g sugar); 3g protein; 0mg sodium; 2% Daily Value (DV) calcium; 6% DV iron

Kids can measure ingredients and mix.

PB&J Muffins

If you like good old-fashioned peanut butter and jelly sandwiches, then you'll *love* these yummy whole-grain muffins! We used buckwheat flour (a rich source of disease-fighting flavonoids), natural creamy peanut butter, and instead of sugar-packed jelly, fruit spread (fruit must be listed as the first ingredient on the label). The result is a muffin that makes a nutritious, on-the-go, energy-packed breakfast or after-school snack. If nut allergies are a concern, use SunButter (made with sunflower seeds) instead of peanut butter and enjoy a new flavor.

ingredients

1½ cups buckwheat flour

⅓ cup packed brown sugar

2 tablespoons ground flaxseeds

1 tablespoon baking powder

¼ teaspoon sea salt

1 cup low-fat (1%) milk

½ cup vanilla low-fat yogurt

½ cup natural creamy peanut butter

1 tablespoon vanilla extract

1 large egg

¼ cup fruit spread

directions

1. Preheat oven to 400°F. Line 12 muffin cups with paper liners.

2. In a large bowl, stir together buckwheat flour, brown sugar, flaxseeds, baking powder, and salt. Add milk, yogurt, peanut butter, vanilla, and egg. Stir until blended.

3. Spoon batter into prepared muffin cups, filling each about ⅔ full. Spoon 1 teaspoon fruit spread onto batter in each cup. Spoon remaining batter on top to cover fruit spread.

4. Bake for 18–20 minutes or until tops of muffins are lightly browned. Cool on a wire rack.

Makes 12 servings (1 muffin per serving)

Nutrition Facts per serving: 180 calories; 7g fat (1g sat fat, 4g mono, 2g poly, 0g trans fat); 15mg cholesterol; 21g carbohydrate (3g fiber, 11g sugar); 6g protein; 210mg sodium; 2% Daily Value (DV) vitamin A; 6% DV calcium; 4% DV iron

Kids can spoon batter and add fruit spread to muffin cups.

Berrilicious Risotto

This berry-packed and very delicious take on creamy risotto will lure you out of bed and keep your digestive system regular because it's a good source of fiber. We added a lot of berries, which are high in antioxidants, and agave nectar to sweeten it up—the perfect weekend treat for the whole family. With flaxseed oil as a finishing touch, we made sure it was heart healthy too!

ingredients

5 cups water

1 cup arborio rice

1 cup enriched original rice milk

2 tablespoons agave nectar

2 tablespoons flaxseed oil

2 teaspoons vanilla extract

1 cup raspberries

1 cup strawberries, sliced

¼ teaspoon ground cinnamon

directions

1. In a medium saucepan, heat water to boiling over high heat. Reduce heat to low; keep warm.

2. In a large skillet, combine rice, rice milk, and agave nectar and cook over medium heat for 1 minute, stirring. Increase heat to medium-high and stir in 1 cup simmering water. Cook, uncovered, stirring frequently, until water is absorbed. Continue stirring and adding water, 1 cup at a time, and allowing each cup to be absorbed before adding another.

3. Cook until rice is tender and mixture has a creamy consistency, about 25–30 minutes, stirring frequently.

4. Remove from heat and stir in flaxseed oil and vanilla, then raspberries and strawberries. Sprinkle cinnamon on top as the final touch.

5. Serve warm.

Makes 5 servings (1 cup per serving)

Nutrition Facts per serving: 260 calories; 7g fat (0.5g sat fat, 2g mono, 4g poly, 0g trans fat); 0mg cholesterol; 48g carbohydrate (4g fiber, 12g sugar); 4g protein; 30mg sodium; 2% Daily Value (DV) vitamin A; 45% DV vitamin C; 8% DV calcium; 2% DV iron

Kids can slice strawberries using a plastic knife and stir risotto with adult supervision.

Zucchini Muffins

We wouldn't dream of wasting a bit of the zucchini we grow, so here's another way to bake it into a tasty low-fat breakfast. You'll get a head start on your nutrition, as these muffins are a good source of vitamin C and fiber. And we added ground flaxseeds to give your brain an omega-3 jump start!

ingredients

1 cup buckwheat flour

½ cup unbleached all-purpose flour

½ cup old-fashioned oats

¼ cup ground flaxseeds

1 tablespoon ground cinnamon

1 teaspoon baking soda

¼ teaspoon sea salt

1 large egg

1 cup plain nonfat Greek yogurt

½ cup packed brown sugar

1 tablespoon vanilla extract

2 large zucchini (12–14 ounces each), shredded

directions

1. Preheat oven to 350°F. Line 12 muffin cups with paper liners.

2. In a large bowl, stir together flours, oats, flaxseeds, cinnamon, baking soda, and salt. In a medium bowl, beat egg, yogurt, brown sugar, and vanilla until blended.

3. Add wet ingredients and zucchini to the flour mixture and stir until just mixed. Do not overmix.

4. Spoon batter evenly into prepared muffin cups.

5. Bake for 18–20 minutes or until tops of muffins are browned. Cool muffins on a wire rack.

Makes 12 servings (1 muffin per serving)

Nutrition Facts per serving: 140 calories; 2g fat (0g sat fat, 1g poly, 0g trans fat); 15mg cholesterol; 23g carbohydrate (3g fiber, 11g sugar); 6g protein; 140mg sodium; 2% Daily Value (DV) vitamin A; 10% DV vitamin C; 6% DV calcium; 8% DV iron

---

Kids can shred zucchini and spoon mixture into muffin cups.

Blueberry Buckwheat Pancakes

Here's your new favorite pancake recipe. We used buckwheat flour because it's a rich source of flavonoids and fiber, and we added ground flaxseeds to provide omega-3 fatty acids. The antioxidant-packed blueberries are a seasonal fruit, so if it's the off-season, use frozen, or try a cup of pure pumpkin instead, for a comparable antioxidant boost. Drizzle with 100% pure maple syrup or agave nectar, and your white-flour-only pancake lover will definitely make the switch.

ingredients

⅔ cup buckwheat flour

⅓ cup cornmeal

3 tablespoons packed brown sugar

2 tablespoons ground flaxseeds

1½ teaspoons baking powder

1 teaspoon ground cinnamon

½ teaspoon baking soda

⅛ teaspoon sea salt

1 large egg

2 large egg whites

1½ cups low-fat (1%) milk

½ teaspoon vanilla extract

1 cup blueberries

Maple syrup or agave nectar

directions

1. In a large bowl, stir together flour, cornmeal, brown sugar, flaxseeds, baking powder, cinnamon, baking soda, and salt.

2. Add egg, egg whites, milk, and vanilla to flour mixture, and stir until moistened. Add blueberries and stir until blended.

3. Heat a nonstick griddle or large nonstick skillet over medium heat until hot. Pour batter by ¼ cup onto the hot griddle or skillet. Cook pancakes until bubbles form on top, about 4 minutes. Turn over and cook a few minutes longer, until underside is golden. Transfer pancakes to a plate; keep warm. Repeat until all batter is used.

4. Serve with pure maple syrup or agave nectar.

Makes 6 servings (2 pancakes per serving)

Nutrition Facts per serving: 170 calories; 3g fat (0.5g sat fat, 1g mono, 1g poly, 0g trans fat); 35mg cholesterol; 28g carbohydrate (4g fiber, 12g sugar); 7g protein; 320mg sodium; 4% Daily Value (DV) vitamin A; 4% DV vitamin C; 10% DV calcium; 6% DV iron

---

Kids can crack and separate eggs and flip pancakes with adult supervision.

Homemade Vs. Store-Bought: The Facts!

HealthBarn USA's Blueberry Buckwheat Pancakes	Aunt Jemima Frozen Blueberry Pancakes Reference: product package
Ingredients: Buckwheat flour, cornmeal, brown sugar, flaxseeds, baking powder, cinnamon, baking soda, sea salt, eggs, low-fat milk, vanilla, blueberries	**Ingredients:** Enriched wheat flour (flour, niacin [vitamin B3], reduced iron, thiamine mononitrate [vitamin B1], riboflavin [vitamin B2], folic acid [vitamin B9]), water, sugar, blueberry bits (sugar, dextrose, soybean oil, soy protein, dried blueberries, natural flavor, cellulose gum, salt, carrot juice extract [color], blueberry extract [color]), whole eggs, soybean oil, nonfat milk, contains 2% or less of: salt, blueberry puree, baking powder (baking soda, sodium aluminum phosphate), cornstarch, vanilla extract
Nutrition Facts (per serving): 170 calories; 3g fat (0.5g sat fat, 1g mono, 1g poly, 0g trans fat); 35mg cholesterol; 28g carbohydrate (4g fiber, 12g sugar); 7g protein; 320mg sodium; 4% Daily Value (DV) vitamin A; 4% DV vitamin C; 10% DV calcium; 6% DV iron	**Nutrition Facts** (per serving): 260 calories; 6g fat (1g sat fat, 0g trans fat); 25mg cholesterol; 44g carbohydrate (1g fiber, 13g sugar); 7g protein; 460mg sodium; 6% Daily Value (DV) calcium; 10% DV iron
OURS: • 12 ingredients • contains whole blueberries	**THEIRS:** • 27 ingredients • contains processed blueberry bits, with their first ingredient being sugar

Simply Crepes

Kids love making and eating these low-fat, whole-grain crepes as an alternative to bread. Do what we do at the barn: declare it "Crepe Day" and triple the recipe because you'll use these for our Creamy Berry Crepes (page 59) or Salmon and Swiss Cheese Crepes (page 60) for breakfast; Moo Shu Chicken (page 212) for dinner; and Chocolate Banana Crepes (page 239) for dessert. If you don't work your way through the whole batch in one day, refrigerate or freeze the extras!

ingredients

½ cup whole wheat flour

½ cup unbleached all-purpose flour

¼ teaspoon sea salt

6 large egg whites

1 large egg

1 cup low-fat (1%) milk

½ cup water

directions

1. In a large bowl, stir together flours and salt. In a small bowl, whisk egg whites and whole egg. Whisk eggs, milk, and water into flour mixture until well blended.

2. Heat a 10-inch nonstick skillet over medium heat. Ladle ¼ cup of batter into skillet and immediately tilt skillet to coat bottom completely with batter. Crepe should be very thin. Cook crepe until top is set and underside is lightly browned, about 1½ minutes. Turn crepe over and cook for 30 seconds longer or until underside is golden. Transfer crepe to waxed paper. Don't worry if your first crepe is not a success—often the pan is not quite ready. Simply discard and try again.

3. Repeat with remaining batter, stacking crepes between layers of waxed paper. (Crepes can be made ahead; wrap stack tightly in plastic wrap and refrigerate for up to 1 week or freeze for up to 1 month. When ready to use, let wrapped crepes stand at room temperature for 1 hour.)

Makes 12 servings (1 crepe per serving)

Nutrition Facts per serving: 60 calories; 1g fat (0g sat fat, 1g mono, 0g trans fat); 15mg cholesterol; 9g carbohydrate (1g fiber, 1g sugar); 4g protein; 55mg sodium; 2% Daily Value (DV) vitamin A; 4% DV calcium; 4% DV iron

Kids can crack and separate eggs and flip crepes with adult supervision.

Creamy Berry Crepes

These crepes are the real breakfast of champions. They are fun to make and eat and are high in muscle-building protein and loaded with bone-building calcium. Flex those biceps as you grip your pan to make extra crepes, because these go fast at the breakfast table.

ingredients

1 recipe Simply Crepes (page 58)

1 cup plus 2 tablespoons plain nonfat Greek yogurt

1 cup blueberries (or substitute with strawberries or raspberries)

2 tablespoons agave nectar

1½ teaspoons ground cinnamon

directions

1. Spread half of each crepe with 1½ tablespoons yogurt. Top yogurt with 1 heaping tablespoon blueberries, ½ teaspoon agave nectar, and ⅛ teaspoon cinnamon.

2. Fold unfilled side of each crepe over filling, then fold over again, making a triangle.

3. Repeat with remaining ingredients to make 12 crepes in all.

Makes 6 servings (2 crepes per serving)

***

Nutrition Facts per serving: 190 calories; 1.5g fat (0.5g sat fat, 1g mono, 0g trans fat); 35mg cholesterol; 30g carbohydrate (2g fiber, 12g sugar); 13g protein; 130mg sodium; 2% Daily Value (DV) vitamin A; 4% DV vitamin C; 15% DV calcium; 8% DV iron

***

Kids can fill crepes, drizzle agave, sprinkle cinnamon, and fold.

Salmon and Swiss Cheese Crepes

Move over Julia Child! We have cooked up a super crepe loaded with protein, calcium, and omega-3 fatty acids! The flavor is so good that it's hard to stop at one crepe or limit them to breakfast. Enjoy them for lunch and dinner too.

ingredients

9 ounces Steamed Salmon Pouches (page 213)

1 recipe Simply Crepes (page 58)

1½ cups shredded low-fat Swiss cheese (6 ounces)

directions

1. Prepare Steamed Salmon Pouches as recipe directs, then flake 3 pieces with a fork (reserve remaining piece for another day). Start crepes while salmon is cooking.

2. Prepare Simply Crepes as recipe directs.

3. In the same skillet used to cook the crepes, over medium heat, place 1 crepe; top half of it with 2 heaping tablespoons of the flaked salmon and 2 tablespoons of cheese. Once the cheese starts to melt, fold unfilled side of crepe over filling, then fold in half again, making a triangle. Flip crepe over; heat through, about 1 minute. Transfer filled crepe to platter; keep warm.

4. Repeat for all crepes and serve while warm.

Makes 12 servings (1 crepe per serving)

Nutrition Facts per serving: 120 calories; 3g fat (1g sat fat, 1g mono, 1g poly, 0g trans fat); 30mg cholesterol; 10g carbohydrate (1g fiber, 2g sugar); 12g protein; 115mg sodium; 2% Daily Value (DV) vitamin A; 2% DV vitamin C; 15% DV calcium; 6% DV iron

Kids can stuff crepes and fold and flip on griddle with adult supervision.

Farm-Fresh Omelet

If you haven't had a tasty farm-fresh egg, you are really missing out. Egg whites are a complete protein and kids will have fun getting some exercise by whisking them to be super fluffy. We added fresh spinach and parsley from the garden for some greens. Next time you're at the farmers' market, look for eggs!

ingredients

2 large egg whites

1 tablespoon low-fat (1%) milk

1 tablespoon chopped baby spinach

½ tablespoon 50% reduced-fat cheddar cheese, shredded

½ teaspoon chopped fresh parsley leaves

directions

1. In a small bowl, whisk egg whites and milk until well blended. Fold the spinach, cheese, and parsley into the egg mixture.

2. Heat a small nonstick skillet over medium heat. Pour the egg mixture into the skillet and cook for 1–2 minutes or until liquid sets, lifting edges of egg mixture to allow uncooked portion to run underneath. Fold one side of the omelet over to meet the center, then fold the opposite side over the first side to create a trifold. Slide onto a plate to serve.

Makes 1 serving (1 omelet per serving)

Nutrition Facts per serving: 50 calories; 1g fat (0.5g sat fat, 0.5g mono, 0g trans fat); 5mg cholesterol; 2g carbohydrate (0g fiber, 1g sugar); 9g protein; 140mg sodium; 4% Daily Value (DV) vitamin A; 2% DV vitamin C; 6% DV calcium.

Kids can crack, separate, and whisk eggs, shred cheese, and chop spinach and parsley using a plastic knife with adult supervision.

Raspberry Muffins

We love to pick and eat fresh raspberries from the garden, and you will too if you decide to grow your own. These little berries are high in antioxidants that boost the immune system to protect us from getting sick. Don't forget your seasonal food knowledge—if they're not in season, substitute frozen. These muffins contain healthy fats and are a good source of fiber too.

ingredients

1 cup whole wheat flour

½ cup unbleached all-purpose flour

¼ cup ground flaxseeds

1 teaspoon baking soda

1 teaspoon baking powder

¼ teaspoon sea salt

1 cup unsweetened applesauce

½ cup low-fat (1%) milk

¼ cup agave nectar

2 tablespoons canola oil

1 teaspoon vanilla extract

1 cup raspberries, halved

1 tablespoon granulated
   brown sugar

1 teaspoon ground cinnamon

directions

1. Preheat oven to 350°F. Line 12 muffin cups with paper liners.

2. In a large bowl, stir together flours, flaxseeds, baking soda, baking powder, and salt. In a small bowl, use a fork to mix the applesauce, milk, agave nectar, oil, and vanilla until blended. Add wet ingredients to flour mixture and stir just until mixed. Do not overmix. Fold raspberries into batter.

3. Spoon batter evenly into prepared muffin cups.

4. In a cup, mix brown sugar and cinnamon; sprinkle on top of muffins.

5. Bake muffins for 20–25 minutes or until a toothpick inserted in the center of muffins comes out clean. Cool on a wire rack.

Makes 12 muffins (1 muffin per serving)

Nutrition Facts per serving: 140 calories; 4g total fat (0g sat fat, 2g mono, 2g poly, 0g trans fat); 0mg cholesterol; 24g carbohydrate (3g fiber, 9g sugar); 3g protein; 170mg sodium; 6% Daily Value (DV) vitamin C; 4% DV calcium; 6% DV iron

---

Kids can measure and mix ingredients, halve raspberries using a plastic knife with adult supervision, and spoon mixture into muffin cups.

CHAPTER 3

Snacking Outside the Box: Healthy Morning Munchies

RECIPES

Younger kids generally wake up early and pack a lot of action into their day between breakfast and lunch—which is why they're usually hungry and ready for more fuel by the time you're considering a second cup of coffee. Whether a child is still being cared for at home or in day care, or has started attending a full day of school, a quality morning snack is a must for most kids.

At most preschools, morning snacks are a part of the day's routine, just like time on the swings or in the sandbox. Parents sometimes provide the snack, or the school may do so—often the classic "juice and crackers" combo. The idea is that a small amount of food is probably enough to tide over the average three-year-old until lunch.

But when children move up to kindergarten and first grade, they face a longer, more demanding day. In recent years, many schools have recognized that students will be more focused and perform better in class if their energy levels are consistent and their stomachs aren't growling. Though a good breakfast will take care of their main morning energy needs, many schools now allow and encourage kids to bring a "healthy snack" from home that they can consume mid-morning quickly and without a lot of fuss.

Kids and snacks go together like peanut butter and jelly, and food manufacturers have taken note. Companies have targeted the youthful snack market with their 100-calorie "snack packs" of just about everything, with a focus on items like miniaturized versions of bestselling crackers (teeny, tiny Ritz) and cookies (bite-size Oreos). But whether we're talking about creatively marketed individual servings or their whole-package counterparts, these items are rarely nutritious, and the empty carbohydrates they contain won't stave off the hunger pangs of the average six-year-old, much less a growing adolescent.

There was a time when the word "snack" meant "junk" because snacks were often not much more than chips, cookies, and the like (what many of those 100-calorie snack packs contain). The old-school rule of "No snacking between meals!" made some sense, because if the snacks were junk, then there was no reason to eat them. But healthy eaters have always known that healthy snacking—small amounts of well-chosen, satisfying, *real* food from natural ingredients that offer energy and help prevent overeating at the next scheduled meal—has a natural place within a healthy lifestyle. This is especially true for growing kids.

One of the top questions I get from parents at HealthBarn USA is, "What *is* a healthy snack?" Rarely, as you're about to see, will you find the answer to that question in a bag or box! But you and your family will find a bounty of great-tasting answers—portable, nutritious, and delicious options for morning snacks—when you approach smart snacking the way we do at HealthBarn USA.

Giving up the convenience of packaged foods isn't easy if it's the default way of shopping and eating in your house, but it can be done, snack by snack. Take a moment and visualize the contents of your pantry (or go open the cabinets right now), and come up with a ratio of whole foods to processed foods. What percentage is reflected in your kitchen? Is it evenly split, 50/50? Or do you have more processed foods, so that it's more like 30/70? Wherever you fall on this scale, if half or more of your food is packaged and processed, try this: set a goal to move the needle in favor of whole foods by about 20 percentage points over the next few months, and you will dramatically improve the health of the whole family.

The recipes and suggestions here will open your eyes to many delicious whole-food options. And here's an added benefit: when you move your family away from processed foods for snack choices, the same healthy shift will naturally take hold at breakfast, lunch, and dinner.

The First Step in Smart Snacking: Choosing Natural over Artificial Ingredients

It's so simple that it's almost easy to forget. Natural foods come from nature—from the ground or from an animal. Artificial foods come from factories and are man-made. If a food is not made from natural ingredients, then it's artificial and generally not beneficial to the health of a child or an adult. Natural, unprocessed, whole foods contain the essential vitamins and minerals a growing child needs, but artificially flavored and colored snacks have little to offer other than wasteful packaging.

Man-made ingredients and additives like partially hydrogenated vegetable oils, high-fructose corn syrup, and artificial food colorings and flavorings do little to our food except add empty calories. Partially hydrogenated vegetable oils, for instance, may extend the shelf life of a cracker or cookie and may keep it crunchy, but the hydrogenation process (adding hydrogen to vegetable oil so that it takes on a semisolid form, like stick margarine) makes trans fats, which contribute to heart disease, high cholesterol, and obesity. Artificial sweeteners like aspartame and saccharin have been linked to cancer.*

---

* For a detailed list of food additives and their impact on health, see the CSPI's "Chemical Cuisine: Learn About Food Additives," Nutrition Action Health Letter (May 2008), available online at www.cspinet.org/reports/chemcuisine.htm.

Of course, the importance of this differentiation between artificial and natural isn't limited to our kids' snack foods. But when it comes to snack foods, we find a profusion of conveniently packaged products disguised as healthy alternatives, products that contain more artificial ingredients than real ones. Snacks such as granola bars, dried fruit snacks, juice, yogurt, trail mix, muffins, and graham crackers may seem like they would be superior to chips or candy, but a closer look at the ingredients lists on many of these "healthy" foods tells another story. A few examples of what these items may contain:

✦ The yogurt that comes in a tube contains artificial food dyes to make it pink, high-fructose corn syrup, and only a small amount of calcium. It doesn't contain live and active cultures, the good bacteria that keep the digestive tract in tip-top shape.

✦ The graham crackers are made with refined flour, chemical preservatives, and partially hydrogenated fats (trans fats) to extend shelf life. If the serving size for the food item contains 0.5g or less of trans fat, then the manufacturer can state "0g trans fat" in the nutrition facts and on the front panel. But if you eat more than one serving of the food, you are certainly getting trans fats in your diet, and they have been proven to cause heart disease.

✦ The granola bars have so much added sugar that your child might be better off with a Snickers bar.

✦ The juice is usually a "juice beverage" or "juice drink," with only a small percentage of *real* juice—not much better than artificially flavored sugar water or a can of soda.

It's time to stop looking at our food—in this case, the "healthy" snack foods that make so many claims—from the *outside,* including the packaging that surrounds it, and start looking at what's *inside.* (For further discussion of some of the claims made on food packages, see the box on page 72, "Can You Believe Everything You Read?") At HealthBarn USA, I teach families to go beyond the buzz words on the front of the package—including phrases like "all-natural"—and even the nutrition facts, which are not as revealing as the information you'll find in the ingredients list.

A product's ingredients list is the only place on the packaging where manufacturers are legally bound to itemize what is in the product. They must list the contents in order of predominance, which means that the first ingredient is the main one and the remaining ingredients are listed in descending order based on the amount used (the last ingredient being the least in terms of content). This is not marketing; this is fact. The ingredients list is where you'll read the true story of what's in your food and learn how natural (or artificial) it really is.*

I want to help you and your children become more aware of the differences between natural and artificial foods, a distinction that is often hard to see when we're faced with so many confusing choices on a typical grocery store trip. At HealthBarn USA we play a game called "Supermarket Spy Kids," a fun way to increase our knowledge about natural versus artificial. You can re-create this activity with your kids (see the "Hands-On Family Fun" section on page 68) so that a trip to the grocery store will be nothing less than an adventure—one that will make all of you healthier and happier. Your family will never shop for snack foods (or breakfast, lunch, and dinner items) quite the same way!

REAL-LIFE RESULTS:
Junior Detective Uncovers Food Fraud!

Benjamin, a six-year-old Sprout (and spy) at HealthBarn USA, has become such an ingredients expert that he regularly unmasks unhealthy products, not just at the supermarket. "At dinner my parents put A1 steak sauce on the table. I decided to be a supermarket spy kid at home and found out that the steak sauce has high-fructose corn syrup. I told my mom to throw it out immediately and she did!"

What if your spy is a double agent? One day at the barn, Jake, another Sprout, read all the ingredients of Kellogg's Strawberry Fruity Snacks. He and the rest of his class determined that it was loaded with artificial ingredients and off the list of acceptable snacks. Still, Jake was tempted . . . until another Sprout pointed out that if he ate it they'd all be in the Junk Barn—not the HealthBarn. "The JUNK Barn! Who wants to go there?" another Sprout said. "You're right!" Jake agreed. Nothing like a little positive peer pressure!

---

* Note that the standardized nutrition facts label, which many consumers zero in on, highlights calories and fat, but that's only part of the story. Any nutrition label can be manipulated to look healthier than it is by making the serving size small.

Supermarket Spy Kids

This revealing game, which involves "detecting" the natural versus artificial ingredients in many of our foods, is loads of fun for children and parents alike. Many nutrition educators teach kids how to read the standardized nutrition facts labels on packages for fat, calories, and sugar content to determine whether foods are healthy. But numbers and phrases like "percentage of calories from fat" rarely mean much to kids (or adults!), who struggle to place these facts in the context of their daily diets. They'll be quick to tune out if it's just a numbers game.

hands-on family fun

A far more effective technique is to do what we do at the HealthBarn USA and teach kids to "spy" on ingredients to determine what's natural and what's not, and to understand why natural is the better choice for our bodies.

Younger children who are just learning to read may need help with some words when it's time to read through ingredients (though even adults will be stumped by "butylated hydroxyanisole," an additive known as BHA and found in items like potato chips). Older kids will do fine, even if the words are difficult to pronounce. Assure them that if the words are that challenging, they are probably describing an ingredient that is artificial!

WHAT YOU NEED: Two sheets of paper and a marker; a package of fresh strawberries; a strawberry-flavored "fruit roll-up" (you'll need the ingredients list from the package);* the HealthBarn USA Supermarket Spy Sheet in the back of this book; a clipboard (recommended) and pencils for each player.

---

* You can use any real fruit and fruit-flavored snack you have on hand. The idea is to contrast the real fruit with an item that is artificially fruit-flavored. We use strawberries and flavored fruit roll-ups at HealthBarn USA.

1. **WHAT YOU'LL DO:** Show your kids the difference between natural versus artificial ingredients. Start with natural: On a sheet of paper, draw a picture of a tree with grass beneath it. Add a cow or chicken. (Don't worry if your cow looks like Fido—as long as your kids know what the animal figures represent, it's fine!)

WHAT KIDS WILL DO: In response to your picture, ask them to name as many foods as they can think of which could come from this "natural" scene, like foods that grow on trees (apples, lemons, pears, oranges) or in the ground (lettuce, carrots, zucchini, corn, herbs), that come from a cow (milk, yogurt, cheese, meat), and that come from a chicken (eggs, chicken).

2. **WHAT YOU'LL DO:** Show your kids where artificial ingredients come from. On your other sheet of paper draw a square building and label it "factory"—add some smoke stacks and people (stick figures will do) to represent workers.

WHAT KIDS WILL DO: In response to this picture, ask them what kinds of foods come out of a factory. You can give them a big hint: snacks that come in a bag or box or any foods that don't look like foods that come from the ground or from animals are artificial. Let them come up with ideas for foods laden with artificial ingredients such as Oreos, barbecue potato chips, GoGurt, cookie- or candy-inspired cereal, or Lunchables.

Continued on page 70

Now, ask them to think about this question and then answer it: Which type of ingredients—natural or artificial—contain the vitamins and minerals that keep our bodies healthy and strong, like calcium for strong bones and teeth? The answer: natural!

3. WHAT YOU'LL DO TOGETHER: Show the kids the container of strawberries and the package of strawberry-flavored fruit roll-ups. Let the kids tell you what these two items have in common—strawberry flavor or scent? Red color? Anything else? Now, let them answer this question: What's different about them, besides how they look and feel? The answer: ingredients!

Let your children read the ingredients (perhaps with help) on the strawberry fruit roll-ups. Ask them if they know how the snack got its red color and strawberry smell and taste. The answer is in those big words on the ingredients list—the artificial ingredients. Can they find any natural ingredients in the listing? Now, compare the roll-ups to the fresh strawberries—their ingredients? Just strawberries, 100 percent pure, from nature (in most cases there is no label).

You can do this exercise with many other items, including a bottle of pure water and a product like Vitamin Water; a container of 100% real fruit juice with a juice drink or fruit punch; Nesquik chocolate milk versus low-fat white milk; jelly versus fruit spread; microwave popcorn versus corn kernels; fresh turkey breast compared to processed, packaged turkey slices; real cheddar cheese versus a product like Cheetos or another cheese-flavored item; a 100% whole wheat cracker and some Goldfish crackers; different varieties of peanut butters, jarred tomato sauces, and cereals— the possibilities are endless, but the results will always be the same. Foods that come from nature have naturally occurring vitamins and minerals that are good for our bodies. Foods made with artificial ingredients are rarely beneficial.

4. GO SHOPPING WITH YOUR SPY: Once you feel that your child grasps the difference between foods from nature and foods from a factory, she'll be able to look at ingredients lists herself to "spy" on the artificial ingredients and search out natural ones (again, young readers will need assistance). Bring your junior detective to the supermarket to do some spying. But first, give her these handy clues about unmasking artificial foods. In general, they usually:

- Contain ingredients that are hard to read and difficult to pronounce.

- Use ingredients with numbers and abbreviations, like YELLOW #4 or BHT.

- Have ingredients consisting of few recognizable or simple foods like milk, apples, sugar, or eggs.

- Have an ingredients list that is several lines long (shorter is better!).

- Are available in flavors that don't sound like they come from nature, like GoGurt's "Cool Cotton Candy" variety. Or, even trickier, have names that sound natural—with words like "fruity" in the title—but have ingredients that don't match up with the natural-sounding name. For example: a "fruit" snack may contain food dyes that turn the product yellow like a lemon or purple like a berry, but no real lemons or berries at all. Is there truth in the name of that food? Unravel the mystery by spying on the ingredients!

Challenge her to find at least five natural foods, including those she could have for a morning snack, in your local market and record the information on her HealthBarn USA Supermarket Spy Sheet. True, the store manager may give your kid a funny look if she's walking around with a clipboard and frowning over a box of Cheez-Its, but maybe he'll ask what you're doing, listen up, and start stocking more foods with natural ingredients, instead of the artificial ones!

For now, let your newly minted food detective help you put the good stuff in the grocery cart and keep the junk out. This involvement will make her feel invested in the positive changes you're making in how your family eats. You are living with a supermarket spy kid, and snack time—as well as breakfast, lunch, and dinner—will be healthier and better than ever.

Can You Believe Everything You Read?

Here are some popular products and the health claims their manufactures make on the packaging. While they technically comply with labeling laws, in my opinion these companies are stretching the truth, or at least only giving consumers one part of it. Before you put these items in your shopping cart, look at the whole truth by reading the ingredients list.

Pop-Tarts—"baked with real fruit." Fruit is listed as the sixteenth ingredient, and many more follow.

Hawaiian Punch—"made with natural fruit juices." Water and high-fructose corn syrup are the first two ingredients; juice makes up only 5 percent of the content.

General Mills Milk 'n Cereal Bars—"filling made with real milk." Ingredients for the filling are sugar, palm kernel oil, lactose, nonfat milk, and dried sweetened condensed milk. So, yes it does contain "real milk" but it's mixed with many other things!

Wonderbread—"soft, delicious, nutritious." All versions of Wonderbread include this tag line, even their "classic" Wonderbread—which contains high-fructose corn syrup and has 0 grams of fiber per slice. (One positive: one slice contains 15 percent of the daily value of calcium.)

Chef Boyardee (most varieties)—"no preservatives." True, there are no preservatives—but it does contain high-fructose corn syrup and food dye.

Wishbone salad dressings—"naturally helps better absorb vitamins A & E from salad with the oils in Wishbone," with an asterisk afterward. The asterisk was hard to find, but the fine print reads: "vs. salad without dressing." Vitamins A and E are fat-soluble vitamins, meaning that they dissolve in fat, so of course the oil in the dressing will help absorption! The dressing also contains the preservative MSG.

As I said, these manufacturers, technically, are telling the truth, but you have to look beyond their claims and at the ingredients for the total story. A product may trumpet that it's a "good source" of calcium or vitamin C, but it may also be an excellent source of unnecessary additives and other junk that cancel out any health benefits.

Morning Snack Solutions: Naturally Easy

At the end of this chapter, you'll find some tasty recipes for morning snacks, including kid-tested foods that children can make on their own or help prepare, like our fantastic and portable Soft Pretzels (great to take to school) and Homemade Fruit Roll-Ups, complete with a fun-to-eat dipping sauce. Because weekday morning snacks are often eaten in a classroom or other group setting, teachers and caregivers prefer low-fuss, no-mess, easy-to-eat foods.* Perhaps your child's school or day care has even sent out a list of snack ideas, though sometimes the suggestions—like yogurt-in-a-tube or 100-calorie snack packs—are anything but healthy.

Below you'll find some options that can go where your kids go, including school. Hand this list to your supermarket spy kid and let them help you choose natural items at the store.**

Below are some ideas for combo snacks, or you can mix and match items from the categories you'll find at the end of this idea list. The goal is hunger-busting combinations. Many of the recipes at the end of this chapter, like Banana Chocolate Chip Mini Muffins, also combine whole grains, protein, and healthy fat.

Combo Snacks

◆ hummus with fresh veggies and whole-grain crackers or chips such as pita chips

◆ tasty dips and dressings with veggies, like our Creamy Herb Dip, Chickpea Delight, or Creamy "Ranch" Dressing

◆ fresh fruit with vanilla yogurt and our homemade granola

◆ whole-grain graham crackers with peanut butter or SunButter

◆ half a peanut butter or SunButter sandwich on whole wheat bread

---

* Most schools, day care centers, camps, and other places where children regularly eat together observe strict nut-free policies in order to protect those children who may suffer from nut allergies. Though I have included nuts and nut butters in this chapter as healthy morning snacks, I realize it may not be possible for a child to bring them from home to school or elsewhere.

** The most hunger-satisfying snacks combine whole grains with lean protein and a little healthy fat (you need all three to fuel up properly, as with breakfast)—for instance, cheese and whole-grain crackers (and add some fruit or veggies for more fiber and vitamins). These snacks may be a little more elaborate than just a banana, and therefore eating them in a classroom isn't always possible if time is limited. However, whenever there is an opportunity to serve a healthy snack "combo platter," do so—your child will feel more satisfied and energized. (With some prep and a plastic snack container with two or more compartments, combo snacks can go anywhere!)

- whole or cut-up fruit and a handful of almonds
- cheese, grapes, and whole-grain crackers
- Our Banana Chocolate Chip Mini Muffins or our Ginger Snap cookies with a piece of fruit

Put your own combo snacks together from these mix-and-match lists.

Protein for Energy

- a hard-boiled egg, peeled
- edamame beans
- a snack-size portion of fresh turkey breast slices

A Little Healthy Fat Through Calcium-Rich Dairy

- a small container of low-fat yogurt (like Stonyfield vanilla)—not a flavored yogurt tube
- low-fat cheese sticks or slices

Whole Grains for Fiber

- woven wheat crackers (100% whole wheat)
- Doctor Kracker or whole-grain Wasa crispbreads
- a favorite breakfast cereal—Cheerios, Barbara's Puffins, or Kashi Cinnamon Harvest work well as pop-in-your-mouth snacks

Add Fruits and Veggies for Daily Vitamins, Minerals, and More Fiber

- a whole piece of fruit, cut up for younger kids
- small fruits like seedless grapes, or cherries for older kids who can safely handle the pits
- crunchy raw veggies (try a mix) like carrot sticks, celery, sugar snap peas, cucumber slices, bell pepper slices
- grape tomatoes
- dried fruit—unsulfured
- natural (no sugar added) applesauce

You may be wondering why there is no granola bar on this list. Many parents ask me to recommend a healthy one, but generally I find that they are too highly processed to be substituted for real food. Some bars, like Larabar or KIND bars, do pass muster because they are unprocessed, but they are really formulated for adults and kids usually don't like them.

The best option is to make your own, which is why I've included a recipe at the end of this chapter for The Barn Bar. You can also put together an all-natural snack mix (like we do at HealthBarn USA) that includes far healthier ingredients than those you'll find in most commercially produced granola bars or packaged trail mixes.

To make the snack mix: let your child combine semisweet chocolate chips (or dark chocolate chips), unsulfured apricots or other dried fruit, sunflower or pumpkin seeds, and dry whole-grain cereal—just enough to fill a baggie. (For an individual serving, the combined ingredients should fit in the palm of the snacker's hand.) You can also use raw almonds or other nuts, coconut shavings, or any other additional variations your family favors.

Stacey's Tips

Juice—Too Much of a Good Thing?

We know what to eat when we're hungry between meals—good snacks from nature—but what about when we're thirsty? Parents and kids often wonder about this, and many of them consider juice a healthy "snack" that happens to be drinkable. Any well-trained supermarket spy kid would allow all-natural, 100% juice into the shopping cart. But is it a good option?

I know it's hard to escape the juice box (and its cousin, the drink pouch), with its own little straw so conveniently attached. But its popularity (consider the amount of real estate it takes up in your local grocery store) also means that kids today consume a lot of juice, often with their snacks. At one time, juice primarily was limited to orange juice with breakfast or at other meals as a "special" drink. (Raise your hand if you remember drinking grape juice out of a fancy glass at Thanksgiving!)

Now, however, visit any place where kids are allowed to eat and drink—in the classroom or cafeteria, on playgrounds or ball fields, in the backseat of the family car—and you'll spot juice boxes clutched in the hands of children of all ages, particularly when they're snacking on foods like crackers and pretzels. They range from tiny toddler-size boxes that fit in a child's pocket to bigger sizes for bigger kids (that often hold "noncarbonated juice beverages"—an industry term for juice-based drinks that have little to no nutritional value), and they are particularly tempting to parents looking for a packable, portable product because they don't leak and don't need refrigeration.

Pure 100% fruit juice—with *no added sugar*—can be a healthy choice. Orange juice, for example, is a good source of vitamin C, and as mentioned earlier, it is now possible to find calcium- and vitamin D–fortified orange juice. When ascorbic acid is added to apple juice, it also becomes a good C source. However, look closely at that medium-size apple juice box (6.75 ounces). Though it has 100 percent of the daily recommended value for vitamin C, it also has about 100 calories and 18 grams of sugar—the equivalent of more than four teaspoons!* When these otherwise healthy juices are consumed in large quantities, they are no longer healthy.

Juice is naturally high in sugar (fructose, from fruit) and calories. If your child drinks

---

* The four teaspoons of sugar refer to naturally occurring fruit sugar (fructose), not added table sugar. However, though it is not a refined or artificial sugar, fructose and all other natural sugars (such as lactose and glucose) still impact blood-sugar levels in the body.

juice several times a day, she's going to consume more sugar and calories than her body needs. In addition, her preference for sweetened beverages over milk or water could eventually lead to a taste for sugary soda and foods. Very young children can fill up on juice and have less room in their small tummies for more nutritious foods. (As mentioned earlier, this can happen when kids overconsume milk too.)

Unfortunately, the giant cases of juice boxes that so many stores offer tempt families to purchase in bulk—and kids to drink in bulk. The boxes are easy to grab and open, even for the littlest hands (no pouring, no searching for a straw). Convenient? Yes. Healthy? Not when overconsumed. Friendly to the environment? No, because juice boxes (and milk boxes) are usually made of nonrecyclable or hard-to-recycle laminated and/or waxed cardboard, and plastic (for the straw).*

The American Academy of Pediatrics suggests limiting daily juice intake as follows: for children one to six years old: 4–6 ounces; for children seven to eighteen years old: 8–12 ounces. (Note that these are *limits;* there is no daily recommended amount for juice.) At HealthBarn USA I serve kids no more than half a cup of 100% juice as an energy booster before heading out to work in the garden. We also use it in moderation as a natural sweetener in some of our recipes, such as smoothies.

If you're looking for ways to reduce juice consumption, here are some tips:

✦ If a child is thirsty, always offer water first, then low-fat milk or nondairy alternative.

✦ Teach your child that juice is an occasional drink (perhaps limited to breakfast), not one to be sipped all day long.

✦ Offer whole fruit instead of juice. The vitamin content may be similar, but juice offers no fiber.

✦ Dilute juice with ice cold seltzer for a fizzy treat—and treat it as a *treat.*

---

* Some carton packaging may be recyclable, but only in communities equipped to handle these specialized materials. Visit www.recyclecartons.com to find out what type of cartons are recyclable in your area.

pantry pick

Yogurt Offering calcium, protein, live and active cultures (or probiotics) for digestive health, and other beneficial nutrients, low-fat yogurt can be an excellent snack. The yogurt section in your local grocery store is packed with choices, so you'll want to use your knowledge of natural versus artificial ingredients to make the best selections.

Yoplait's popular GoGurt tubes, marketed directly to kids with flavors like a Sponge-Bob themed "Bikini Bottom Berry," have high levels of added sugar (10 grams in one 2.25-ounce tube)—the second ingredient listed after low-fat milk—and no beneficial live and active cultures. Another prominent brand is YoCrunch. Though they do not put their product in a tube, this sugary yogurt contains no live and active cultures and is packaged with a separate serving of candy or cookie toppings, like M&Ms, Nestle Crunch, or Oreo cookies. (A half cup of natural ice cream is a much better choice—as an occasional treat, not a daily snack!)

Drinkable yogurts are yet another incarnation of what can be a healthy food, and they no doubt enjoy popularity because they appeal to shoppers who believe it is easier to buy a smoothie than make one. But what's in it? Homemade smoothies like our Banana Cream Smoothie or Rainbow Swirly Smoothie don't have the artificial ingredients and added sugars you'll find in many of those liquid yogurt products.

In short, beware of packaging gimmicks and flavors that have more in common with candy than they do with what should be a simple and wholesome dairy product. As with cereal packaging, yogurt packaging that features cartoon characters or kid celebrities is frequently packed with artificial stuff that your kids don't need, and that would make a supermarket spy kid dial 9-1-1! Here's what to look for:

Low-fat (not nonfat). Kids need some fat, and low-fat milk is a good source. Also, when fat is completely removed from yogurt, it tends to have higher sugar content. Thick Greek yogurt is becoming increasingly popular and is available in low-fat versions, but at HealthBarn USA we have found that kids won't always go for it (it's not as sweet as regular yogurt). However, we use plain, nonfat Greek yogurt in some of our recipes; it's an excellent substitute for sour cream.

Vanilla. We use vanilla yogurt at HealthBarn USA (we like Stonyfield Organic French Vanilla) because kids like it better than plain, the healthiest option of all. Instead of buying yogurt "with fruit on the bottom" (which a lot of kids don't like anyway because it's lumpy and runny), let kids add their own fresh fruit to vanilla yogurt. The fruit-on-the-bottom yogurts contain a lot of added sugar because the fruit is based in a sweetened syrup.

Live and active cultures. The ingredients should list live and active cultures—the living organisms that convert milk into yogurt during fermentation—because if a yogurt does not contain them, then it's not real yogurt! Also referred to as "good" bacteria or probiotics, live and active cultures keep the digestive tract healthy.

Naturally sweetened (not artificially). Many consumers think yogurt is high in sugar when they review the nutrition facts on the container, but the fact is that milk contains a naturally occurring sugar (lactose). Even yogurt with no added sugar will have some sugar content because of the milk content, and most commercially made yogurts have added sugar in some form in the ingredients list. However, avoid yogurt with man-made sugars like high-fructose corn syrup, or artificial sweeteners like aspartame (used in some reduced-calorie yogurts), which is a chemical, or sucralose, which is the branded artificial sweetener Splenda (both are used often in products claiming "reduced or no sugar").

No artificial colorings or flavorings. You can avoid these artificial ingredients if you avoid yogurt in shades of neon green and turquoise blue, as well as flavors like "banana split explosion." If it doesn't sound like it comes from nature, then most likely its ingredients don't either.

A very short list of ingredients. As always, the shorter that list, the better the food! Yogurt ideally should contain low-fat milk, live and active cultures, some natural sugar, and possibly pectin (a natural gelling agent found in many fruits).

I suggest buying vanilla yogurt in 32-ounce containers. Whether it's being eaten at home or packed for snack, yogurt can be portioned into individual servings. Let kids add fresh fruit as desired and top it as they wish, with flavorful and nutritious natural ingredients like chopped almonds or walnuts, dried fruit, whole-grain crunchy cereals, or ground flaxseed. The large container is more economical and environmentally friendly because it can be reused or, in most cases, recycled.

The Three R's: Reduce, Reuse, and Recycle

You read about the first of our Seven Healthy Habits at HealthBarn USA—**Eat your breakfast!**—in the last chapter. Here's another one: **recycling**—which becomes an even more effective way to protect our earth when we combine it with **reducing** and **reusing** the amount of waste we generate.

An item like the 32-ounce yogurt container just mentioned is a perfect example to share with kids because it illustrates how we can **reduce** the amount of packaging we consume by avoiding buying lots of small plastic containers; we can **reuse** the container to store other foods or items, or for a craft project; and we can **recycle** the container in most communities so that it can be made into another item, like plastic piping.

Turn recycling into a family activity and challenge kids to reduce, reuse, and recycle before they toss it in the trash. For some related activities, see the Get Your Hands Dirty activity in chapter 6 for more on composting and the Real-Life Results tip on page 115 in chapter 4 for setting up a "waste-free lunch day" at school. We share the chart below with kids at HealthBarn USA. Can your kids come up with even more ways to make the "three Rs" a part of their healthy day?

This item . . .	. . . can get recycled into:
Newspapers, magazines	New newspapers and magazines, books, cardboard
Paper milk cartons	New milk cartons
Glass jars and bottles	New glass jars and bottles
Aluminum foil	New aluminum foil, soda cans
Christmas trees	Wood chips—composted and used as mulch in parks
Vegetable scraps	Compost
Plastic water bottles	Fleece for a fuzzy hoodie, stuffing for ski jackets and teddy bears, carpet
Yogurt containers	Flower pots, trash cans, plastic pipes
Plastic bags	Plastic lumber to make decks and fences, backyard furniture
Cardboard boxes	New boxes, paper towels, kitty litter

WHEN IT'S TIME TO CELEBRATE

Classroom Snacks to Share on Birthdays and Holidays

In many schools, bringing in a sweet birthday treat to share with classmates is a tradition, though some schools have banned sugary items like cupcakes or encourage other types of food-free birthday celebrations like bringing in a favorite book to share. We came up with the tradition of the "Birthday Apple" at HealthBarn USA. We set a candle in an apple and serenade the birthday boy or girl. After they make a wish and blow out the candle, we use an apple slicer to share pieces of this favorite fruit. Kids love apples and the novelty of the slicer. Depending on the number of children and the age of the birthday child, you could do this with multiple apples.

If you want to bring in something grander than the birthday apple to your child's classroom, here are our top school-approved recipe picks from the barn:

✦ Popcorn with Brain Butter (bring in the air-popper to pop fresh)

✦ Yogurt Sundaes

✦ Raspberry Crumble

✦ The Perfect Pop

✦ Caprese Salad on a Stick

Beyond birthdays, it seems like there is no end to class parties—Halloween,

Election Day, Thanksgiving, Winter Break, Valentine's Day, St. Patrick's Day, etc.—and requests for snacks. How about bringing fruit, veggie, and cheese kebabs? Set out platters of cut-up fruit and vegetables and cheese cubes and some bamboo skewers and let kids string together their own creations and dip in our Creamy "Ranch" Dressing. (Because skewers have sharp ends, younger children need supervision or the kebabs could be made in advance.)

Our Soft Pretzels are another class favorite. Let your child make them for classmates the day before. They start out soft but get good and crunchy as they cool. Chocolate Ladybugs are another crowd pleaser, as much fun to make as to eat.

Our Sweet Potato Crunchies are a favorite for a school "harvest fest" in the fall, or you can serve them over Thanksgiving holidays when friends and family gather.

All of these snacks—and many more of the recipes in this book—make great party foods outside of the classroom too! When the next child's party rolls around, think about serving up something other than the same old sugar. (See our sleepover party ideas at the end of chapter 7 for even more festive inspiration.) And when it's your family's turn to bring the snacks, do what we do at HealthBarn USA and snack outside the box!

Grow an Organic Garden

I'm hopeful that by now your entire family has grown quite skillful at spotting natural ingredients and blowing the whistle on artificial ones. One excellent way to really bring this lesson home (and out of the supermarket) is to reinforce eating from nature by growing food for your table in your very own organic garden, be it in the ground or in containers. Children (and certainly many adults) love digging in the dirt, and gardening as a family can be a fun, satisfying way to spend time together and get some exercise.

get your hands dirty

There's another benefit of growing fruits, vegetables, and herbs. Growing food organically, without harmful pesticides and chemicals, is a way of protecting our planet and all living organisms. I tell kids: **we can't be healthy unless the soil is healthy.** One way to make this happen is through organic farming methods that can be implemented in a home garden—whether it's a few tomato and strawberry plants on a patio or an entire section of the backyard with four kinds of lettuce, rows of carrots, bountiful bell peppers, zucchini, eggplant, dwarf peach trees, and a pumpkin patch.

If you haven't ever planted and maintained an edible garden, prepare to enjoy the delicious and healthy fruits of your labors. If you're a skilled gardener, why not help another family get a taste (literally) of the wholesome farming lifestyle? Here are the basics we share with garden-planning families at HealthBarn USA:

Pick a sunny spot. Choose an area that gets a lot of direct sunlight throughout the day and has easy access to a water source. Veggies need at least six hours of direct sunlight! (You may need to create a barrier with chicken-wire fencing to discourage garden scavengers such as hungry rabbits and groundhogs.)

Compost. Healthy soil is the key to healthy plants and healthy people, so use compost or an organic fertilizer. To compost, dig a hole in your yard in a sunny place (a good distance from your edible plants), add fruit and vegetable scraps, grass clippings, tea, coffee grinds, and egg shells daily, turn it using a shovel or pitch fork, and you'll have "black gold" in no time. For more instructions on composting, see the Get Your Hands Dirty activity in chapter 6.

Plant what you like to eat. Everyone always asks me, "What should I plant?" Start with what you eat. We begin by reviewing our favorite seasonal recipes loaded with veggies, and then we take an inventory of our seeds to determine what we need to purchase for spring, summer, and fall plantings. If you're a first timer, **Mother Earth News** suggests potatoes, green beans, tomatoes, squash, lettuces, and herbs as some of the easiest (and most satisfying) choices for new gardeners. Some of our favorite things to grow at HealthBarn USA also happen to make great snacks: sugar snap peas, raspberries, cherry tomatoes, strawberries, bell peppers, cucumbers, carrots, and even asparagus!

Know your zone. Check for your region in the USDA Hardiness Zones (visit www.garden.org/zipzone to find your zone by entering your zip code). Once you know your zone, select plants that will thrive in your area.

Buy quality seeds and seedlings. Purchasing high-quality seeds is important for germination because there is nothing worse than planting seeds, waiting, and not having so much as a sprout come up. We recommend organic seeds from Johnny's Selected Seeds (www.johnnyseeds.com) and heirloom seeds (and a variety of unique plants) from the not-for-profit group Seed Savers Exchange (www.seedsavers.org). For seedlings, it's important to buy from reputable local nurseries (preferably one that grows their seedlings from seed) with hardy and well-maintained plants because you'll minimize the risk of introducing diseased plants into your (or your neighbors') garden.

Get the right garden gear. The essentials include shovels (large and small), a hoe, a rake, gloves, and a hat (sunscreen is also recommended). Make sure to get enough gear in the right sizes so the whole family can participate.

Have fun! As with preparing food, when it comes to gardening there are tasks for even the smallest family members. Little ones love to water plants, so find small watering cans they can lift and handle. Harvesting is a big thrill for most kids, especially if they've never picked their own vegetables and fruits—even a handful of tiny berries is a joy. Your garden doesn't have to be picture-perfect, and it will change and mature as the seasons pass. Just get started, get dirty, and get active with family, friends, and neighbors!

The Barn Bar

We learned during a "Supermarket Spy Kid" shopping trip that popular brands of granola bars have lots of strange-sounding ingredients that kids had never heard of (and couldn't pronounce), so we set out to make our own creation using whole grains. Our delicious Barn Bar is high in heart-healthy fats and fiber, and it contains easy-to-read ingredients. Parents like this simple hunger-buster for any time of day, but it's especially good as a morning school snack.

ingredients

2 cups old-fashioned oats

⅔ cup ground flaxseeds

⅓ cup hulled raw sunflower seeds

¼ cup raisins

3 tablespoons brown sugar

1 large egg, beaten

½ cup maple syrup

½ cup canola oil

directions

1. Preheat oven to 325°F. Line a 13 x 9-inch metal baking pan with foil, extending the ends of the foil 2 inches over the short sides of the pan. Grease foil.

2. In a large bowl, combine oats, flaxseeds, sunflower seeds, raisins, and brown sugar. Stir in egg, maple syrup, and oil until well mixed. Transfer mixture to prepared pan and, with wet hands, press into an even layer.

3. Bake for 25–30 minutes or until golden brown. Cool in pan on a wire rack.

4. Once cool, use the foil to transfer the bars to a cutting board. With a serrated knife, cut lengthwise into 8 strips, then cut each strip crosswise in half to make 16 bars. Enjoy right away or store in an airtight container at room temperature for up to 4 days, or freeze for up to 1 month.

Makes 16 servings (1 granola bar per serving)

Nutrition Facts per serving: 190 calories; 11g fat (1g sat fat, 5g mono, 4g poly, 0g trans fat); 10mg cholesterol; 20g carbohydrate (3g fiber, 10g sugar); 4g protein; 10mg sodium; 4% Daily Value (DV) calcium; 6% DV iron

---

Kids can measure and mix ingredients and spread mixture into pan.

Homemade Vs. Store-Bought: The Facts!

HealthBarn USA's The Barn Bar	Quaker Chewy Granola Bars (Chocolate Chip Flavor) Reference: www.quakeroats.com
Ingredients: Old-fashioned oats, flaxseeds, sunflower seeds, raisins, brown sugar, egg, maple syrup, canola oil	**Ingredients:** Granola (whole-grain rolled oats, brown sugar, crisp rice [rice flour, sugar, salt, malted barley extract], whole-grain rolled wheat, soybean oil, dried coconut, whole wheat flour, sodium bicarbonate, soy lecithin, caramel color, nonfat dry milk), semisweet chocolate chips (sugar, chocolate liquor, cocoa butter, soy lecithin, vanilla extract), corn syrup, brown rice crisp (whole-grain brown rice, sugar, malted barley flour, salt), invert sugar, sugar, corn syrup solids, glycerin, soybean oil, contains 2% or less of: sorbitol, calcium carbonate, salt, water, soy lecithin, molasses, natural and artificial flavor, BHT (preservative), citric acid
Nutrition Facts (per serving): 190 calories; 11g fat (1g sat fat, 5g mono, 4g poly, 0g trans fat); 10mg cholesterol; 20g carbohydrate (3g fiber, 10g sugar); 4g protein; 10mg sodium; 4% Daily Value (DV) calcium; 6% DV iron	**Nutrition Facts** (per serving): 100 calories; 3g fat (1g sat fat, 0g trans fat); 0mg cholesterol; 17g carbohydrate (1g fiber, 7g sugar); 1g protein; 75 mg sodium; 8% Daily Value (DV) calcium; 2% DV iron
OURS: • 8 ingredients	**THEIRS:** • 39 ingredients • package claims "Made Without High-Fructose Corn Syrup"—however both corn syrup and corn syrup solids appear in the ingredients list • contains sorbitol, an artificial sweetener • artificial flavors and preservatives added

Soft Pretzels

Making pretzels at home is a fun activity for the whole family. We added whole wheat flour to the mix to increase our intake of whole grains. The longer they cool the crunchier the pretzels become, but you can also enjoy them warm and soft, straight from the oven. For a sweet variation, skip the optional sea salt topping and mix up a light dip with ½ teaspoon cinnamon and ¼ cup agave nectar, then dunk away!

ingredients

- ½ cup plus 1 tablespoon water
- 1 envelope active dry yeast (2¼ teaspoons)
- ½ teaspoon honey
- 1 cup whole wheat flour
- ⅓ cup unbleached all-purpose flour
- 1 teaspoon sea salt plus additional for sprinkling
- 1 large egg white

directions

1. Preheat oven to 400°F. Grease 2 large baking sheets.

2. Heat ½ cup water to 105°–115°F. In a medium bowl, combine warm water, yeast, and honey; stir until yeast dissolves. Let stand until foamy, about 5–10 minutes.

3. With a wooden spoon, stir in flours and 1 teaspoon salt to make a soft dough.

4. Turn dough onto floured surface and knead for 1–2 minutes or until smooth (it should look a little dry when it's ready).

5. Divide the dough into 10 equal pieces. Roll each piece of dough into a rope 10–12 inches long. Twist each rope into a loop-shaped pretzel; press the ends lightly to seal. Place pretzels on prepared baking sheets.

6. In a small bowl, whisk the egg white and remaining 1 tablespoon water; use this egg wash to brush pretzels. If you like, lightly sprinkle salt over egg wash coating on pretzels.

7. Bake the pretzels for 10–12 minutes or until golden brown. Transfer to a wire rack to cool slightly, about 5 minutes. Serve warm.

Makes 10 servings (1 pretzel per serving)

Nutrition Facts per serving: 70 calories; 0g fat; 0mg cholesterol; 14g carbohydrate (2g fiber, 0g sugar); 3g protein; 60mg sodium; 8% Daily Value (DV) iron

---

Kids can roll and shape pretzels and brush with egg wash.

Chocolate Ladybugs

There is nothing better than freshly picked strawberries, so when they're in season, bring some home. They are not only sweet and delicious, but also loaded with immune-boosting vitamin C. Strawberries make a great snack on their own, or you can add a dose of antioxidants by making Chocolate Ladybugs, a low-fat treat that takes just minutes to create. We use semisweet chocolate chips to create the spots on our "bugs."

ingredients

5 medium strawberries

20 semisweet chocolate chips

directions

1. Cut leaves and tops off strawberries, then cut each strawberry in half lengthwise.

2. With fingers, gently push 2 chocolate chips, pointy side down, into rounded side of each strawberry half to create the ladybug's spots.

Makes 2 servings (5 strawberry halves per serving)

Nutrition Facts per serving: 35 calories; 1.5g fat (1g sat fat, 0g trans fat); 0mg cholesterol; 6g carbohydrate (1g fiber, 5g sugar); 1g protein; 0mg sodium; 30% Daily Value (DV) vitamin C

Kids can halve strawberries using a plastic knife with adult supervision, and can press in chips.

Homemade Chocolate Milk

Kids love chocolate milk, but every good supermarket spy knows that it's packed with added sugar and artificial ingredients. At HealthBarn USA, the children challenged us to come up with a natural version of one of their favorite tastes—and we rose to the occasion. We whipped up this yummy, low-fat, calcium-rich concoction with cocoa powder, which is rich in antioxidants. Since it's made with rice milk, even nondairy drinkers can indulge. (Parents love it too!)

ingredients

1 quart enriched vanilla rice milk, chilled

5 teaspoons unsweetened cocoa powder

2½ teaspoons agave nectar

directions

In a blender, place rice milk, cocoa, and agave nectar; cover and blend until well mixed, about 1 minute.

Makes 5 servings (1 cup per serving)

Nutrition Facts per serving: 120 calories; 2g fat (0g sat fat, 1g mono, 1g poly, 0g trans fat); 0mg cholesterol; 24g carbohydrate (0g fiber, 12g sugar); 1g protein; 85mg sodium; 8% Daily Value (DV) vitamin A; 25% DV calcium; 2% DV iron

---

Kids can add all ingredients and blend.

Mini Potato Leek Frittata,
page 47

Chocolate Ladybugs,
page 87

PB&J Muffins,
page 53

Veggie Sushi
Hand Roll,
page 126

TLT Wrap,
page 120

Pasta Fagioli with Mini Meatballs,
page 128

BBQ Turkey Pizza,
page 195

*Coconut Shrimp with
Pineapple Herb Dipping Sauce,
page 204*

Raspberry Crumble,
page 236

Turkey Burgers with
Sweet Oat Rolls,
page 216

Pizza Potato Skins,
page 169

No-Bake White Mac and Cheese,
page 228

Yum! Yum! Dumplings, page 201

Homemade Vs. Store-Bought: The Facts!

HealthBarn USA's Homemade Chocolate Milk	Nestle Nesquik Chocolate Low-fat Milk Reference: www.nesquik.com
Ingredients: Vanilla rice milk, unsweetened cocoa powder, agave nectar	**Ingredients:** Low-fat milk with vitamin A palmitate and vitamin D3 added, sugar, less than 2% of: cocoa processed with alkali, calcium carbonate, cellulose gel, natural and artificial flavors, salt, carrageenan, cellulose gum
Nutrition Facts (per serving): 120 calories; 2g fat (0g sat fat, 1g mono, 1g poly, 0g trans fat); 0mg cholesterol; 24g carbohydrate (0g fiber, 12g sugar); 1g protein; 85mg sodium; 8% Daily Value (DV) vitamin A; 25% DV calcium; 2% DV iron	**Nutrition Facts** (per serving): 170 calories; 2.5g fat (1.5g sat fat, 0g trans fat); 10mg cholesterol; 29g carbohydrate (<1g fiber, 28g sugar); 8g protein; 160mg sodium; 10% Daily Value (DV) vitamin A; 40% DV calcium; 2% DV iron; 25% DV vitamin D
OURS: • 3 ingredients	**THEIRS:** • 10 ingredients • artificial flavors added

Ginger Snaps

These crunchy cookies are hard to keep in the cookie jar because they're a family favorite at HealthBarn USA, and they're sure to be a hit in your house too. If ginger is not your favorite flavor, go without and enjoy a molasses snap instead. Pack them with low-fat milk or milk alternatives such as soy, rice, or almond milk for a yummy school snack—and be prepared to share the recipe when the other parents ask for it!

ingredients

1 large egg

1 cup packed brown sugar

¾ cup extra-virgin olive oil

½ cup dark molasses
   (Blackstrap is best!)

1 cup whole wheat flour

¾ cup unbleached all-purpose flour

¼ cup ground flaxseeds

2 teaspoons baking soda

1 teaspoon ground cinnamon

1 teaspoon ground ginger

directions

1. Preheat oven to 350°F.

2. In a large bowl, whisk together egg, brown sugar, oil, and molasses. In a small bowl, stir together flours, flaxseeds, baking soda, cinnamon, and ginger.

3. Add the flour mixture to wet ingredients and stir together until well mixed.

4. Cover the bowl with plastic wrap and refrigerate for a minimum of 30 minutes or until dough is firm enough to roll into a ball without sticking to your fingers.

5. Scoop dough by 1 heaping teaspoonful at a time, and with the palms of your hands roll dough into a ball. Repeat with remaining dough, placing balls 2 inches apart (they will spread out!) on an ungreased baking sheet.

6. Bake cookies for 8–10 minutes or until edges of cookies are brown. Let cookies cool on the baking sheet before removing.

Makes 26 servings (2 cookies per serving)

Nutrition Facts per serving: 140 calories; 7g fat (1g sat fat, 5g mono, 1g poly, 0g trans fat); 5mg cholesterol; 19g carbohydrate (1g fiber, 11g sugar); 2g protein; 110mg sodium; 6% Daily Value (DV) calcium; 10% DV iron

---

Kids can stir ingredients, roll out dough balls, and place them on the cookie sheet.

Creamy Herb Dip

Our versatile herb dip is made with fresh basil, rosemary, chives, and mint from the garden, so it's packed with disease-fighting phytonutrients! Get dipping with your favorite raw seasonal vegetables, pita chips, or whole wheat crackers for even more health-boosting vitamins, minerals, and fiber.

ingredients

¼ cup loosely packed fresh basil, rosemary, chive, and mint leaves mixture

1 clove garlic

1 pint low-fat cottage cheese

¼ teaspoon sea salt

¼ teaspoon freshly ground black pepper

Sliced raw vegetables and/or pita chips

directions

1. Place herbs and garlic in a food processor; pulse until finely chopped.

2. Add cottage cheese, salt, and pepper and pulse until herbs are evenly distributed through cottage cheese.

3. Spoon dip into a small bowl; cover and refrigerate for at least 2 hours or up to 4 days.

4. Serve with raw seasonal vegetables and/or pita chips.

Makes 14 servings (2 tablespoons per serving)

Nutrition Facts per serving: 25 calories; 0g fat (0g trans fat); 0mg cholesterol; 1g carbohydrate (0g fiber, 1g sugar); 4g protein; 140mg sodium; 2% Daily Value (DV) calcium; 2% DV iron

Kids can add ingredients to food processor and pulse.

Chickpea Delight

Here's a recipe that parents love too, because it makes the perfect appetizer for any special occasion or dinner party. Serve our Chickpea Delight spooned into endive leaves, topped with cherry tomatoes and drizzled with extra-virgin olive oil. When the party's over, pack this homemade alternative to hummus in your child's snack bag with sliced veggies or pita chips.

ingredients

1 can (15 ounces) low-sodium chickpeas (garbanzo beans), drained and rinsed

¼ cup loosely packed fresh chives (or other fresh herb combination from the garden)

¼ cup extra-virgin olive oil

¼ teaspoon sea salt

⅛ teaspoon freshly ground black pepper

1 clove garlic

Sliced raw vegetables and/or pita chips

directions

1. In a food processor, place chickpeas, chives, oil, salt, pepper, and garlic. Pulse until ingredients are well blended and mixture is smooth.

2. Serve with raw seasonal vegetables and/or pita chips.

Makes 12 servings (2 tablespoons per serving)

Nutrition Facts per serving: 80 calories; 5g fat (1g sat fat, 4g mono, 1g poly, 0g trans fat); 0mg cholesterol; 6g carbohydrate (1g fiber, 0g sugar); 2g protein; 20mg sodium; 2% Daily Value (DV) vitamin C; 2% DV calcium; 2% DV iron

Kids can add ingredients to food processor and pulse.

Banana Chocolate Chip Mini Muffins

Ahh, the irresistible aroma of homemade banana bread! Our recipe takes that old classic and boosts the fiber content by using whole wheat flour, and adds kid-pleasing semisweet chocolate chips for extra antioxidants (and happiness). "It's the best snack ever," say the HealthBarn USA taste testers. Your kids will give these a thumbs up too.

ingredients

1⅔ cups whole wheat flour

¼ cup ground flaxseeds

1 teaspoon baking soda

¼ teaspoon baking powder

¾ cup packed brown sugar

⅓ cup unsweetened applesauce

⅓ cup water

3 large egg whites

3 ripe medium bananas, mashed

⅓ cup semisweet mini chocolate chips

directions

1. Preheat oven to 350°F. Line 28 mini muffin cups with paper liners.

2. In a large bowl, stir together the flour, flaxseeds, baking soda, and baking powder. In a medium bowl, use a fork to stir together the brown sugar, applesauce, water, and egg whites until blended. Stir in bananas.

3. Add wet ingredients to the flour mixture and stir just until blended. Do not overmix. Fold in chocolate chips.

4. Spoon the batter evenly into the prepared muffin cups. Bake for 10–12 minutes or until a toothpick inserted in the center of the muffins comes out clean. Cool on a wire rack.

Makes 28 servings (1 muffin per serving)

Nutrition Facts per serving: 90 calories; 1.5g fat (0g sat fat, 0.5g mono, 0.5g poly, 0g trans fat); 0mg cholesterol; 17g carbohydrate (2g fiber, 9g sugar); 2g protein; 60mg sodium; 2% Daily Value (DV) vitamin C; 2% DV calcium; 2% DV iron

Kids can peel and mash bananas and spoon batter into muffin cups (and eat some extra chocolate chips!).

Homemade Fruit Roll-Ups

Your kids will never ask for another box of Fruit Roll-Ups after they've tried the real thing. Light and refreshing, this simple snack loaded with the antioxidant superstars vitamins A and C makes eating fruit fun and nutritious (and messy, which kids really love)!

ingredients

Vanilla Sauce

3 large egg yolks

2 tablespoons agave nectar

1 cup low-fat (1%) milk

2 tablespoons cornstarch

½ teaspoon ground cinnamon

Roll-Ups

½ pint strawberries, sliced

Juice of 1 orange

1 teaspoon vanilla extract

2 ripe mangoes, peeled, sliced

4 kiwifruits with skin, sliced
 (¼-inch thick)

12 (8½-inch diameter) rice paper
 wrappers

Nutrition Facts per serving: 120 calories; 2g fat (1g sat fat, 1g mono, 0g trans fat); 45mg cholesterol; 23g carbohydrate (1g fiber, 8g sugar); 3g protein; 25mg sodium; 15% Daily Value (DV) vitamin A; 60% DV vitamin C; 4% DV calcium; 2% DV iron

---

directions

1. To prepare Vanilla Sauce, in a small bowl, whisk the egg yolks and agave nectar until blended. In a small saucepan, whisk together milk and cornstarch. Cook over medium heat until mixture thickens and boils, about 5 minutes, stirring constantly. Boil for 1 minute, stirring.

2. Whisk a small amount of hot milk mixture into yolk mixture. Gradually pour the yolk mixture back into milk mixture in saucepan, stirring rapidly to prevent lumping. Cook over low heat, stirring constantly, for about 3 minutes or until mixture is very thick and coats the back of a spoon well.

3. Pour the sauce into a small bowl and sprinkle with cinnamon. Cover and refrigerate until roll-ups are ready to serve.

4. To prepare Roll-Ups, toss strawberries with orange juice and vanilla in a bowl, set aside.

5. Fill a 9-inch diameter shallow pan with about 1 inch of cool water. Soak 1 rice paper wrapper in water until it becomes pliable, about 20 seconds. Carefully remove wrapper from water and place flat on cutting board or plate (not a paper plate—they will stick) smoothing out edges as best you can.

6. About one-third of the way up from bottom of wrapper, place 2 slices of mango side-by-side; top with 4 slices strawberry, then 2 slices kiwifruit. Fold the bottom of the wrapper over fruit, then fold sides over toward center and pull tightly. Roll up tightly from bottom to top. Set aside and repeat until all wrappers and fruit are used.

7. Plate the Fruit Roll-Ups and top with Vanilla Sauce.

   Makes 12 servings (1 roll-up with sauce per serving)

   Kids can fill rice paper and make roll-ups.

Homemade Vs. Store-Bought: The Facts!

HealthBarn USA's Homemade Fruit Roll-Ups	Betty Crocker Fruit Roll-Ups (strawberry flavored) Reference: www.bettycrocker.com
Ingredients: Strawberries, orange juice, vanilla extract, mangoes, kiwis, rice paper wrapper, egg yolks, agave nectar, low-fat milk, cornstarch, cinnamon	**Ingredients:** Pears from concentrate, corn syrup, dried corn syrup, sugar, partially hydrogenated cottonseed oil, contains 2% or less of: citric acid, sodium citrate, acetylated monoglycerides, fruit pectin, dextrose, malic acid, vitamin C (ascorbic acid), natural flavor, color (red 40, yellow 5, yellow 6, blue 1)
Nutrition Facts (per serving): 120 calories; 2g fat (1g sat fat, 1g mono, 0g trans fat); 45mg cholesterol; 23g carbohydrate (1g fiber, 8g sugar); 3g protein; 25mg sodium; 15% Daily Value (DV) vitamin A; 60% DV vitamin C; 4% DV calcium; 2% DV iron	**Nutrition Facts** (per serving): 50 calories; 1g fat (0g sat fat, 0g trans fat); 0mg cholesterol; 12g carbohydrate (7g sugar); 0g protein; 55mg sodium; 10% Daily Value (DV) vitamin C
OURS: • 11 ingredients	**THEIRS:** • 17 ingredients • contains partially hydrogenated oils (aka trans fat) • does not contain strawberries but is strawberry flavored • contains food dyes for color

Creamy "Ranch" Dressing

We love a delicious ranch dressing to top a fresh salad or as a dip for seasonal vegetables, but the traditional versions are usually high in saturated fat. We came up with a creamy alternative that delivers a rich and savory taste, but that's made with guilt-free ingredients, including fresh chives. Start pouring, dipping, and enjoying.

ingredients

½ cup low-fat buttermilk

¼ cup plain nonfat Greek yogurt

1 tablespoon chopped fresh chives

1 tablespoon cider vinegar

¼ teaspoon sea salt

¼ teaspoon freshly ground
    black pepper

1 clove garlic

directions

1. Place all ingredients in a food processor. Pulse until mixture is smooth and creamy.

2. If not using dressing right away, pour into a container, cover, and refrigerate for up to 4 days.

   Makes 8 servings (2 tablespoons per serving)

Nutrition Facts per serving: 15 calories; 0g fat (0g trans fat); 0mg cholesterol; 1g carbohydrate (0g fiber, 1g sugar); 1g protein; 35mg sodium; 2% Daily Value (DV) calcium; 2% DV iron

---

Kids can add ingredients to food processor and pulse.

Homemade Vs. Store-Bought: The Facts!

HealthBarn USA's Creamy "Ranch" Dressing	Hidden Valley Original Ranch Salad Dressing Reference: www.hiddenvalley.com
Ingredients: Low-fat buttermilk, nonfat Greek yogurt, chives, cider vinegar, sea salt, pepper, garlic	**Ingredients:** Soybean oil, water, egg yolk, sugar, salt, cultured nonfat buttermilk, natural flavors (soy), spices, less than 1% of: dried garlic, dried onion, vinegar, phosphoric acid, xanthan gum, modified food starch, monosodium glutamate, artificial flavors, disodium phosphate, sorbic acid and calcium disodium EDTA as preservatives, disodium inosinate, and disodium guanylate
Nutrition Facts (per serving): 15 calories; 0g fat; 0mg cholesterol; 1g carbohydrate (1g sugar); 1g protein; 35mg sodium; 2% Daily Value (DV) calcium; 2% DV iron	**Nutrition Facts** (per serving): 140 calories; 14g fat (2.5g sat fat, 0g trans fat); 10mg cholesterol; 2g carbohydrate (1g sugar); 1g protein; 260mg sodium; 2% Daily Value (DV) vitamin C
OURS: • 7 ingredients	**THEIRS:** • 21 ingredients • contains MSG (monosodium glutamate) • artificial flavors and multiple preservatives added

CHAPTER 4

It's in the Bag: Lunches They Will Love

RECIPES

THE MAIN COURSE

THE GARDEN

THE CRUNCH

THE TREAT

I grew up in a busy household with two sisters, and all three of us took our lunch to school. Every morning we'd grab our lunches off the kitchen counter and rush off to school. A few hours later, we'd open those brown bags and know instantly which of our parents had made our lunches. Would it be the oozing cream cheese and jelly sandwich flattened by the big apple placed on top? Or was it to be the perfectly packed turkey sandwich, accompanied by apple slices, chopped carrots, and an encouraging or sweet note? Believe it or not, our dear mom (excellent at cooking and many other things) was the messy sandwich maker while Dad was the Martha Stewart of bagged lunches! Not what you'd expect—but there was a reason for this, and there's a lesson that you can take away.

Mom didn't like making lunches, and Dad loved it. For her, it was yet another meal chore—hard on the heels of breakfast and its dishes—that she had to tackle during the course of her own busy day, with dinner looming on the horizon. For Dad, it was a fun task that provided a break from his hectic routine. He enjoyed being creative and applying his tendency to be neat and orderly to preparing nourishing food for his girls. He loved using his sense of humor to come up with kindhearted and silly notes that we always looked forward to.

Dad *wanted* to make lunch—and on those mornings when he couldn't and Mom *had* to, let's just say that the Antine sisters could taste the difference.

Here's the moral of my family story: if you view making your child's lunch as a much-detested chore, then *get someone else to do it*. Like my sisters and me, your child will know. If she is old enough to make it herself, then let her go for it. (If you keep the good stuff on hand, then she'll be able to assemble a healthy lunch with no problem.) If he's still too young to pull it together, enlist your partner or an older sibling to help. It's that simple.

Lunch—not dinner—is the meal that causes the most stress for families with school-age children. For five days of the week, kids eat in a setting that is largely out of a parent's control. Even if children bring their lunch from home (as I always recommend) rather than purchase it from the hit-or-miss school cafeteria, parents never know for sure what food their kids consume—not to mention share, trade, or toss in the garbage. However, with a little bit of thought and preparation (by someone who *wants* to do it), you can ease your worries by creating well-planned, appealing lunches your child will happily eat!

You may think your lunch-making days will end with school buses and backpacks, and perhaps they will—but consider this. My middle sister, Elyse, grew up to become an elementary school teacher and continued to take many a lunch to school. (Teachers always steer clear of cafeteria food!) She lived with my parents right before she got married, and on the last day of classes before her wedding, years after he'd made that first, perfectly packed lunch that was the envy of her classmates, Dad delighted her with one last brown-bag creation, prepared with love—and complete with a handwritten note to put a smile on her face.

Growling Stomachs and Growing Pains: Why Kids Need Healthy Lunches

Well before the noon hour, the smells of the school cafeteria are wafting through the hallways of your child's school and into the classrooms. (And let's admit it—when you're starving, even mystery meat from the cafeteria smells good!) Many young students have already had three or four classes before they get to eat their next meal, and breakfast probably happened about an hour before they even got to first period. A balanced breakfast and a healthy mid-morning snack will help stave off hunger—but only to a point. (More than one teacher has wondered if her kids are chewing on their pencils at noon because they're ready for lunch!)

Working life for adults often requires later lunch hours. Many of us with busy schedules have disciplined ourselves to eat lunch when we have the time, not when our bodies tell us we need to eat. But beware of sending your body into a starvation state because you need to take another call, extend the meeting another hour, or send another email: you'll make up for it by overeating at lunch. A late lunch is often not a healthy one!

Adults can push the limit, but growing kids need to eat a healthy lunch at an appropriate hour. The midday meal should fuel them for the rest of their day—through the long afternoon of classes and after-school activities (both physical and mental), and into the evening until dinner.* When children are faced with such full days, it's important that they get what their minds and bodies need at lunch (and in most schools, as children grow older, the lunch hour gets a bit later—so more is riding on a solid breakfast and a smart morning snack). There's another factor to take into consideration: most kids don't usually get a lunch "hour"—it's more like a combined forty-minute lunch and recess period. If you're a kid and you know that the sooner you finish eating lunch, the sooner you can get outside for recess, you're going to either eat quickly or not eat enough!

---

* An after-school snack, which is the subject of the next chapter, can extend the benefits of a good lunch.

So, here's your challenge as a parent: Can you create a variety of easy-to-make, appealing lunches five times a week that satisfy your child's nutritional needs and taste really, really good?

As you're about to see, the answer is as easy as counting to five.

The Lunchbox Blueprint

I'm a big believer in variety, but when parents tell me, "I need new lunch ideas!" I tend to rely on *the same five elements* every time I pack a lunch. Within these five categories there is plenty of room for creativity, but if you stick to the same components when you fill a lunchbox, you will never be at a loss for what to offer.

Here's what to pack:

1. the main course

2. the garden

3. the drink

4. the crunch

5. the treat

Below, I'll give you some suggestions under each category to get you started, and you'll also find recipes at the end of this chapter (and elsewhere in the book) for additional items. Think of these five categories as a lunchbox blueprint that you can refer to week after week.

Don't forget to involve the hungry young eater who carries the lunchbox! Share this blueprint with your child and let him come up with his own ideas, with the main "rule" being that foods come from nature and are made with ingredients that fit into a healthy day of eating. Depending on his age, let him play a role in choosing foods at the market and assembling his own lunch. As with all meals and snacks, if he has a hand in making it (even if it's just voicing an opinion), he's more likely to eat it!

Finally, a little organization will go a long way on a rushed morning. Many items can be prepared and packed the night before, like crunchy veggies, a portion of whole-grain crackers, or a beverage. Sandwiches can get soggy, depending on the filling, so assembly might be better in the morning. Don't spend precious morning minutes scrambling for an ice pack or looking for plastic bags and napkins. If your child is old enough, put him in charge of laying out lunch supplies the night before, perhaps while he's readying his backpack for the next day.

1. The Main Course

The main course is the centerpiece of lunch, be it a sandwich, wrap, or other entrée, or a hearty soup or salad. Perhaps you're in the habit of reflexively thinking "sandwich" when you think "lunch," but the main course provides you with an opportunity to mix it up a little. If your child loves pasta, why not pack up a container of leftover Spinach Pesto Pasta or Pasta and Sweet Peas? If it's cold outside and soup is always a hit, a thermos full of Creamy Broccoli Soup or Pasta Fagioli and Turkey Meatballs is sure to please. Our Veggie Sushi Hand Roll makes an excellent packed lunch. If sandwiches are favorite standbys, check out the recipe for our TLT Wrap, and see the box "Beyond the Bread" below for more suggestions.

Some More Ideas:

✦ Serve hot and cold soups with slices of whole-grain bread or woven wheat crackers. Try Doctor Kracker flatbreads and crackers and Wasa whole-grain crispbreads.

✦ If you have a cheese lover, pack a café-style "cheese sampler" with a variety of cheeses, grapes, unsulfured dried fruits, and whole wheat crackers (almonds or walnuts are also a healthy addition, but it may not be possible for your child to bring nuts into school).

✦ Try wraps or pita bread instead of sandwiches, using whole wheat lavash.

✦ Make extra Simply Crepes and fill with cheese and sliced grapes, egg salad, or fresh turkey, shredded lettuce or cabbage, and tomato.

2. The Garden

Eating fruits and vegetables is another one of our Seven Healthy Habits at HealthBarn USA, and getting them into a lunchbox is ridiculously simple.

Your child may prefer a whole piece of fruit like a banana, or whole cherry tomatoes that she can pop in her mouth. Or, she may like it better if the fruit or veggies (served raw for maximum crunch) are sliced and combined in a salad. Consider adding a small container of HealthBarn USA's Creamy "Ranch" Dressing to go with veggies, or our White Bean Dip or Green Edamame Dip. Experiment with freezing grapes and berries and then packing them—by lunchtime, they're still icy cold with a bit of crunch. Keep sliced fruit looking fresh by squeezing a bit of lemon or lime juice onto it before packing.

Beyond the Bread: Rethinking the Sandwich

Sure, kids like sandwiches and they frequently make a perfectly healthy main course for lunch. But when you think about it, if you pack your child a sandwich every single day for her entire tenure in the school lunchroom—well, imagine a kid's version of the film **Groundhog Day** every time she opens her lunchbox. It's also a lot of bread, which some kids don't particularly love, and which isn't always a reliable source of whole grains, as I explained in our breakfast chapter.

Below are some ideas for sandwiches, but I also recommend that you consider offering these same spreads and fillings with a serving of whole-grain crackers, crispbreads, and flatbreads, which don't get soggy or have the bulk of bread (Wasa and Doctor Kracker brands are a big hit with the kids at HealthBarn USA), as well as on whole-grain lavash or in a whole wheat pita. Another tip: when you pack the whole-grain item separately from the spread or filling, a child can assemble her own lunch and thus get a little more control over what and how she is eating. Ever wonder why Lunchables are so popular? It's because Oscar Mayer cleverly packages all the ingredients separately in those little divided trays so that kids can assemble their own meals. Providing the fixings from home is a much better deal nutritionally (not to mention financially). Pack up individual items in bento box–style plastic trays or containers, which keep the crispy items separate from the moist ones and allow kids to eat foods their way. (You can find divided individual or interlocking food containers in stores like Target or Walmart, or visit www.laptoplunches.com for many more options.)

Pack the following fillings or spreads with your child's favorite whole grain or use these suggestions to spark your own ideas. Some are new twists on old favorites; all are kid-tested and get the thumbs up from HealthBarn USA. (You'll want to supplement some of the lighter all-veggie selections with additional protein.)

- Organic peanut butter or SunButter and banana wheels (slices) on whole wheat bread
- Almond butter or SunButter and pure fruit spread (tastes great on whole wheat raisin bread)
- Sliced turkey, avocado, or White Bean Dip on crispbread (choose one or combine)
- Classic egg salad, tuna salad, or chicken salad (made with olive oil mayo); fresh turkey or roast beef slices
- Sliced low-fat cheddar and sliced apples with flatbread
- Low-fat cream cheese on celery sticks, served with raisins and nuts
- Whole wheat pita, filled with our Quinoa Falafel with yogurt sauce

Some More Ideas:

A crisp and crunchy red and yellow pepper medley; zucchini spears; green beans; sweet peas; broccoli florets; edamame shelled or in pods; shredded carrots with raisins (try our Carrot Halwa Dip); whole-grain creations with fruit and veggies such as Harvest Wheat Berry Salad and Bulgur Tabbouleh; berries; sliced cantaloupe; watermelon cubes; apple and pear slices. Try our Hydration Salad, with its irresistible and thirst-quenching mix of cantaloupe, honeydew, cucumbers, lime, and sea salt.

3. The Crunch

Don't let potato chips be the default "crunch" in lunch! (If you're concerned about weight gain, a recent headline-making study found that potato chips top the list when it comes to foods responsible for adding unwanted pounds.) Most kids want a little something—perhaps slightly salty—to bite into, especially if they're having a wrap or sandwich as their main course. Stacy's pita chips, Lundberg rice chips, Food Should Taste Good sweet potato chips and multigrain chips, and Plocky's The Original Three Grain tortilla chips and Beanitos (gluten-free) are our top salty picks.

Fortunately, baked (not fried) chips are now widely available, as are low-sodium varieties, but even some "veggie chips" (sold as a potato chip alternative) can pack a lot of fat and sodium. If you do have a stubborn chip eater who won't go cold turkey when she's eating her sandwich, start by switching to baked chips, and choose tortilla chips over potato for less saturated fat. (And take your child to the chip aisle to play a game of Supermarket Spy Kids; the endless ingredients lists on a package of "flavored" potato chips will do the work for you!)

Some More Ideas:

Baked pita chips; dried fruit and raw nuts (again, be aware of the nut policy at your child's school, camp, or day care); air-popped popcorn (see Popcorn with Brain Butter); whole-grain pretzels (see our Soft Pretzel recipe); soynuts; rice crackers.

4. The Drink

Water and low-fat milk or nondairy alternatives are the healthiest drinks of choice (see chapter 2 for specific recommendations on milk, and regarding juice see the Stacey's Tips segment "Juice—Too Much of a Good Thing?" in chapter 3), but 100% juice, a fruit smoothie, or a drinkable yogurt are also welcome additions. If you purchase premade smoothies and drinkable yogurts at the grocery store, look over the ingredients list carefully to make sure it's as natural as possible. Our yogurt guidelines in the "Pantry Pick" section in chapter 3 also apply to commercially made smoothies and drinkable yogurts. Another drink option is our double-thumbs-up Homemade Chocolate Milk.

5. The Treat

The treat is optional, but it's a nice (and sweet) way to round out a weekday lunch, and it can be healthy too. If you purchase prepared applesauce, fruit cups, or fruit leathers, read ingredients to avoid added sugars, syrups, and preservatives. And consider adding a note every once in a while—those notes my dad wrote to me were sweeter than any dessert!

Some More Ideas:

Fruit cups in natural juices; applesauce; natural fruit leather; yogurt-covered raisins; whole-grain animal crackers; all-natural graham crackers; HealthBarn USA's homemade Ginger Snaps, Chocolate Pudding, Blueberry Rice Pudding, or Raspberry Crumble.

Protein Power: Putting Some Punch in Their Lunch

Kids need some protein at every meal, preferably lean protein from lunchbox-friendly foods like fresh-roasted turkey, peanut butter, beef, chicken, fish, beans, milk, and yogurt. Protein is essential for muscle and organ growth, and it helps keep hunger at bay. When I talk to kids about protein, I emphasize its role in building and maintaining muscle, because they always get the connection between muscles and strength. Of course, even though kids love to flex their biceps in classic strongman fashion, protein is also vital for the development and maintenance of the heart—which is, after all, a muscle.

At HealthBarn USA, we like to do an activity called Protein Power, and you can do a less-structured version of this lesson at home. The goal is twofold: to get kids to identify natural protein sources that contribute to their health, and to show them that protein comes not just from animal sources but from plant sources as well.

Stacey's Tips

"I Made My Own Lunch! Is It Healthy? And Can I Try the School Cafeteria Food Tomorrow?"

If your child wants to make lunch on her own, encourage her efforts and make her job easier by keeping good food on hand. At HealthBarn USA, we tell kids that if they can answer "yes" to the simple questions below, they've successfully made a healthy lunch!

Is it natural?

Are the grains whole grains?

Does it contain fruits or vegetables?

Does it have protein to help your muscles grow?

Does it have bone-building calcium?

Does it contain a healthy fat?

If your child is making his own nutritious lunch, that's an excellent achievement. However, you may get some push back about "hot lunch" at school, which just about every kid wants at some point. (You may even be in the process of weaning your child off of a steady diet of school cafeteria food, and I know that can be a challenge—but it's one worth taking on.) School cafeterias, in some districts, are striving for healthier choices, and recent federal legislation (the Healthy School Meals Act) is designed to raise the standards of school lunch menus. Still, the food you make for your child at home is going to be far healthier, lower in fat and sodium, and much more natural than what your child will encounter in most lunch lines. The good news is that change is happening around the country, and schools are even taking the initiative by planting gardens (see the Get Your Hands Dirty feature "Starting a Schoolyard Garden" below) and serving the harvest to students, just like we do at HealthBarn USA.

So, if your child is begging to eat the food on "Pizza Friday" or on "Breakfast for Lunch" day, should you let him? Kids want to fit in, particularly as they get older, and lecturing your child on why the microwaved meatball hero with fries is "bad" probably won't work—particularly if his friends regularly eat school lunches. To him, you're just criticizing his peers. Instead, continue to help him learn what foods are artificial versus natural, and challenge him to find the natural choices on the school menu. Don't make school lunch the forbidden fruit; the occasional Pizza Friday won't do any lasting damage. Chances are that if he tastes cafeteria food after a steady diet of delicious foods from nature, brought from home, he'll understand why it's better to rely on his lunchbox than the lunch line.

Encourage older kids to watch the eye-opening documentary *Food, Inc.,* a powerful film that reveals precisely where our food comes from, including how animals are raised and crops are grown. My thirteen-year-old nephew Jack used to argue with his mom, who wanted him to skip the cafeteria and bring a healthy lunch from home, but Jack insisted on eating the school lunch—until he watched *Food, Inc.* Now he brings his lunch from home every day. Once you see the film, if you haven't already, you'll know why. For more information on *Food, Inc.* (including educational materials for parents and teachers), visit the film's official website, www.foodincmovie.com.

Start by asking your child to think about what foods come from animals and explain that nearly all of those foods will naturally be packed with protein. They will probably be quick to come up with meats like beef and poultry, but remind them that fish, milk, cheese, eggs, and yogurt are also animal products.

Next, explain that it's a little more challenging to come up with plant-based protein sources, but that plants can also provide this important nutrient. If your child has gotten involved in shopping and cooking, then he may be aware of some plant protein foods. Here are the examples we usually use at HealthBarn USA: beans; nut butters like peanut and almond; soy, rice, or almond milk; edamame; and seeds and grains like quinoa. Include the Rainbow Quinoa Salad for a protein-packed lunch.

At HealthBarn USA we let the kids put together a collage of protein-power foods, which they glue onto paper plates or onto a diagram of a flexed muscle. You may want to let your child create her own visual reminder of protein foods. Either way, the idea is to help kids grasp the essential role that protein plays in a healthy day of eating.

When Meat Is on the Menu

When we grow and harvest our own food, it's easy to see the connection between what's on our plate and where it comes from. When you discuss animal- versus plant-based sources of protein, you may find yourself having to answer questions about where the meat comes from, particularly from older kids (including any child

who has ever read *Charlotte's Web* or seen the movie and worried about the fate of Wilbur). Only you as the parent can decide what and how much information to give your child about how animals are raised for food. Obviously, factors like your child's age and your own views on the topic will play a big role.

At HealthBarn USA, on the way to harvesting veggies at the garden, the kids see many farm animals. They play with the goats and sheep, check out the lone chicken in the pig pen, and then, inevitably, they ask what happens to the pigs. "Bacon and pork chops," we tell them. Some are horrified and saddened, while others don't blink; they like to eat bacon and pork (and hamburgers and chicken) and they accept the reality. Sometimes, a child will be so put off by the facts of farm life ("That's gross!" is a common refrain) that she will declare herself to be a vegetarian from here on out. These different reactions are normal, and they highlight the importance of experiencing our food sources—both animal and vegetable—in a hands-on way. Whether we shop at a big supermarket or a local farmers' market, knowing where our food comes from and how it is produced helps us to make the right decisions for ourselves and our families.

I met one child at HealthBarn USA who became a vegetarian—within a family of meat eaters—because she'd seen a carcass hanging in a butcher shop and became very upset. She was a true animal lover and decided at that moment that eating meat was no longer something she could do. Her mother told me, "But it's weird and awkward—we eat meat in our home." I told this parent that it was important to honor her child's decision and that the next best step in this journey was to make sure her daughter ate well through a nutritious plant-based diet. And that's what this mom decided to do.

If you are a meat eater and have a child who declares, "I'm now a vegetarian," don't ridicule her, pressure her, or make it difficult for her to eat well. Gently remind your child that this decision doesn't mean she can subsist on pasta, and offer her guidance and resources on putting together healthy meals and snacks so that her growing body will get the protein and other nutrients it needs.

Identifying as a vegetarian may just be a phase, or it may be the beginning of a choice she'll make for life. Either way, it shows that she's made the connection between what's on her plate and where it comes from, and is working toward becoming an equal participant in what she eats.

Our thumbs-up vegetarian recipe picks are:

♦ Quinoa with Kale and Walnuts

♦ Indian Veggie Medley

♦ Eggplant Parmesan Towers

♦ Quinoa-Stuffed Peppers

♦ Veggie Stir-Fry with Soba Noodles

♦ Sweet Potato Gnocchi with Basil Pesto

♦ Quinoa Falafel

♦ Vegan bonus: Veggie Sushi Hand Roll, Veggie Chili, Italian-Style Lentil Soup

♦ You'll also find a week's worth of vegetarian menus on page 261.

When kids think their meat and produce originate in the supermarket, we are doing them a disservice. To grow into healthy eaters, our kids need to be educated about our food system—including the good, the bad, and the ugly—so that they can make educated choices about the food they eat as they grow into healthy adults. One great place to start is *The Omnivore's Dilemma for Kids* by Michael Pollan. Pollan has adapted his groundbreaking book for adults into an intelligent and provocative but readable book for young people.

Not all kids are ready to hear about factory farms, pesticides, genetically modified crops, and how big agribusiness is squeezing out independent farmers, but some are mature enough to grasp the issues, and eventually all kids deserve to know the whole story of where our food comes from. Their eating habits and preferences will have a major impact on the future of the world's food supply, and if they make informed choices now, they can bring about important and positive changes in how our food is produced—changes that many of today's adults are not willing to make.

Staying Healthy on the Inside: Fiber from Whole Grains

Getting enough dietary fiber isn't just a concern for adults. Kids need it too! Constipation is not an unusual problem among kids. When I look closely at the diets of children who suffer from it, it's clear that they are hardly eating any veggies or whole grains. The "bulk" of their diets is coming from highly processed foods with no fiber and low nutrition.

Buying Quality Meat

Choose the most natural and unprocessed deli meats you can find in your market. Many packaged, mass-produced sandwich meats are loaded with high levels of sodium, preservatives like MSG, artificial coloring, nitrites and nitrates, and other unnecessary additives. These products are designed for a longer shelf life, but it's best to buy items like fresh-roasted turkey from the deli counter or look for high-quality packaged meats from companies like Applegate Farms. Boar's Head, one of the largest producers and distributors of deli meats, now offers an "all-natural" line of products that are minimally processed and made with no artificial ingredients. Look for meats from animals raised on vegetarian diets and without the use of antibiotics or hormones (check the labels).

If you're purchasing beef or poultry to cook at home, look for quality natural meats from local farmers or small producers, as opposed to large-scale processors. (Make friends with your butcher, who can tell you where the meat comes from.) It's well documented that independent and reputable farms can enforce and maintain higher standards in their treatment of animals as well as their meat production than giant agribusiness can. Many local farmers' markets have vendors who specialize in high-quality, naturally raised meat. Niman Ranch meats, available in nearly all parts of the country, are also a good choice.

You will probably pay more for organic or natural meats, but if you're concerned about what your family eats, it's worth the extra cost. Fortunately, due to consumer demand, many club stores and other large chains now sell such meats nationwide at affordable prices.

Fiber is essentially any type of carbohydrate that our bodies cannot break down and digest. Healthy sources of fiber include whole grains, fruits, and vegetables. Fiber is a major factor in helping us "stay regular" as our grandparents would say, but it's also an effective ally in the prevention of serious illnesses like heart disease, diabetes, and certain cancers. It's hard to look at the average active child and think about those "grown-up" problems, but the fact is that most kids simply don't get enough of this important dietary component. One study estimates that only 45 percent of four- to six-year-olds and 32 percent of seven- to ten-year-olds eat adequate amounts of fiber.*

---

* Jeffrey S. Hampl, Nancy M. Betts, and Beverly A. Benes, "The Age+5 Rule," *Journal of the American Dietetic Association* 98, no. 12 (1998): 1418–1423.

The amount of daily fiber each person needs depends on gender, weight, caloric intake, age, and other factors. In general, healthy adults should get at least 20 grams per day, but pregnant women, for instance, need closer to 30 grams. Kids' needs, of course, also vary, but I, like many nutritionists, rely on a fairly simple method for calculating dietary fiber needs in children between the ages of four and ten known as the "Age+5" rule. Simply take your child's age (assuming she falls into that range), and add five. A seven-year-old should get 12 grams of fiber, a ten-year-old 15 grams, and so on. Keep in mind that when you up the fiber, you must increase the water intake or all the good stuff will get stuck too!

The Whole Story on Whole Grains, Just for Kids

At HealthBarn USA, we keep our fiber information simple for kids. We don't get into long calculations about how much we need in grams, nor do we go into great detail about soluble versus insoluble fiber. (That information may be interesting and useful to you, like the fiber calculation method above, but it doesn't grab the attention of most children!) Instead, we talk about how foods from nature like fruits, veggies, and whole grains contain loads of good fiber, and how, by contrast, artificial and processed foods like refined white flour and sugar don't help us stay healthy, inside *or* out.

As I mentioned earlier, it's very hard to find a loaf of commercially baked whole-grain bread that will meet fiber needs but that doesn't have a lot of extra stuff like added sugars and preservatives. That's why I prefer to introduce whole grains through other sources, like quinoa or brown rice, which many of our recipes incorporate. (Fruits and vegetables, which you'll hear more about in our next chapter, should also be daily go-to fiber sources.)

Below are some FAQs about whole grains that you can share with your child. If you have whole grains in any form at home (and I hope you've been putting them in your grocery cart by now), make sure your child knows what they look like and use some props to show the difference between refined and whole grains.* (Some kids may even be hearing "hole" grains—not "whole" grains—so help them to understand what you're talking about.) Handling an actual wheat berry or a popcorn kernel, or examining the difference between a scoop of white flour and a scoop of

---

* At HealthBarn USA, we display these items for refined grains: white rice, white bread, spaghetti (unless it's whole-grain pasta), pizza crust, chocolate chip cookie. You could also use pretzels and chips. For whole grains, we show them brown rice, whole wheat bread, quinoa, oatmeal, popcorn, wheat berries, and our HealthBarn USA oatmeal cookies and granola.

whole wheat flour (or a slice of white versus wheat bread), is a "whole" lot more fun and interesting than just reading about it!

Finally, here's a tip from parents who've successfully gotten their families to eat more whole grains. Don't "hide" whole grains in the pantry, as if they were a mystery ingredient. Store them in glass jars on the counter so everyone can see them (and so they're easy to use). Curious kids will ask, "What are those?" and you can start the conversation.

So, what's a whole-grain food anyway? Why does it matter?

A whole-grain food is a food made from all three parts of a grain seed—the bran, the endosperm, and the germ. When you eat foods made from all three parts of a whole grain, it makes you feel full and you know when to stop eating. Whole grains help you digest your food better, so your insides are healthier too! Whole grains can be ground into flours that are used to make other foods, or they can be eaten (whole!) on their own.

Is there such a thing as a "part-grain" food?

Sort of. The opposite of whole grain is called "refined" grain—like refined flour, which is in a lot of processed foods (such as white bread, cookies, pretzels, and chips) that don't contain many ingredients from nature. The problem with refined grains is that they only use part of the grain; they leave the good stuff out. The nutrition your body needs is in the bran, the endosperm, and the germ.

Why do they take the good parts out of the grain?

Because the food manufacturers want to make products that will go to the stores and sit on a shelf for a while and still taste fresh when they're finally out of the bag

or box. Unfortunately, they make that happen by refining and ruining the healthy whole grain. For example, there is a healthy kind of oil that is found in the germ of a grain, but over time that oil will go bad. Food manufacturers know that if they take away all or part of the germ, then the oil will also be removed and can't make a cookie or cracker taste stale. However, the more they refine or process the grain, the more they remove the beneficial parts containing fiber, nutrients, and vitamins. The cookie or cracker may be crunchy, but it has little nutritional benefit for our bodies.

Can you tell if a grain is whole or refined just by looking at it?

One hint is color. Refined grains look white (like white bread or the inside of a pretzel), and whole grains are more brown, like a slice of whole wheat bread.

Do whole grains taste different from refined grains?

Whole grains taste wonderful! They are naturally nutty and delicious. Refined grains don't have much flavor on their own—the flavors you taste come from added ingredients that aren't good for your body, like too much sugar or salt, or artificial flavorings.

What are some whole grains I might like to eat?

Do you like oatmeal cookies? Pizza? Popcorn? All of these can be made with whole grains, and you'll find recipes for foods like that right here in this book. Look for grains like the ones listed in the following chart next time you go to the grocery store and play Supermarket Spy Kids. Put more of these whole grains in your shopping cart and in your tummy, and you'll stay healthy inside and out!

Grains to Put on Your Shopping List

Do you bypass those cylinders of grains sold in the bulk section at your local market? A lot of shoppers do because they are unfamiliar with how to use whole grains, except for perhaps the rolled oats or brown rice, but there is a whole world of delicious whole-grain eating to be had! If you're not sure what to do with that bag of bulgur once you get it home, the chart on the next page from the Whole Grains Council makes cooking with whole grains simple. And buying your grains in bulk cuts down on the cost of these super foods and helps reduce packaging waste, so everyone wins—including the planet.

In recent years I have received an increasing number of requests from families for gluten-free dishes. You'll find a number of thumbs-up recipes in these pages for snacks and meals that can be part of a gluten-free diet (as well as a week's worth of gluten-free menus on page 260), including:

◆ Rainbow Swirly Smoothie

◆ Sweet Berry Polenta

◆ Veggie Sushi Hand Roll

◆ Mike's Sicilian Stew

◆ Spinach Pesto Pasta (with your favorite gluten-free pasta)

◆ Hydration Salad

◆ Mango and Peach Salsa with corn chips

◆ Pesto-Stuffed Cherry Tomatoes

◆ Rainbow Quinoa Salad

To 1 cup of this grain:	Add this much water or broth:	Bring to a boil, then simmer for:	Amount after cooking:
Amaranth	2 cups	20–25 minutes	3½ cups
Barley, hulled	3 cups	45–60 minutes	3½ cups
Buckwheat	2 cups	20 minutes	4 cups
Bulgur	2 cups	10–12 minutes	3 cups
Cornmeal (polenta)	4 cups	25–30 minutes	2½ cups
Couscous, whole wheat	2 cups	10 minutes (heat off)	3 cups
Kamut grain	4 cups	Soak overnight, then cook for 45 minutes	3 cups
Millet, hulled	2½ cups	25–35 minutes	4 cups
Oats, steel cut	4 cups	20 minutes	4 cups
Pasta, whole wheat	6 cups	8–12 minutes (varies by size)	Varies
Quinoa	2 cups	12–15 minutes	3+ cups
Rice, brown	2½ cups	25–45 minutes (varies by variety)	3–4 cups
Rye berries	4 cups	Soak overnight, then cook 45–60 minutes	3–4 cups
Sorghum	4 cups	25–40 minutes	3 cups
Spelt berries	4 cups	Soak overnight, then cook 45–60 minutes	3 cups
Wheat berries	4 cups	Soak overnight, then cook 45–60 minutes	3 cups
Wild rice	3 cups	45–55 minutes	3½ cups

Courtesy Oldways and the Whole Grains Council, www.wholegrainscouncil.org.

REAL-LIFE RESULTS:

Kids Make a Huge Dent in Nation's Landfill Crisis!

Did you know that your child is capable of generating up to sixty-seven pounds of lunch-related waste every year? Think about it—all those paper napkins, plastic bags, foil, juice boxes, milk cartons, plastic utensils and straws, empty chip bags, yogurt containers, and other food packages really add up (and may even outweigh your child). According to WasteFreeLunches.org, the average elementary school sends 18,760 pounds of garbage into landfills and incinerators each year!

Some schools, however, are pushing back by taking their lunchtime recycling to a whole new level, with "waste-free lunch day" contests. Schools can create their own teams, rules, and prizes, but here's one basic way to play this environmentally oriented game: Kids, divided into teams by grade or homeroom, compete to generate the **least** amount of landfill trash by using lunchboxes instead of brown paper bags, reusable containers instead of plastic bags, cloth napkins, real silverware, and water bottles or other beverage containers instead of juice boxes and milk cartons. After lunch period is over, teams divide their garbage into recyclable materials (plastic yogurt containers, water bottles, etc.), waste suitable for the compost pile, reusable items for storage (nonsoiled plastic bags), and nonrecyclable trash. (Easy-access recycling containers and a schoolyard compost bin are important!) After they've sorted their garbage, teams weigh the remaining nonrecyclable trash and tally up the results over the course of a week or a month (or even a day). The team with the least amount of garbage wins!

Not only does this program reduce waste, but it also saves money and encourages healthy eating: uneaten food, rather than contributing to the garbage and penalizing the team, can go back into the lunchbox (perhaps to be eaten as a healthy after-school snack); out of a desire to reduce waste, families will purchase items like yogurt in more economical large containers and pack individual servings in reusable containers; prepackaged meals like Lunchables, which are loaded with processed foods, immediately become less appealing because they involve so much wasteful packaging. (If your family is playing the Supermarket Spy Kids game and reading ingredients labels, Lunchables and similar foods are definitely off the shopping list by now!)

If you are interested in helping your child's school set up a waste-free lunch day, visit www.wastefreelunches.org and share the information with your child and her school.

Starting a Schoolyard Garden

Do you want to really help children make the connection between the food they eat and where it comes from? Then help start an edible garden at the one place where kids spend so many of their waking hours: school! In recent years, school gardens have become increasingly popular, in part due to the nationally renowned Edible Schoolyard Project pioneered by chef Alice Waters. Waters not only created gardens where students grow fruits, vegetables, herbs, and grains; she also got students into the kitchen to prepare meals with their harvest and serve them to their peers in the school cafeteria.

get your hands dirty

Every school has its own hierarchy, and you may find yourself presenting to a school board, a parent-teacher group, or a principal, teachers, and other staff. But remember that kids can often get attention for issues like this in a way that adults cannot. Schools are used to hearing from parents asking for things all the time; as a result, they may not be responsive to yet another adult with yet another request. However, if a kid takes the podium and makes the case for a garden with a well-thought-out plan, there may just be butter beans next to the basketball court come next May.

Eighth-grader Samantha Aboody, who was one of the first Young Harvesters to enroll at the barn when it began in 2005, and who is now a counselor-in-training at HealthBarn USA, successfully spearheaded the efforts to break ground for a garden at her New Jersey middle school. She offers the tips listed below to any kids and parents who may be interested in doing the same. At every step of the way, keep your child and other students who may be interested involved with the process—even the fundraising!

Get support from someone at school. Secure the support of an advocate at school, like a teacher who will back your efforts. In Samantha's case, her principal was newly arrived from another school where he'd started a garden for the kids and was eager to re-create the project. She got additional support from two science teachers who were interested in using the garden as an extension of their classroom, to teach kids about plant cycles and growing seasons.

Have a plan—a garden plan, that is. Samantha had some specific ideas about where the garden could be located at her school and what should go in it. (She wanted a mix of easy-to-grow herbs, some manageable veggies and small fruits, and flowering plants that would attract butterflies.) She also considered the possibility of raised beds, the pros and cons of a compost pile at school, what supplies and tools her garden brigade would require, whether or not they'd need fencing to keep out the local deer population, and other details specific to the site.

Samantha's ideas may inspire you. As she learned, making a garden plan for a school is not unlike figuring out what you'd like to put in your own backyard. Figure out what you want and why you want it. Make a list of plants that could work, determine how they could be used and enjoyed by the school, and listen for feedback. Is it your hope (and that of the school) that the children can grow foods to harvest and serve in the school cafeteria? How many plants will be edible or serve a practical use? Will it be totally organic? What about incorporating native plants into the landscape to fit in with your local ecosystem? Of course, the needs and wishes of your school will influence the answers to these kinds of questions, and the school will have to determine how a garden could fit into its regular curriculum.

Whether your plans are simple or ambitious, broad-strokes or detailed, be prepared with something to present to your audience.

Get as much help as you can. Samantha enlisted the help of other students, as well as teachers and parents. The more helping hands you have, the faster you can turn the earth and make it go from dirt to dream. Samantha used emails and word of mouth to send out her calls for volunteers. One parent offered to build all the raised beds, others loaned garden tools, and those who had neither expertise nor materials gave something just as valuable: their time.

Starting a schoolyard garden doesn't have to be expensive but it's not entirely free (unless you are lucky enough to have all the materials donated or to receive a grant to cover the costs). Consider how much money you'll need to raise and encourage fellow volunteers (including the students) to brainstorm fundraising ideas.

Samantha's parting advice? "Don't give up!" For more information and helpful suggestions, as well as ideas from other schools around the country, visit www.sustainabletable.org/schools/projects.

A Seed Worth Saving

Most kids think of seeds as something they spit out—watermelon seeds, peach pits, cherry stones, and others. While lots of seeds are inedible, kids are often surprised to discover that strawberries, for example, have their seeds on the outside; that seeds can travel many miles through the air and water; and that you won't grow an apple tree in your tummy if you accidentally swallow a seed!

Seed facts like these help children make the connection between the earth and the foods that it offers us. Even in our children's increasingly high-tech learning environments, nothing beats the thrill of planting a dried bean in a dirt-filled paper cup and watching it sprout!

hands-on family fun

The next time you eat an avocado, save the pit. With your help, have your child insert two or three toothpicks into the thickest part of the pit (in the middle). Fill a small jar with water and rest the pit on top (the toothpicks should be placed so that the pit is partially but not totally submerged in the water). Put it in a sunny windowsill and in a few weeks you can watch your avocado plant sprout roots, then leaves, and grow! Depending on what zone you live in, you can move your plant into the ground or into a pot once it's large enough. If you are fortunate enough to harvest an avocado from your tree, turn it into our Holy Green Guacamole!

Some families have luck with planting other types of seeds, such as peach pits and beans. When I was a child, my mom and I saved and sprouted avocado pits, and the leafy results never failed to amaze me. At the same time I learned about how we grow plants for food and why saving seeds is vital to the cycle of life. It's fun to see what happens when we put a part of our food back into the ground that it sprang from, and it's a true lesson for your child in maintaining a sustainable food supply.

WHEN IT'S TIME TO CELEBRATE

A Picnic Lunch, Indoors or Out!

During the school year, your children eat their lunch in a noisy cafeteria, and you probably eat yours (a bit more quietly) at work or at home. When there is down-time on the weekend or over the summer months, or during school holidays, why not share a special lunch with your kids and enjoy this meal as a family?

Everyone loves a picnic, and with these rain-or-shine, easy-to-pack foods, you can eat lunch in the great outdoors or on the living room floor inside a homemade fort. Let your kids get involved in picking foods (and even making decorations and planning games), or surprise them with a special midday meal. You can also do a simple brown-bag lunch with all your favorites—remember the main course, the garden, the crunch, the drink, and the treat—and just head to the nearest park bench!

A Perfect Picnic in the Park: Put together a classic picnic basket of warm weather foods, complete with a red checkered picnic blanket to spread out on the grass. Try our recipes for Holy Green Guaca-mole and Mango and Peach Salsa with pita chips, TLT Wraps, Turkey Burgers with Sweet Oat Rolls, and Ginger Snaps. Don't forget the watermelon!

Beach Party Blow-Out: Kids love Sponge Bob, but have you seen how he makes those greasy Krabby Patties? Keep the Bikini Bottom theme, but set sail for deliciously healthy food with Green Edamame Dip, Steamed Salmon Pouches, Coconut Shrimp with Pineapple Herb Dipping Sauce, Citrus and Herb Shrimp Kebabs, Hydration Salad, and Chocolate Ladybugs.

Mamma Mia, That's Yummy! Go Italian all the way, with White Bean Dip, Caprese Salad on a Stick, Pesto-Stuffed Cherry Tomatoes, Garden-Fresh Pasta, and Grilled Peach Sensation. Serve your feast outside and eat under the sun, Tuscan style. Buon Appetito!

Around the World, One Plate at a Time: At HealthBarn USA we love to make fantastic foods inspired by other cultures. Travel around the world without leaving your hometown, with recipes for our Chinese Chicken Rice Bowl, Veggie Pad Thai, Veggie Stir-Fry with Soba Noodles, Indian Veggie Medley, and our Carrot Halwa Dip.

TLT Wrap

The bacon, lettuce, and tomato sandwich is an American classic, but the average BLT is high in calories, saturated fat (the "bad" stuff for your heart), and sodium. We remade this favorite into a healthier option, without sacrificing the flavor. Turkey bacon is a lean protein and it's so satisfying that you'll never go back to regular bacon again! This wrap is high in vitamins A and C, two antioxidants that help keep our immune systems strong.

ingredients

4 slices turkey bacon (4 ounces)

2 whole wheat lavash flatbreads or 2 (11-inch) whole wheat wraps

4 teaspoons olive oil mayonnaise

4 Romaine lettuce leaves

2 tomatoes, cut into ¼-inch chunks

directions

1. Cook bacon as label directs; drain on paper towels. Set aside.

2. Unfold lavash. Cut each lavash crosswise in half to make 4 pieces in total. Place 1 piece on a plate or flat surface.

3. Spread 1 teaspoon mayonnaise evenly over one narrow end of lavash, covering about half of it. Place 1 lettuce leaf on mayonnaise at end of lavash (so it's easy to roll). Fill the spine of the lettuce leaf with ¼ of tomatoes; top with 1 slice bacon.

4. From the filling end, tightly roll lavash in jelly-roll fashion. If you like, cut the wrap in half.

5. Repeat to make 4 wraps in all.

Makes 4 servings (1 wrap per serving)

Nutrition Facts per serving: 150 calories; 7g fat (0.5g sat fat, 1g mono, 4g poly, 0g trans fat); 25mg cholesterol; 14g carbohydrate (2g fiber, 2g sugar); 9g protein; 320mg sodium; 15% Daily Value (DV) vitamin A; 20% DV vitamin C; 2% DV calcium; 8% DV iron

Kids can fill lavash and roll wraps.

Pasta and Sweet Peas

Garden-fresh sweet peas make this high-fiber recipe a favorite at the barn. This delicious pasta dish is good served hot or cold, so it's a popular leftover with kids for the lunchbox. It's high in vitamin C to keep the immune system in top form.

ingredients

1 package (13.25 ounces) whole wheat penne or rotelle pasta

2 tablespoons extra-virgin olive oil

1 large Spanish onion, thinly sliced

1 clove garlic, minced

2 large tomatoes, cut into 1-inch cubes

¼ cup water

1 teaspoon chopped fresh oregano leaves

⅛ teaspoon sea salt

⅛ teaspoon freshly ground black pepper

1 cup fresh peas, shelled, or 1 cup frozen peas, thawed

⅓ cup (1.5 ounces) shredded low-moisture, part-skim mozzarella cheese

2 tablespoons freshly grated Parmesan cheese

Spanish onions are readily available and sweeter than a regular onion.

directions

1. In a large saucepot of boiling water, cook pasta as label directs. Drain pasta and set aside.

2. Heat oil in a large nonstick skillet over medium heat. Add onion and cook until soft and translucent, about 10 minutes, stirring occasionally. Add garlic and cook for 30 seconds, stirring.

3. Add tomatoes, water, oregano, salt, and pepper and cook, uncovered, until tomatoes are very soft, about 10 minutes, stirring occasionally. Stir in pasta and peas and simmer 5 minutes to blend flavors and cook peas.

4. Remove saucepan from heat; stir in mozzarella and Parmesan.

Makes 10 servings (1 cup per serving)

Nutrition Facts per serving: 210 calories; 5g fat (1g sat fat, 2g mono, 1g poly, 0g trans fat); 5mg cholesterol; 35g carbohydrate (5g fiber, 5g sugar); 8g protein; 65mg sodium; 8% Daily Value (DV) vitamin A; 20% DV vitamin C; 8% DV calcium; 8% DV iron

---

Kids can take tomato quarters and chop into cubes and chop oregano using a plastic knife with adult supervision.

Spinach Pesto Pasta

The secret ingredient in this pesto is raw sunflower seeds instead of the traditional pine nuts, which are more expensive and higher in fat. We also use spinach instead of basil, and whole wheat pasta so that it's high in fiber. This pasta dish is a favorite lunch item with kids because it tastes so good, and it's popular with parents because it's so good for kids! Spinach is easy to grow, so this is the perfect recipe for anyone interested in starting a school or backyard garden. If you have a shovel in one hand, make sure you have a fork in the other, because this pesto dish disappears quickly!

ingredients

1 package (13.25 ounces) whole wheat penne or rotelle pasta

2 cups packed baby spinach leaves

¼ cup hulled raw sunflower seeds

¼ cup freshly grated Parmesan cheese

¼ teaspoon sea salt

¼ teaspoon freshly ground black pepper

1 clove garlic

2 tablespoons extra-virgin olive oil

2 tablespoons low-sodium vegetable broth (or water)

directions

1. In a large saucepot of boiling water, cook pasta as label directs. Reserve ½ cup of the pasta cooking water, then drain pasta. Set pasta aside in a large bowl.

2. In a food processor or blender, combine the spinach leaves, sunflower seeds, Parmesan, sea salt, pepper, and garlic; pulse until finely chopped. With the processor running, gradually add the oil and broth through feed tube to form a smooth, thick mixture.

3. Add spinach pesto to pasta in a bowl and toss until evenly coated. If mixture is too thick, stir in enough reserved pasta cooking water to reach the desired consistency.

Makes 8 servings (1 cup per serving)

Nutrition Facts per serving: 240 calories; 7g fat (1g sat fat, 3g mono, 2g poly, 0g trans fat); 0mg cholesterol; 37g carbohydrate (5g fiber, 2g sugar); 8g protein; 75mg sodium; 4% Daily Value (DV) vitamin A; 2% DV vitamin C; 6% DV calcium; 10% DV iron

Kids can add pesto ingredients to food processor and pulse.

Crustless Veggie Quiche

For lunch, brunch, or dinner, this colorful quiche, full of vitamin C, not only looks beautiful but tastes great too! We went crustless to lighten the calories and saturated fat, but you won't miss out on any of the flavor. Serve with whole-grain toast squares or with a green salad for a quick and satisfying meal. To keep the recipe seasonal, switch up the veggies.

ingredients

2 large eggs

2 large egg whites

½ (16-ounce) container reduced-fat cottage cheese (1 cup)

⅔ cup (2.5 ounces) shredded 50% reduced-fat cheddar cheese

¼ cup low-fat (1%) milk

¼ cup buckwheat flour or whole wheat flour

½ teaspoon baking powder

¼ teaspoon sea salt

1½ teaspoons olive oil

1 medium zucchini (10 ounces), cut into ¼-inch dice

½ medium red onion, cut into ¼-inch dice

½ red bell pepper, cut into ¼-inch dice

2 medium Yukon Gold potatoes, unpeeled and cut into ¼-inch dice (1 cup)

¼ cup chopped fresh dill

directions

1. Preheat oven to 350°F. Grease 12 muffin cups.

2. In a large bowl, with whisk, beat eggs and egg whites until fluffy. Whisk in cottage cheese, cheddar, milk, flour, baking powder, and salt; set aside.

3. In a large nonstick skillet, heat oil over medium heat. Add zucchini, onion, red pepper, potato, and dill and cook until all vegetables are tender, about 10 minutes, stirring occasionally. Stir vegetable mixture into egg mixture.

4. Ladle quiche mixture evenly into prepared muffin cups (filling will come almost to top). Set the pan in the middle of the oven. Bake for 20–25 minutes or until egg mixture puffs up and knife inserted in quiches comes out clean. Cool for 2 minutes, then loosen edges with sharp knife and scoop them out of the pan one by one. (They will deflate somewhat after cooling.)

5. Serve warm or at room temperature.

Makes 12 servings (1 quiche per serving)

Nutrition Facts per serving: 80 calories; 3g fat (1g sat fat, 1g mono, 0g trans fat); 35mg cholesterol; 7g carbohydrate (1g fiber, 2g sugar); 7g protein; 170mg sodium; 8% Daily Value (DV) vitamin A; 25% DV vitamin C; 8% DV calcium; 4% DV iron

---

Kids can crack and separate eggs; shred cheese; take strips of zucchini and pepper and dill and chop them using a plastic knife with adult supervision.

HealthBarn-O's Pasta

This baked pasta dish is so irresistible you'll think we traveled to Italy to get the recipe. We took the idea of SpaghettiOs but improved it so much that it tastes like it came out of a Sicilian *cucina*. It's high in protein, fiber, iron, and vitamins C and A. Parents give it the thumbs up because it's easy to make, plus the leftovers freeze very well.

ingredients

1 package (1 pound) anelletti pasta or small pasta shells

¾ pound ground beef (93% lean)

1 tablespoon olive oil

1 medium onion, coarsely chopped

3 cloves garlic, minced

1 can (28 ounces) crushed tomatoes

1 cup water

¼ cup coarsely chopped fresh basil leaves

1 teaspoon chopped fresh rosemary leaves

¼ teaspoon freshly ground black pepper

2 cups frozen peas

½ cup plain dried bread crumbs

4 tablespoons shredded low-moisture, part-skim mozzarella cheese (1 ounce)

2 tablespoons freshly grated Parmesan cheese

Nutrition Facts per serving: 290 calories; 5g fat (1g sat fat, 2g mono, 1g poly, 0g trans fat); 15mg cholesterol; 48g carbohydrate (5g fiber, 2g sugar); 15g protein; 200mg sodium; 15% Daily Value (DV) vitamin A; 15% DV vitamin C; 8% DV calcium; 20% DV iron

directions

1. In a large saucepot of boiling water, cook pasta as label directs. Drain pasta and set aside in a large bowl.

2. Heat a large skillet over medium-high heat. Add ground beef and cook, breaking up meat with side of spoon, until browned. Drain off excess fat. Spoon beef into a bowl and set aside.

3. In the same skillet, over medium heat, in 1 tablespoon of oil, cook the onion until soft and translucent, about 10 minutes, stirring occasionally. Add garlic and cook 30 seconds, stirring. Add tomatoes, water, basil, rosemary, and pepper; heat to boiling over high heat. Reduce heat to low; simmer uncovered for 5 minutes.

4. Return beef to the skillet; add peas and simmer uncovered for 5–7 minutes.

5. Add beef and tomato mixture to the pasta and mix well.

6. Preheat oven to 400°F. Grease the bottom of a 13 x 9-inch baking pan and sprinkle with 1 tablespoon of bread crumbs.

7. Spoon half of pasta mixture into pan; top with 2 tablespoons mozzarella and 1 tablespoon Parmesan. Repeat with remaining pasta mixture and cheeses.

8. Sprinkle the remaining bread crumbs on top. Cover with foil and bake for 15–20 minutes. Remove the foil and bake for 5–7 minutes longer to brown top.

9. Remove from the oven and let stand 10 minutes before serving.

Makes 10 servings (1 cup per serving)

Kids can layer pasta and cheese in the pan and top with bread crumbs.

Homemade Vs. Store-Bought: The Facts!

HealthBarn USA's HealthBarn-O's Pasta	Campbell's SpaghettiOs (original flavor) Reference: product package
Ingredients: Anelletti pasta, 93% lean ground beef, olive oil, onion, garlic, crushed tomatoes, water, basil, rosemary, pepper, peas, bread crumbs, part-skim mozzarella cheese, Parmesan cheese	**Ingredients:** Water, tomato puree (water, tomato paste), enriched macaroni product (wheat flour, niacin, ferrous sulfate, thiamine mononitrate, riboflavin, folic acid), high-fructose corn syrup, contains less than 2% of: salt, enzyme-modified cheddar cheese (cheddar cheese [cultured milk, salt, enzymes, calcium chloride], water, disodium phosphate, enzymes), flavoring, potassium chloride, vegetable oil (corn, cottonseed, canola, and/or soybean), enzyme modified butter (milk), skim milk, paprika extract, citric acid
Nutrition Facts (per serving): 290 calories; 5g fat (1g sat fat, 2g mono, 1g poly, 0g trans fat); 15mg cholesterol; 48g carbohydrate (5g fiber, 2g sugar); 15g protein; 200mg sodium; 15% Daily Value (DV) vitamin A; 15% DV vitamin C; 8% DV calcium; 20% DV iron	**Nutrition Facts** (per serving): 170 calories; 1g fat (0.5g sat fat, 0.5g poly, 0g trans fat); 5mg cholesterol; 35g carbohydrate (3g fiber, 11g sugar); 6g protein; 600mg sodium; 10% Daily Value (DV) vitamin A; 4% DV vitamin C ; 2% DV calcium; 10% DV iron
OURS: • 14 ingredients	**THEIRS:** • 27 ingredients • contains high-fructose corn syrup

Veggie Sushi Hand Roll

We love this twist on sushi for lunch! This nutrient-packed hand roll is easy to make and loaded with colorful veggies instead of fish for first-time sushi eaters. It's low in fat but full of fiber and iron, and it's an excellent way to get vitamins A and C.

ingredients

2¾ cups short-grain brown rice

4 cups water

¼ cup unseasoned rice vinegar

1 carrot

1 cucumber, unpeeled

1 red bell pepper

1 yellow bell pepper

½ cup fresh chives

10 sheets nori (seaweed)

Low-sodium soy sauce for dipping
    (optional)

directions

1. Place the rice in a coarse-mesh sieve and rinse with cold running water until water runs clear. Shake out excess water.

2. In a large saucepan, combine rice and water; heat to boiling over high heat. Reduce heat to low; cover and simmer for 40 minutes or until rice is tender and water is absorbed. Remove from heat; let stand, covered, for 10 minutes. Transfer rice to a bowl and sprinkle with rice vinegar; toss and let cool.

3. Meanwhile, peel the carrot and cut into matchsticks. Cut the unpeeled cucumber lengthwise in half; discard seeds. Then cut cucumber into matchsticks. Slice peppers into matchsticks. Cut chives to match the length of the vegetables. All vegetables should be about the same length and thickness. Cut each nori sheet in half crosswise.

4. To prepare sushi, hold the nori in one hand, shiny side down. Dip your free hand in a small bowl of water to prevent sticking. Using your wet hand, shape ¼ cup rice into a ball and place on the left side of nori sheet. Spread the rice to a ¼-inch thickness, leaving about a 1-inch border of nori on the sides. With your finger, make a crosswise "well" in the center of rice where vegetables will go.

5. Place 1–2 sticks of each vegetable (carrot, cucumber, peppers, and chives) in the well and tightly press vegetables together. (Let kids pick combos of their favorites, but making colorful sushi is the goal!)

6. To roll sushi, start with bottom left edge of the nori and bring it up on a diagonal to the center of the rice and vegetable. Start rolling the sushi to the right to create a cone shape, using your free hand to tuck it all together tightly. With your fingertip, place a drop of water on the outside bottom corner of the nori to hold the sushi together.

7. Repeat steps 4–6 with remaining ingredients.

8. Place sushi rolls on a platter and serve with low-sodium soy sauce for dipping, if you like.

Makes 10 servings (2 hand rolls per serving)

Nutrition Facts per serving: 220 calories; 2g total fat (0g sat, 1g poly, 0g trans fat); 0g cholesterol; 46g carbohydrate (3g fiber, 2g sugar); 6g protein; 50mg sodium; 25% Daily Value (DV) vitamin A; 90% DV vitamin C; 4% DV calcium; 10% DV iron

---

Kids can make their own roll using prepared ingredients.

Pasta Fagioli with Mini Meatballs

This classic Italian recipe is popular with kids because it combines two favorite and fun-to-eat foods: soup and meatballs! The turkey meatballs make a great family activity and the cannellini beans transform the broth into a creamy, delicious concoction. Make a big pot of it and your kids will be sure to fill up their thermoses for a tasty and nutritious school lunch loaded with fiber, vitamins A and C, and iron.

ingredients

Mini Meatballs

¾ cup bulgur wheat

2½ cups water, divided

3 slices whole wheat bread, cut into 1-inch pieces

4 large egg whites

3 cloves garlic, minced

1½ pounds ground turkey (99% lean)

½ cup freshly grated Parmesan cheese

1½ teaspoons chopped fresh oregano leaves

¼ teaspoon sea salt

¼ teaspoon freshly ground black pepper

Soup

2 tablespoons olive oil

4 carrots, chopped

4 celery stalks, chopped

1 medium onion, chopped

2 cloves garlic, minced

2 cans (15 ounces each) low-sodium white kidney beans (cannellini), drained and rinsed

1 quart reduced-sodium chicken broth

1 can (8 ounces) no-salt-added tomato sauce

2 plum tomatoes, cut into ¼-inch dice

¼ cup loosely packed fresh parsley leaves, chopped

1 cup Israeli couscous

directions

1. Preheat oven to 425°F. Line a rimmed baking sheet with foil and lightly grease.

2. Prepare the Mini Meatballs: In a medium bowl, combine bulgur and 1½ cups water. Let soak 20 minutes.

3. In another medium bowl, combine bread with remaining 1 cup water. Let soak a few minutes; drain and squeeze out excess liquid.

4. In a large bowl, add egg whites, bulgur, bread, garlic, turkey, Parmesan, oregano, salt, and pepper; mix together with hands just until well blended but not overmixed. Shape mixture by rounded tablespoons into 45 mini meatballs and place on the prepared baking sheet.

5. Bake meatballs for 10–12 minutes, until lightly browned and cooked through; remove from oven and set aside.

6. Prepare the Soup: In a large saucepot, heat oil over medium heat. Add carrots, celery, onion, and garlic and cook until vegetables are soft, about 10 minutes, stirring occasionally.

7. Meanwhile, on a plate, mash half of the beans with a fork; set aside.

8. To the vegetables in the saucepot, add the whole beans, broth, tomato sauce, tomatoes with their juice, and parsley; heat to boiling over high heat. Reduce heat to low; simmer for 5 minutes.

9. Add uncooked couscous, meatballs, and mashed beans; cook over medium heat for 8–10 minutes or until couscous is al dente.

10. Spoon 1 cup of soup into each of 15 bowls; sprinkle with additional Parmesan, if you like.

Makes 15 servings (1 cup soup per serving)

Nutrition Facts per serving: 230 calories; 4g fat (1g sat fat, 2g mono, 0g trans fat); 20mg cholesterol; 28g carbohydrate (6g fiber, 4g sugar); 20g protein; 330mg sodium; 60% Daily Value (DV) vitamin A; 10% DV vitamin C; 8% DV calcium; 10% DV iron

---

Kids can shape meatballs and mash beans.

Quinoa Falafel

Falafel tastes terrific, but it's traditionally deep-fried, which means it's much higher in fat than we'd like. So we reworked this Mediterranean classic and came up with a pan-fried version that got the thumbs up from the kids at the barn. Our falafel packs a punch of protein, thanks to the quinoa. Serve these flavorful patties in a pita pocket with yogurt sauce for a boost of calcium.

ingredients

Falafel

½ cup quinoa

1 cup water

1 can (15 ounces) chickpeas (garbanzo beans), drained and rinsed

1 large egg, beaten

1 clove garlic, coarsely chopped

1 cup loosely packed fresh flat-leaf parsley leaves

Juice of ½ lemon

½ teaspoon grated fresh lemon peel

¼ teaspoon ground cumin

¼ teaspoon ground coriander

¼ teaspoon sea salt

½ cup whole wheat panko bread crumbs

3 (4-inch) whole wheat pitas, warmed

Yogurt Sauce

½ small cucumber, coarsely shredded

1 cup plain low-fat yogurt

¼ cup chopped fresh mint leaves

Juice of ¼ lemon

½ teaspoon grated fresh lemon peel

⅛ teaspoon ground coriander

⅛ teaspoon sea salt

⅛ teaspoon freshly ground black pepper

directions

1. Prepare the Falafel: Rinse the quinoa with cold running water; drain. In a medium saucepan, heat water to boiling over high heat; stir in quinoa. Reduce heat to low; cover and simmer for about 15 minutes or until liquid is absorbed. Spread quinoa on a sheet pan to cool.

2. In a food processor, combine beans, egg, garlic, parsley, lemon juice, lemon peel, cumin, coriander, and salt. Pulse until just pureed.

3. In a bowl, stir the bean puree and quinoa until well blended. Shape bean mixture into six 1-inch-thick patties. Place panko in a shallow bowl or pie plate; add patties, turning to coat. Set aside.

4. Lightly grease a large nonstick skillet; heat over medium-high heat. Carefully add patties to skillet and cook about 6 minutes or until browned on both sides and heated through, turning over once.

5. Prepare the Yogurt Sauce: Squeeze as much liquid out of shredded cucumber as possible. In a small bowl, combine cucumber, yogurt, mint, lemon juice, lemon peel, coriander, salt, and pepper.

6. To serve, cut each pita in half. Fill each half with 1 patty and drizzle yogurt sauce evenly over patties.

Makes 6 servings (1 half pita per serving)

Nutrition Facts per serving: 240 calories; 4g fat (1g sat fat, 1g mono, 1g poly, 0g trans fat); 35mg cholesterol; 42g carbohydrate (6g fiber, 4g sugar); 11g protein; 370mg sodium; 20% Daily Value (DV) vitamin A; 35% DV vitamin C; 15% DV calcium; 20% DV iron

Kids can shape bean mixture using their hands and coat in panko to make falafel; and they can make yogurt sauce.

Hydration Salad

Put down the Gatorade and Vitamin Water! We've concocted a natural fruit and veggie salad that's loaded with vitamins A and C and a lot of water to keep us hydrated all day long, at school or on the playing field. The lime, rich in citric acid, helps keep this super salad fresh for up to 4 days in the refrigerator.

ingredients

½ medium honeydew melon, peeled and cut into 1-inch chunks

½ medium cantaloupe, peeled and cut into 1-inch chunks

½ small seedless cucumber, unpeeled and cut into 1-inch chunks

Juice from 1 lime

⅛ teaspoon sea salt

directions

1. In a large bowl, combine melons and cucumber. Add lime juice and salt and toss to mix well.

2. Serve in bowls or large cups to go.

Makes 8 servings (1 cup per serving)

Nutrition Facts per serving: 45 calories; 0g fat (0g trans fat), 0mg cholesterol; 12g carbohydrate (1g fiber, 10g sugar); 1g protein; 35mg sodium; 25% Daily Value (DV) vitamin A; 50% DV vitamin C; 2% DV iron

Kids can cut melon wedges and cucumber strips into smaller chunks using a plastic knife with adult supervision; and they can squeeze limes (and suck on them afterward!) and pinch sea salt.

Zany Zucchini Soup

We love this soup at any time of the year, but especially when zucchini is in season. It's a good source of vitamins A and C as well as calcium to keep growing bodies strong throughout the school day. Pack it for lunch because it's satisfying served hot *or* cold!

ingredients

- 3 cups low-sodium vegetable or chicken broth
- 3 medium zucchini (10 ounces each), cut into 1-inch chunks
- ¼ cup chopped fresh basil leaves
- ¼ cup chopped fresh chives, divided
- ¼ teaspoon sea salt
- ¼ teaspoon freshly ground black pepper
- ½ cup (2 ounces) shredded 50% reduced-fat cheddar cheese

directions

1. In a medium saucepan, place the broth, zucchini, basil, 2 tablespoons of chives, salt, and pepper; heat to boiling over high heat. Reduce heat to low and simmer, uncovered, until the zucchini is tender, 7–10 minutes.

2. Pour half of the mixture into a blender; cover, with center part of blender cover removed to let steam escape, and blend until pureed. (Or, use an immersion blender and puree in the saucepan.)

3. Pour soup into a bowl and repeat with remaining mixture. Return all soup to saucepan and heat over medium heat, slowly stirring in cheese until cheese melts and soup is smooth. Do not boil or soup may separate.

4. Serve soup hot topped with the remaining 2 tablespoons of chives or cover and refrigerate for up to 4 days to serve cold.

Makes 5 servings (1 cup per serving)

Nutrition Facts per serving: 60 calories; 2g fat (1g sat fat, 0g trans fat); 5mg cholesterol; 6g carbohydrate (2g fiber, 3g sugar); 5g protein; 190mg sodium; 10% Daily Value (DV) vitamin A; 35% DV vitamin C; 10% DV calcium; 6% DV iron

Kids can take zucchini strips and cut them into chunks and can chop herbs using a plastic knife with adult supervision.

Creamy Broccoli Soup

We typically avoid "creamy soups" because they are usually high in saturated fat, but *our* creamy soup—healthy and slimmed down—is most definitely an exception. Sip a serving of this light but filling low-fat soup for calcium and vitamins A and C.

ingredients

1 tablespoon olive oil

1 medium onion, chopped

2 cloves garlic, minced

1 tablespoon whole wheat flour

2 cups water

3 cups broccoli florets

2 medium white potatoes, peeled and coarsely chopped

1 cup low-fat (1%) milk

¼ teaspoon sea salt

¼ teaspoon freshly ground black pepper

½ cup (2 ounces) shredded 50% reduced-fat cheddar cheese

½ cup finely chopped chives

directions

1. In a large saucepan, heat the oil over medium heat. Add onion and cook until tender and translucent, 7–10 minutes, stirring occasionally. Stir in garlic; cook 30 seconds, stirring.

2. Add flour to the vegetable mixture and cook for 1 minute, stirring constantly. Gradually stir in water and cook, stirring, until mixture boils and thickens slightly, about 5 minutes.

3. Add the broccoli and potatoes; heat to boiling. Reduce heat to low; cover and simmer for 20 minutes or until broccoli and potatoes are fork-tender. Remove saucepan from heat.

4. Pour about ⅓ of soup into blender; cover, with center part of cover removed to let steam escape, and blend until pureed. (Or, use an immersion blender and puree in saucepan.)

5. Pour soup into a large bowl and repeat in batches with remaining mixture. Return all soup to saucepan; stir in milk, salt, and pepper and heat through over medium heat.

6. To serve, ladle soup into 9 soup bowls; top with cheddar and chives divided evenly among the bowls.

Makes 9 servings (1 cup per serving)

Nutrition Facts per serving: 90 calories; 3g fat (1g sat fat, 1g mono, 0g trans fat); 5mg cholesterol; 13g carbohydrate (2g fiber, 3g sugar); 5g protein; 80mg sodium; 20% Daily Value (DV) vitamin A; 60% DV vitamin C; 10% DV calcium; 6% DV iron

Kids can break broccoli into florets with hands; shred cheese; and chop chives using a plastic knife with adult supervision.

Green Edamame Dip

The edamame give this dip its green color; the flaxseed oil and walnuts make it a good source of healthy fats. Serve with baby carrots, celery sticks, and bell pepper slices, or use it as a spread in a whole wheat wrap or sandwich with your favorite fillings.

ingredients

1 cup fresh or frozen (thawed) shelled edamame (soybeans)

¾ cup walnuts

½ cup loosely packed fresh parsley leaves

¼ cup plus 2 tablespoons plain low-fat yogurt

1 teaspoon flaxseed oil

¼ teaspoon sea salt

1 small clove garlic

Sliced raw vegetables and/or pita chips

directions

1. In a food processor, place all ingredients except sliced vegetables and pita chips. Pulse until ingredients are well blended and mixture is smooth.

2. Serve with cut-up vegetables or pita chips, or cover and refrigerate for up to 4 days.

Makes 13 servings (2 tablespoons per serving)

Nutrition Facts per serving: 60 calories; 5g fat (0g sat fat, 1g mono, 3g poly, 0g trans fat); 0mg cholesterol; 3g carbohydrate (1g fiber, 1g sugar); 2g protein; 20mg sodium; 6% Daily Value (DV) vitamin A; 6% DV vitamin C; 2% DV calcium; 4% DV iron

Kids can measure and add ingredients to food processor and pulse.

Veggie Chili

This nutrient-packed veggie chili is easy to make, great for sharing with friends and family, and full of seasonal vegetables. The beans are a good source of protein and iron as well as fiber. Dig in to a bowl of the best for lunch or dinner.

ingredients

2 tablespoons olive oil

1 sweet onion, such as Vidalia, chopped

1 green bell pepper, chopped

1 jalapeño chile, seeded and chopped (optional)

2 ounces mushrooms, sliced

2 cloves garlic, chopped

2 tablespoons chili powder

8 medium tomatoes (4 pounds), coarsely chopped

2 cans (15 ounces each) low-sodium red kidney beans, drained and rinsed

directions

1. In a large saucepot, heat the oil over medium heat. Add onion, green pepper, and jalapeño (if using) and cook for 5 minutes, stirring occasionally. Add mushrooms and cook for 5 more minutes, or until vegetables are tender. Stir in garlic and chili powder; cook for 1 minute.

2. Add the tomatoes with their juice and the beans; heat to boiling. Reduce heat to low; cover and simmer for 50–55 minutes.

Makes 10 servings (1 cup per serving)

Nutrition Facts per serving: 170 calories; 4g fat (0g sat fat, 2g mono, 1g poly, 0g trans fat); 0mg cholesterol; 28g carbohydrate (8g fiber, 5g sugar); 9g protein; 140mg sodium; 8% Daily Value (DV) vitamin A; 50% DV vitamin C; 4% DV calcium; 15% DV iron

---

Kids can take strips of bell pepper (not the jalepeño!) and tomatoes and chop using a plastic knife with adult supervision.

White Bean Dip

For those of you who love to dip into something really yummy, break out the sliced veggies or pita chips. This natural dip can also do double-duty as a spread for sandwiches, instead of mayo or mustard. The vitamin C will boost your immune system while the omega-3 fatty acids will benefit your heart and memory!

ingredients

1 can (19 ounces) low-sodium, white kidney beans (cannellini), drained and rinsed

¼ cup chopped fresh parsley leaves

¼ cup chopped fresh chives

2 tablespoons extra-virgin olive oil

1 tablespoon flaxseed oil

Juice of 2 lemons

2 teaspoons water

¼ teaspoon sea salt

½ teaspoon freshly ground black pepper

1 clove garlic

Sliced raw vegetables and/or pita chips

directions

1. In a food processor, place all ingredients except vegetables and pita chips. Pulse until ingredients are well blended and mixture is smooth.

2. Serve with cut-up vegetables or pita chips, or cover and refrigerate for up to 4 days.

Makes 10 servings (2 tablespoons per serving)

Nutrition Facts per serving: 80 calories; 5g fat (1g sat fat, 2g mono, 1g poly, 0g trans fat); 0mg cholesterol; 8g carbohydrate (2g fiber, 1g sugar); 3g protein; 30mg sodium; 4% Daily Value (DV) vitamin A; 10% DV vitamin C; 2% DV calcium; 6% DV iron

Kids can measure and add ingredients to food processor and pulse.

Rainbow Quinoa Salad

This fresh and flavorful creation uses whole-grain quinoa (pronounced *keen-wah*), which is the only grain that naturally contains protein. The combination of vitamin C and iron in this recipe is really important, because your body uses the vitamin C to help absorb the iron. Feta cheese is really tasty, but if you prefer, substitute goat cheese. Get the kids involved in chopping, measuring, and mixing because this recipe is a fun family activity and a great meal to pack for lunch!

ingredients

2 cups quinoa

3 cups water

1½ tablespoons extra-virgin olive oil

1 tablespoon minced shallot

Juice of ½ a lemon

1 teaspoon sherry vinegar

1 teaspoon chopped fresh dill

¼ teaspoon sea salt

1 cup cherry tomatoes, quartered

½ yellow bell pepper, cut into ¼-inch dice (½ cup)

1 small unpeeled Kirby cucumber, cut into ¼-inch dice (½ cup)

¼ cup (1 ounce) crumbled feta cheese

The short, versatile Kirby cucumber is used for both slicing and pickling. It's small, with bumpy yellow or green skin. Like the English cucumber, it has a thin skin and inconspicuous seeds. They have more flesh and fewer seeds and they are super crunchy— but a regular cucumber will do as well.

directions

1. Rinse the quinoa with cold running water and drain.

2. In a large saucepan, heat water to boiling over high heat. Stir in quinoa. Reduce heat to low; cover and simmer for about 15 minutes or until liquid is absorbed. Uncover and fluff quinoa with fork. Set aside to cool to room temperature.

3. In a large bowl, whisk together the oil, shallot, lemon juice, vinegar, dill, and salt. Add tomatoes, pepper, cucumber, and feta, and toss to mix. Gently stir in quinoa.

Makes 7 servings (1 cup per serving)

Nutrition Facts per serving: 240 calories; 7g fat (1g sat fat, 3g mono, 3g poly, 0g trans fat); 5mg cholesterol; 36g carbohydrate (3g fiber, 1g sugar); 8g protein; 95mg sodium; 4% Daily Value (DV) vitamin A; 40% DV vitamin C; 6% DV calcium; 25% DV iron

Kids can take bell pepper and cucumber strips and chop; quarter cherry tomatoes; and chop dill using a plastic knife with adult supervision.

Popcorn with Brain Butter

Popcorn is the ultimate whole-grain snack food, but often its nutritional value is compromised by the microwave and movie theater versions. We've remade this much-loved snack by using an air popper to pop the corn kernels and then adding flaxseed oil instead of butter. Flaxseed oil's yellow color looks like butter, but this healthy fat rich in omega-3 fatty acids protects our hearts and sharpens our brains. Add a few pinches of sea salt to taste and munch away.

ingredients

¼ cup popcorn kernels

1 tablespoon flaxseed oil

¼ teaspoon sea salt

directions

1. Place popcorn kernels in an air popper and pop following manufacturer's directions.

2. In a medium bowl, drizzle flaxseed oil over popped corn and sprinkle with salt; toss to coat evenly.

Makes 4 serving (1 cup per serving)

Nutrition Facts per serving: 70 calories; 4g fat (0g sat fat, 1g mono, 2g poly, 0g trans fat); 0mg cholesterol; 8g carbohydrate (2g fiber, 0g sugar); 1g protein; 30mg sodium; 4% Daily Value (DV) iron

Kids can fill the popper, drizzle flaxseed oil on popcorn, and pinch sea salt.

Homemade Vs. Store-Bought: The Facts!

HealthBarn USA's Popcorn with Brain Butter	Jolly Time's Blast O Butter Microwave Popcorn Reference: www.jollytime.com
Ingredients: Popcorn kernels, flaxseed oil, sea salt	**Ingredients:** 100% whole-grain pop corn, partially hydrogenated soybean oil, salt, natural and artificial flavors, annatto for coloring, soy lecithin
Nutrition Facts (per serving): 70 calories; 4g fat (0g sat fat, 1g mono, 2g poly, 0 g trans); 0mg cholesterol; 8g carbohydrate (2g fiber, 0g sugar); 1g protein; 30mg sodium; 4% Daily Value (DV) iron	**Nutrition Facts** (per serving): 150 calories; 12g fat (3g sat fat, 4g trans fat); 0mg cholesterol; 19g carbohydrate (9g fiber, 0g sugar); 3g protein; 340mg sodium; 6% Daily Value (DV) iron
OURS: • 3 ingredients	**THEIRS:** • 7 ingredients • contains partially hydrogenated oils resulting in 4g trans fat per serving • artificial flavors added

Zucchini Sticks

Zucchini fries? Yes! We use zucchini instead of potato and cover it in panko bread crumbs mixed with Parmesan cheese and fresh chopped herbs. Then, we bake these instead of frying, making them low in saturated fat. You can truly enjoy these delicious "fries," a good source of vitamin C, without the guilt. This recipe works very well with eggplant too. Experiment with any of your favorite veggies.

ingredients

3 medium zucchini (10–12 ounces each)

1 large egg

1 large egg white

1½ cups whole wheat panko bread crumbs

½ cup freshly grated Parmesan cheese

¼ cup ground flaxseeds

1 tablespoon finely chopped fresh parsley leaves

¼ teaspoon sea salt

¼ teaspoon freshly ground black pepper

directions

1. Preheat oven to 400°F. Grease a large baking sheet.
2. Cut each zucchini in half lengthwise; scoop out seeds. Cut each half zucchini in half again crosswise, then cut into ¼-inch-wide sticks.
3. In a pie plate or bowl, whisk egg and egg white until blended. In another pie plate or bowl, stir together panko, Parmesan, flaxseeds, parsley, salt, and pepper.
4. Dip the zucchini sticks into the egg mixture, then into the panko mixture to coat. Place zucchini on prepared baking sheet.
5. Bake zucchini until crisp and golden, about 25 minutes, turning over halfway through baking.

Makes 12 servings (½ cup per serving)

Nutrition Facts per serving: 70 calories; 3g fat (1g sat fat, 1g mono, 1g poly, 0g trans fat); 20mg cholesterol; 8g carbohydrate (1g fiber, 1g sugar); 4g protein; 100mg sodium; 4% Daily Value (DV) vitamin A; 15% DV vitamin C; 4% DV calcium; 2% DV iron

Kids can dip zucchini sticks in egg mixture and panko to coat and can place them place on the baking sheet.

Harvest Wheat Berry Salad

Put some crunch in your lunch (or dinner) with this sweet and satisfying whole-grain salad that's full of fiber, healthy fats, vitamin A, and iron. The extras travel well in a lunchbox!

ingredients

2 cups water

1 cup hard wheat berries

2 carrots, shredded (½ cup)

½ cup dried cranberries or raisins

⅓ cup chopped walnuts (optional)

¼ cup thinly sliced scallions

1 tablespoon extra-virgin olive oil or walnut oil

1 tablespoon balsamic vinegar

1½ teaspoons cider vinegar

1 teaspoon chopped fresh dill

⅛ teaspoon sea salt

directions

1. In a medium saucepan, combine water and wheat berries; heat to boiling over high heat. Reduce heat to low; cover and simmer for 40 minutes or until wheat berries are tender but still firm to the bite. Drain wheat berries; set aside to cool slightly.

2. In a large bowl, stir together wheat berries and all the remaining ingredients.

Makes 6 servings (½ cup per serving)

Nutrition Facts per serving: 210 calories; 7g fat (1g sat fat, 3g mono, 3g poly, 0g trans fat); 0mg cholesterol; 34g carbohydrate (5g fiber, 8g sugar); 5g protein; 20mg sodium; 30% Daily Value (DV) vitamin A; 2% DV vitamin C; 2% DV calcium; 10% DV iron

---

Kids can shred carrots and slice scallions and chop dill using a plastic knife with adult supervision.

Bulgur Tabbouleh

This wheaty tabbouleh gets added crunch from garden-fresh cucumbers. Loaded with heart-healthy good fat, antioxidants, and fiber, it's also easy to make.

ingredients

1½ cups boiling water

1 cup bulgur wheat

Juice of 2 lemons

3 tablespoons extra-virgin olive oil

⅛ teaspoon sea salt

1 clove garlic, finely chopped

1 cup grape or cherry tomatoes, halved

1 medium unpeeled cucumber, cut into ¼-inch dice

1 cup chopped fresh parsley leaves

1 cup chopped fresh chives

½ cup chopped fresh mint leaves

¼ cup (1 ounce) crumbled feta cheese

Pita chips and/or whole wheat crackers

directions

1. In a large bowl, pour boiling water over the bulgur, stirring to mix. Cover and set aside until water is absorbed, about 30 minutes.

2. Stir lemon juice, oil, salt, and garlic into bulgur. Add tomatoes, cucumbers, parsley, chives, mint, and feta, and gently toss to mix well. Cover and refrigerate at least 1 hour to blend flavors or up to 4 days.

3. Serve chilled or at room temperature with pita chips or whole wheat crackers.

Makes 10 servings (½ cup per serving)

Nutrition Facts per serving: 110 calories; 5g fat (1g sat fat, 4g mono, 1g poly, 0g trans fat); 5mg cholesterol; 14g carbohydrate (4g fiber, 1g sugar); 3g protein; 55mg sodium; 20% Daily Value (DV) vitamin A; 30% DV vitamin C; 4% DV calcium; 6% DV iron

---

Kids can juice lemons; halve grape tomatoes and dice cucumber strips using a plastic knife; and chop herbs, with adult supervision.

Chocolate Pudding

Instant pudding, step aside! This tasty, low-fat snack or dessert is made with all-natural ingredients like cocoa and milk, not the laundry list of artificial ingredients you'll get in instant pudding. It's quick and easy to make, and it provides a good source of calcium. Add sliced fruit (we like bananas) to make it an even healthier snack.

ingredients

⅓ cup granulated sugar

¼ cup unsweetened cocoa powder

3 tablespoons cornstarch

⅛ teaspoon sea salt

2 cups low-fat (1%) milk

½ cup water

2 teaspoons vanilla extract

directions

1. In a medium saucepan, stir sugar, cocoa, cornstarch, and salt until blended; gradually stir in milk and water.

2. Cook over medium heat until mixture thickens and boils, about 20 minutes, stirring constantly. Boil for 1 minute, stirring. Remove from heat; stir in vanilla.

3. Pour the pudding into 6 small dessert bowls. Cool slightly at room temperature; serve warm. If not serving right away, cover with plastic wrap on top of pudding to prevent a film from forming and refrigerate until chilled, about 30 minutes or up to 3 days (good luck keeping them in the refrigerator!).

Makes 6 servings (½ cup per serving)

Nutrition Facts per serving: 110 calories; 2g fat (1g sat fat, 1g mono, 0g trans fat); 5mg cholesterol; 20g carbohydrate (1g fiber, 15g sugar); 4g protein; 55mg sodium; 4% Daily Value (DV) vitamin A; 10% DV calcium; 8% DV iron

Kids can measure and add ingredients and stir pudding on stove with adult supervision.

Homemade Vs. Store-Bought: The Facts!

HealthBarn USA's Chocolate Pudding	Snack Pack Pudding (chocolate flavor) Reference: product package
Ingredients: Sugar, unsweetened cocoa powder, cornstarch, sea salt, low-fat milk, water, vanilla extract	**Ingredients:** Water, nonfat milk, sugar, modified cornstarch, vegetable oil (contains one or more of the following: palm oil, partially hydrogenated palm oil, sunflower oil, partially hydrogenated soybean oil), cocoa (processed with alkali), less than 2% of: salt, calcium carbonate, sodium stearoyl lactylate, artificial flavors, color added
Nutrition Facts (per serving): 110 calories; 2g fat (1g sat fat, 1g mono, 0g trans fat); 5mg cholesterol; 20g carbohydrate (1g fiber, 15g sugar); 4g protein; 55mg sodium; 4% Daily Value (DV) vitamin A; 10% DV calcium; 8% DV iron	**Nutrition Facts** (per serving): 120 calories; 3g fat (1.5g sat fat, 0g trans fat); 0mg cholesterol; 21g carbohydrate (2g fiber, 14g sugar); 1g protein; 130mg sodium; 10% Daily Value (DV) calcium; 4% DV iron
OURS: • 7 ingredients	**THEIRS:** • 14 ingredients • contains partially hydrogenated oils (sources of trans fat) • added artificial flavors and colors

CHAPTER 5

Afternoon Appetites: Satisfying Snacks That Won't Spoil Dinner

RECIPES

chool's out but that doesn't mean the day is done. For many kids, it's still in full swing as they head home or on to after-school activities that will keep them busy until bedtime. They might have piano lessons, karate, homework, or sports practice—but lunch was hours ago. Whether they choose Legos over lacrosse or softball instead of singing in the chorus, kids all have one thing in common when that dismissal bell rings—they are hungry and they need high-quality fuel to get them through the afternoon. Keep your child's energy level high with naturally delicious snacks that are fun to eat and simple to prepare.

Mini-Meals: Hunger-Busting Snacks That Do the Trick

Some of the ready-to-go morning snacks in chapter 3 will do just fine for kids who need portable food. But, if a child comes home before heading out again, now is your best chance to serve up snacks that function as mini-meals—substantial combinations of whole grains, a little lean protein and healthy fat, and fruits and/or veggies. A peanut butter spread on an apple or on whole wheat bread beats an artificially flavored yogurt-in-a-tube or a refined sugar–packed granola bar any afternoon!

Don't balk at offering something that seems like a meal in itself (such as a sandwich or wrap, a bowl of homemade soup, or even a snack-size portion of healthy dinner leftovers). Any well-rounded snack that leaves a child (or an adult) satisfied is a good snack. A handful of pretzels, on the other hand, isn't balanced nutrition. That's why the recipes at the end of this chapter include items that sound like lunch or dinner, such as our Whole Wheat Pita Pizzas or Caprese Salad on a Stick, Pesto-Stuffed Cherry Tomatoes, or dips like our Holy Green Guacamole or Spinach and Artichoke Dip.

Here are some more after-school snacking tips that will help you and your child bridge the hunger gap until dinnertime, simply and healthily:

✦ *Stock up on the good stuff.* You already know that keeping good food on hand for meals is a must for a healthy day of family eating. Make sure there's enough for after-school snacking too. When you keep your kitchen full of fresh fruits, low-fat yogurt, whole grains, and healthy fats (and free of processed, artificial foods), you make it much easier for your child to make good choices.

✦ *Let the kids cook something up.* If your child is old enough, she can make many of the recipes in this book herself, or she can get involved with preparing them.

Kids in the Kitchen: Fighting BAC!

That's BAC as in bacteria, something we don't want in the kitchen! When kids are starting to cook on their own, it's important for them to practice kitchen hygiene basics and to understand the connection between foodborne illnesses and common bacteria that can be spread in a home kitchen when we're not careful. Take a moment and share these tips with your young chefs:

Wash. Scrubbing your hands and hard surfaces like countertops helps Fight BAC!

Separate. Raw meat can contain a lot of bacteria. It's important to keep it away from other foods to Fight BAC!

Cook. Cook foods to the proper temperature to Fight BAC! Use a thermometer to make sure your food is cooked enough by checking the internal temperatures:

- Whole cuts of beef, lamb, veal, and pork: 145°F
- Poultry (ground, too!): 165°F
- Ground meat (beef, pork, lamb, veal): 160°F
- Fish: 145°F or until the flesh is opaque

Chill. Keeping foods refrigerated at the right temperature helps Fight BAC! The refrigerator temperature should be 40°F or below.

Make it easy for your child to "Fight BAC"* by stocking your kitchen with plenty of washable cutting boards. Use color-coded plastic cutting boards to prevent cross-contamination of foods. For instance, use green for fruits and veggies, red for meats, etc. Also, have lots of soap and scrubbing pads, easy-to-access food storage containers, a working meat thermometer (they should know how to use it), and any other tools to make it simple for them to cook safely.

---

* "Fight BAC!" is part of a food safety program produced in conjunction with the USDA, among other partners. For more information on other food safety measures, visit their website at www.fightbac.org.

Fixing no-cook snacks or those that require almost no cooking is a great way for a kid to feel comfortable and independent in the kitchen. Some tasty places to start: our EZ-Make Cookies, Banana Cream Smoothie, and The Perfect Pop.

✦ *Offer water first.* Though some kids are downright ravenous when they get home from school, before you offer them food, offer them water—because often

REAL-LIFE RESULTS:
Ravenous Kids Offered Donuts During Carpool!

Chris recently came to me with a sticky situation—literally **sticky,** because donuts were involved—and asked for advice. Her kids play travel soccer and regularly carpool with another teammate's family to travel the long distances required by their away games. When Chris drives, she makes sure there's good food in the car for the trip home, plus plenty of water. When the other family drives, they routinely stop at a drive-through donut shop on the way home and "treat" the kids to sugary snacks and drinks.

Chris's kids usually partake. They know it's not healthy, but the team spirit apparently has a hold over them, even in the car. But more importantly, they are starving and donuts are the only game in town. Chris would like the other parent to bypass the fried dough altogether, but is afraid to offend this family for questioning their choices—plus, she really wants to stay in the carpool. "Should I speak up?" Chris asked me. "I am afraid I'll come off like some kind of spoil-sport and a food fanatic if I tell them not to take my kids for a greasy sugar rush. I'm worried they'll think we're being rigid and weird, but I don't want my children putting that junk in their bodies, particularly after they've just played hard and need good nutrition."

The quick-fix solution is that her kids should travel with enough healthy food to eat after the game, even when Chris isn't driving—perhaps fruit, yogurt, a sandwich, homemade oatmeal cookies, HealthBarn USA's all-natural snack mix—nourishment to hold them over on the car trip home. If they are eating good foods from nature, then gradually it will be easier and easier for them to say no to the donuts and eat their own stash of delicious and more satisfying items brought from home.

However, this brings up a bigger issue that parents and children encounter when they start to eat more healthfully, not just at home but in the company of others. Why are people made to feel bad when they try to make a healthy choice? In the case above, why is this mom stressing out about asking that her kids not be given donuts? Why do her kids cave in? Certainly, some of this anxiety stems from social pressure (it's easier to just get along, right?), but all too often the person making the healthy choice winds up feeling like the spoil-sport or the no-fun bad guy.

The next time you're wrestling with feeling uneasy about insisting on a healthy choice for your children, particularly if doing so goes against what everyone else is choosing, think about it this way: if someone offered your kids a ride in a speedy convertible without seat belts, you'd say no—and you would hope that you've given them enough common sense to say no when you're not there to guide them. A donut may not seem as life-threatening as a risky thrill ride, but when you look at what eating food like that does to the body over time, it is.

Food choices are values choices. Stand up for what you believe in, and teach your children the importance of doing the same.

they're as parched as they are hungry. Before they guzzle milk or juice to quench their thirst, make sure they get some old-fashioned hydration. If you and your pediatrician are concerned about your child's weight or if overeating is a worry, drinking a glass of water before snacking can also help to curb hunger and reduce calorie intake.

School-age children head in many different directions when the school day is done, and where they snack may impact what they eat:

If kids go straight from school to another activity. Pack smart snacks and water for the car ride to softball, piano, or wherever your child is headed. It takes some effort and planning (and you have to make peace with kids eating in the car), but it's better than the alternatives: the fast-food drive-through, or the first bag of cheese doodles that enters your starving child's field of vision! A well-meaning coach, parent, or friend may show up with snacks that are less than satisfying or healthy, but if your child has satisfied her hunger with good food from home, you have little to worry about.

Don't forget our all-natural snack mix (see page 75 in chapter 3), an excellent energy-packed portable snack with dark or semisweet chocolate, unsulfured dried fruit, whole-grain cereal, sunflower seeds, and nuts, that's especially great for a sports practice or game. Let your child help you mix up a batch at the beginning of the week and parcel it out into single servings (a handful), ready to take to after-school activities.

If kids go into an aftercare program for a few hours. Put something extra in your child's backpack or lunchbox that will take the edge off of those afternoon hunger pangs and energize them until they get home. A well-rounded after-school day care program usually involves physical activity and homework, so make sure your child has enough fuel to keep up. Find out what kind of snacks, if any, are offered at your child's aftercare program; sometimes it isn't much more than packaged cookies and fruit punch. As with lunch, it's almost always better to bring food from home, and it's a no-brainer to add an extra half-sandwich, a piece of fruit, and a healthy treat like our double-thumbs-up EZ-Make Cookies to a lunchbox. (Tip: Make sure your child knows the extras are for snacking, not lunch!)

If kids go to a friend's house. This is tricky, particularly if you have an older child who wants to fit in with his buddies. But don't give up. If you're teaching your child to eat the HealthBarn USA way, he'll realize that while it's tempting to eat the forbidden fruit (that is to say, junk food), ultimately all those artificial ingredients are going to make him feel physically bad. If your child's friends like to come to your house, that's all the more reason to keep the kitchen free of processed food and full of fresh items. And who knows—your child's buddy could go home and ask his parents to keep more apples on hand and to get that recipe for Popcorn with Brain Butter.

If your kids come straight home. As mentioned above, keep high-quality grab-and-go foods and ingredients on hand and, for older kids, encourage them to make their own snacks (and clean up after themselves!). For young kids who aren't racing off to an activity or burdened with a homework load, an afternoon playdate in the family kitchen with a parent or caregiver and a friend or sibling can be fun and tasty, particularly if the result is Spinach and Artichoke Dip or our Pizza Potato Skins.

It's especially easy to fall into the 100-calorie snack pack rut in the afternoons—manufacturers have designed them to be convenient, so that kids can grab them right out of the package, with no cooking or prep needed. Unfortunately, they're almost always processed foods, full of artificial ingredients. If you don't buy them to stock your snack drawer, you don't need to worry about these foods finding their way into your kids' diet.

Energizing with Exercise: Afternoons Are for Being Active!

Regular exercise is a major component of a healthy lifestyle, and another one of our Seven Healthy Habits for kids and families. Unfortunately, because so many American schools have upped classroom instruction time in recent years, the once-daily gym class many of us grew up with is no longer daily, and recess—often tacked onto lunch—is usually brief. Most parents would agree that children don't get as much "running around time" as their generation did, particularly as kids hit the tween years.

Furthermore, while lots of children participate in activities like soccer and baseball at young ages, as they grow older and these sports become more elite, many kids who don't make the travel teams and the A teams drop out and are left without a regular physical activity. In addition, cash-strapped schools can't support as many sports teams as they once did.

Game Day!

Whether or not your child likes organized sports, joining a team and wearing a jersey with a number isn't the only way to get some exercise. The trick—for kids as well as adults—is to make fitness fun, not a chore. As those of us who've started and abandoned gym routines know all too well, when exercise becomes dull and difficult to incorporate into our day (put on the special clothes, go to the special location, be at the class at a special time), we don't stick with it.

Children are usually big on spontaneity, and this very quality can keep them active and fit. When your child has a friend or two over and the weather is good, send them outside (in fact, make "outside time" a major part of every playdate). Within no time, they'll find some heart-pumping exercise to engage in, whether it's hide-and-seek, tag, or something involving throwing or kicking a ball.

Let them set up a backyard obstacle course. Give them sidewalk chalk to mark start/finish lines and let them race—running, hopping on one foot, speed-walking, backward-walking, relays, or any other way that works for them. If they like doing this, add stop watches and a clipboard (just like a real coach!) for more fun.

Keep some inexpensive, old-school sports equipment on hand, like jump ropes, Frisbees, and Hula-Hoops, and give kids the freedom and space to make up their own games. The money you spend on one computer game can buy a backyard's worth of healthy, wholesome fun.

Don't forget the seasonal standbys: take them biking and swimming in the summer, and find outside activities in the winter too! Adults tend to look outside at the cold (and snow) and throw another log on the fire; but with the right gear, kids will get out into the cold and generate their own heat. Set the tone for staying active, even if it means putting on a pair of long underwear!

If you have a budding dancer on your hands, ballet and tap aren't the only options, particularly if you have a son. Zumba—the very popular Latin-inspired dance fitness program—has been successfully adapted for kids; you can find alternative dance classes like Zumba and hip-hop for kids at local YMCAs and other venues. Kids also seem to love doing yoga. At HealthBarn USA, we are crazy about "Yoga Pretzels"—kid yoga poses based on the popular card deck of the same name. The deck features colorful and clearly drawn illustrations of basic yoga poses, adapted for children.[*]

For more inspiration on how to get kids moving, visit www.letsmove.gov, an initiative launched by First Lady Michelle Obama that is dedicated to helping adults improve the health of children through healthy lifestyle choices—including exercise that is **fun**.

---

[*] Tara Gruber and Leah Kalish, *Yoga Pretzels: 50 Fun Yoga Activities for Kids and Grown-Ups* (Cambridge, MA: Barefoot Books, 2005).

On top of this, consider the amount of time kids spend in front of a TV or computer screen. According to a 2010 study conducted and published by the Henry J. Kaiser Family Foundation, kids ages eight to thirteen spend six hours per day (even on school days) on "media consumption" (combined "screen time" for TV, computer, and video games).* When you consider those numbers, it's no mystery why today's children have record-high levels of obesity and weight-related health problems.

Limiting screen time for kids is as important and crucial a health concern as diet. The same study showed that when parents imposed limits—any limits—on their kids' media consumption, that six hours a day dropped by about three hours. The rules that you set in your household are your call, but here are some recommendations from the National Institutes of Health, who want to help parents and kids shift the balance in a healthier direction.

Work to limit screen time to no more than two hours a day. Kids need at least an hour of physical activity a day. Lots of time in front of a TV or computer will cut into that active time.

Don't put a TV in your child's bedroom. Kids with sets in their bedrooms generally watch at least an hour more of TV per day than kids without.

When your child does watch TV, turn commercial breaks into action-packed breaks. Encourage younger ones to get up and "move it, move it" and have a dance-off. Or, set a kitchen timer for two minutes and see who can jump rope without missing. Or come up with another friendly but physical competition. Another benefit—they won't watch the commercials!

Older ones may roll their eyes at that last suggestion, but if video games are their thing, Wii, XBox Kinect, and other gaming consoles are all designed to get players off the couch and get heart rates pumping through physical movement and fun competitions. Wake-boarding, fencing, and dance parties—all taking place in your living room. Sure, real downhill skiing is preferable to virtual downhill skiing, but take advantage of technology and choose video games that will require more muscle movement than thumbs on the remote!

---

* Victoria J. Rideout, Ulla G. Foehr, and Donald F. Roberts, "Generation M2: Media in the Lives of 8- to 18-Year-Olds," Henry J. Kaiser Family Foundation (January 2010), available online at www.kff.org/entmedia/upload/8010.pdf.

Stacey's Tips

Satisfying the Athlete's Appetite

You may not have any worries when it comes to your child getting exercise if he or she is an Olympian in training. If you have a sporty kid who can't get enough lacrosse, soccer, tennis, softball, swimming, or whatever their passion may be, then they are burning up plenty of calories. The question is, what are they eating to replenish their fuel?

I've worked with many kids who've struggled with their weight—and many of them have been active athletes who are under- or overweight because they aren't eating right. For a quick burst of energy, their go-to food may be gummy bears and a sports drink. But when that sugar high wears off, the energy vanishes in a flash. Boys who want to bulk up to "make weight" may be doing it with fried eggs and greasy bacon, forgoing fresh fruits and vegetables, whole grains, and leaner protein choices for foods high in fat and cholesterol. Some girls, if told to shed a few pounds, tend to stop eating altogether.

Many sports, like baseball and football, involve a lot of standing around in the field or on the sidelines, or sitting on the bench. Yet, kids develop the habit of eating as if they were at the NFL training table, spurred on by adults (coaches and parents alike) who want them to perform. They also get into the habit of quenching their thirst with high-calorie sports drinks, which are marketed straight to kids as if consuming them will enhance their athletic performance, when in truth water is the best choice. Ironically, unhealthy snacks and sugary, caloric drinks that appear at practices and events generally cancel out the benefits of exercise. When kids continue to eat and drink like this as they grow into young adults (consuming far more calories than they are expending), weight-gain is inevitable, especially if they stop playing their chosen sport or staying active.

If your child plays sports, a healthy day of eating is a must, starting with breakfast. Our Sweet Potato Pancakes and Rainbow Swirly Smoothie offer more energy-generating, muscle-building nutrition to young athletes than bacon and eggs or a bowl of cereal. Pack a lunch and snacks with afternoon practice in mind—that extra peanut butter sandwich and piece of fruit could mean one more goal or one more perfect pitch. If you'll be at practice or at the game, bring a large, cold watermelon (or slice it into chunks at home) to share with the team. Watermelon is sweet and hydrating, and most kids love it.

And make a game-plan for dinner too (which we'll discuss in the next chapter). On busy weeknights after practices or games, kids come home hungry and head for something quick—often a high-fat, high-sodium microwavable meal, particularly if everyone else has already eaten. An otherwise fit young athlete came to me with hypertension, which was brought on by a diet of these salt-packed heat-and-eat meals. A busy after-school sports schedule can mean eating at odd times, like a snack in the car at 5:00 P.M. and dinner at 10:00 P.M., but joining the team doesn't automatically mean your kids have to eat microwave junk, Nutella on white bread, greasy pizza, Chinese takeout, or Pop-Tarts. Your child might win the game, but if he eats too much of that food, he'll lose out on good health, and eventually, performance.

Unless the weather is crummy or a kid is under the weather or just too pooped after a hard day at school, weekday afternoons should be a time for combining fun with physical activity, whether it's walking the dog, riding a bike, getting out on the playing field, or tending to the family garden. As with food, when parents and other adults in a household set a positive and healthy example, kids will take note. If you want your child to be active, look at your own attitudes and habits and make sure you're walking the walk (literally!) when it comes to regular exercise. If you're a

Eating in Season, Shopping at the Farmers' Market

You already know that **eating lots of fruits and veggies** is one of HealthBarn USA's Seven Healthy Habits (see chapter 4 for more on this topic), but teaching children to choose seasonal produce is as important as choosing healthy foods in the first place. Take an afternoon (or a weekend morning) with your child and head for a local farmers' market where they can get a firsthand look and a delicious taste of what's in season.*

get your hands dirty

At HealthBarn USA, in addition to our own garden, there is a family-owned farm market a stone's throw away from our classroom with a wide range of just-picked produce. We make regular "field trips" (a two-minute walk!) to check out what's being harvested at Abma's Farm and sold in their market. We also talk to the kids about why buying locally grown foods is so important:

Seasonal produce tastes better than out-of-season. Even better, locally grown seasonal produce doesn't travel far from the farm to your table, so it's picked when it's ripe, not before it's ready.

When food is shipped from far away, the costs to the environment are high. Consider the fuel it takes to ship a tomato to Boston from Mexico in January, and the fertilizer it took to make that tomato grow in winter—and after all that it just doesn't taste as good as garden tomatoes in August.

---

* If you're looking for farmers' markets in your community, visit www.sustainabletable.org/shop/seasonal for information on where and when. You can also bring the farmers' market to your front door if you join a local CSA—Community Supported Agriculture—organization. Members pay a fee and in return receive delivery of locally grown produce and other ingredients. For more information on CSAs and to find one in your community, visit www.localharvest.org, which is also a good resource for locally produced meat, dairy, and other products.

dedicated exerciser, you may prefer working out on your own, but if you're trying to get kids up and out, then take the time to hike, bike, walk, run, climb, jump, dance, and move together—as a family.

Children should know that moving our bodies is a must, but what we put into our bodies is, of course, just as important. I played competitive softball throughout my youth and into my teens. When I went away to college, though, I put my pitcher's mitt on the shelf and moved to Spain to study for a semester abroad.

Buying local means you support local businesses. You're not only getting great-tasting in-season produce that is better than what you'll find in a big supermarket; you're also contributing to the health of your local economy.

Locally grown often means organically grown. If you buy from small, local farmers, it's easier to locate organic produce. (Many will advertise the fact that their produce is organically grown, but if you're not sure, just ask!) Large, industrial growers often use pesticides because it's the only way to manage huge fields and orchards. But independent farmers with less land (and no corporate ownership) have more opportunities to farm organically.*

Samantha, one of our HealthBarn USA counselors-in-training, is committed to eating natural, seasonal foods—not just because she's a healthy eater but because it simply tastes so much better. She was thinking about how kids approach snacking and pointed out that if given a choice between an imported strawberry in winter or an artificially flavored strawberry fruit snack, "Most kids would take the artificial snack over the real fruit because an out-of-season strawberry just doesn't taste good." Remember that the next time you're contemplating a peach and your kids are still wearing their winter coats!

---

* If you are wondering whether to purchase organic or conventionally grown produce, visit the website for the Environmental Working Group, a nonprofit consumer organization that has compiled a list of "clean" produce that generally does not need to be purchased as organic, and "dirty" fruits and veggies that often have high levels of pesticide residues. Go to www.foodnews.org for their complete "Dirty Dozen" and "Clean Fifteen" listings, as well as for a free downloadable app that you can consult while you're shopping.

I returned, well . . . broad. I couldn't fit into a bridesmaid's dress for a cousin's wedding—it had fit perfectly before I'd gone on my European eating tour. As if I needed further confirmation that I'd gained weight, my sweet Italian grandfather, who used to tell me that I was too skinny, took one look at me upon my return and said, "You look great!"

Though my pitching days were done, I knew I needed to get moving—so I jumped on my bike. I rode everywhere. I rode for hours. I rode and rode and rode, determined to pedal away my unwanted souvenirs. And it worked. But I also recognized the role of diet, and I fixed that too, returning to more normal portions and consistent patterns (no more midnight tapas!), and eating more healthfully.

One of my heroes is the late Jack LaLanne, the fitness guru who worked out for two hours a day well into his nineties, and who died just a few years shy of his 100th birthday. It's an old-fashioned metaphor, but he used to say that exercise was the "king" and healthy food was the "queen." They were equally important, but honoring one and ignoring the other made them both powerless. If your goal for your family is lifelong good health, remember Jack's royal equation of exercise *and* diet.

Secrets for Helping Your Kid Eat Fruits and Vegetables

We make trying fruits and vegetables fun at the barn. Every week when the kids (of all ages) arrive they are greeted with the tagine, a covered cooking vessel from Morocco that we use to hide our fruit or vegetable of the week. We offer up clues about its color, how it's grown, and how it helps our bodies; when they correctly guess the answer, we lift the lid off the tagine, they all try it, give it a thumbs up, down, or to the side, and get a sticker for trying. Even the pickiest of eaters usually comes around eventually—the peer pressure, in this case, is positive support. The rule is that if the fruit or veggie gets a thumbs down, they don't have to finish it—and that rule has to be honored to build trust.

A lot of kids (and adults) will go for fruit before they choose veggies, perhaps because fruits are generally sweeter. You may be in the habit of keeping more fresh fruit in your kitchen than you do fresh vegetables, in part because you may serve fresh fruit more frequently (at breakfast and lunch, and as a snack) than you do fresh veggies, which we often think of as something to be served cooked (or worse, overcooked) and with dinner. Fruit might also dominate in the produce competition perhaps because "eat your vegetables" sounds more like an

The Seasonal Food Game

Growing seasons across the country can vary widely, but for the most part, fresh vegetables and fruits are most plentiful in the warmer months of spring, summer, and into fall, with winter being the season for produce that stores well (apples, potatoes, root vegetables) or for frozen or preserved bounty from the garden. Plug in your state at www.sustainabletable.org/shop/seasonal to find out what's in season where your family lives.

At HealthBarn USA, we play a trivia game featuring seasonal food facts. If you make a habit of visiting the farmers' market with your kids, they'll soon get a good sense of what's in season, and this little Q&A game will help them continue to make the connection. Read the hint, and see if your child can guess the name of the food and when it's generally harvested (with an emphasis on the northeast United States) to eat.

- I grow in the ground, and am the most popular vegetable among Americans. (Potatoes—summer/fall)

- I have a reputation for curing many different diseases. Vampires hate me. I taste great in Italian food. (Garlic—summer)

hands-on family fun

- Olympic athletes in Roman times would eat me to purify their blood. If you try cutting me, I might make you cry! (Onions—spring, summer)

- You can make juice, jelly, or even wine out of me. But I hope you will eat me fresh—because I make a great snack! (Grapes—fall)

- I grow in leaves and in heads. (Lettuce—spring, summer, fall)

- I am the only fruit with my seeds on the outside. (Strawberries—spring)

- I am a native of China, but now I grow all over the United States. Georgia is my favorite state. (Peaches—summer)

- Even though my leaves are poisonous, my stalks make delicious pies! (Rhubarb—spring)

- Most people think that I'm a vegetable, but I'm actually a fruit. In fact, I'm the biggest fruit there is! (Pumpkins—fall)

- There are more than two hundred species of me. I grow on bushes. (Raspberries—summer, fall)

- St. Patrick's Day is my favorite day of the year, because I am a very popular choice for dinner on that day. (Cabbage—spring, summer, fall, winter)

- I'm a leafy green and the lutein that I give you helps your eyes to see things well. (Spinach—spring, fall)

- If you cut me down the middle, you will see a star shape. (Apples—fall)

- I can be spicy or sweet. I can also be red, green, yellow, orange, or purple. (Peppers—summer)

pantry pick

Flaxseed **Big Benefits in a Little Package.** Flaxseed—in oil form, as well as ground—is an ingredient we reach for regularly at HealthBarn USA. Packed with beneficial omega-3 fatty acids, in oil form this "good fat" is yellow in color and is the "brain butter" we drizzle on our famous popcorn (Popcorn with Brain Butter). You'll see flaxseed oil in our recipes for dips, like our White Bean Dip, and salad dressings, like Flaxseed Oil Dressing and Raspberry Vinaigrette. Ground flaxseed adds an extra nutritional kick to recipes like our crispy Zucchini Sticks as well as to baked goods like Chocolate Zucchini Cupcakes and our Crunchy Granola with Walnuts. At breakfast, you'll see it in our pancake recipes, our Whole-Grain Breakfast Cookies, Raspberry Muffins, and our Rainbow Swirly Smoothie. We've added it in lunches and dinners too, like our No-Bake White Mac and Cheese.

Kids like the subtle but nutty flavor of flaxseed, and it's an easy nutritional add-on to so many foods (think wheat germ). Sprinkle it in ground form on whole-grain cereal or in yogurt; drizzle a little oil over roasted veggies. You'll find many ways to add it to your family's favorite foods. Look for flaxseed oil and whole or ground flaxseed (brown or golden) in most supermarkets. Though you'll find ground seed, which is convenient, I prefer to buy it whole and grind as needed (in a small coffee grinder). The seed begins to oxidize as soon as it is ground and can lose some of its omega-3 potency. Ground seed is preferable to whole because the whole seed will usually pass through the body undigested; your family will get the most nutritional benefits from a freshly ground batch.

Flaxseed oil is meant as a finishing oil and not a cooking or baking oil, because heat will cause the omega-3s to breakdown. In ground seed form, however, its omega-3s can withstand high heat and therefore can be used in baked goods.

At HealthBarn USA, we introduce kids to flaxseed oil through our Popcorn with Brain Butter recipe. They love the notion of a "brain butter" that makes them super smart! One young boy, however, once raised his hand and told me he wasn't so sure about trying this new kind of popcorn. Was it the flavor, I wondered? His unfamiliarity with a strange-sounding seed? No. "I'm already smart!" he said. He went on to eat a few servings anyway, and he's probably even smarter now!

old-fashioned punishment than it does like an invitation to indulge in something that can be both delicious and healthy!

Ultimately, eating plenty of **both** is the real goal. Serve some with every meal, keep them on hand for snacking, and you'll get there.

Fruit: A Sweet You Can Always Let Them Eat

Even kids who shun vegetables are more open-minded when it comes to fruit (most kids, anyway—I admit I've seen some tough cases!), probably because of its natural sweetness. Your challenge may not be getting your child to eat fruit, but getting her to eat a **variety** of it. Many kids will eat red apples, for instance, but not green, or they'll eat any variety of apple but no pears. Some will eat bananas, but won't consider peaches. They may like seedless clementines, but flip out when they are served a cut-open grapefruit with seeds still intact.

Some of these preferences naturally fade as kids and their palates mature (and when they learn to do things like spit out seeds or accept the tickly texture of peach fuzz). Besides waiting it out, here are a few things you can do now:

Keep brown and bruised off the menu. Fruit comes in many colors, but brown is probably not its most appealing shade. I do suggest serving cut-up apple slices, for instance, but squeezing a little lime or lemon juice on cut-up fruit like apples, pears, and peaches will help keep their color. If fruit is overripe or on the brink, use it for smoothies and not the lunchbox. No kid wants to be the one with the oozing, scary brown banana! (But boy oh boy, it's perfect for Banana Chocolate Chip Mini Muffins!)

Treat a pear like a peapod. Some of the tips for veggies, below, work for fruits, too—like keeping them cool and crisp, serving easy-to-eat choices (peeled or cut if needed), and providing a dip (try our Pumpkin Pie Dip with sliced apples and pears). Pack fruit carefully so that it doesn't bruise or leak its juice.

Make sure it tastes the way it's supposed to taste. If your child spits out a nice-looking piece of fruit, it may be unripe and sour, or flavorless. This is another reminder to buy produce in season and avoid items that are shipped from far away. They are picked when they're rock-hard and have not had adequate time to develop their flavor, and they often stay that way.

Cook with fruit. Make fruit an ingredient when preparing recipes to explore different flavors and interesting ways of eating them. Try the Sweet Fruit Pancake Tacos, the Grilled Peach Sensation, and the Homemade Fruit Roll-Ups.

Veggies: How to Get Kids to Eat More of 'Em

You shouldn't just want your child to eat her vegetables; you should want her to *enjoy* them. That's how she'll get hooked on eating them for life! Here are some tips from the barn:

Keep them crunchy. Serve vegetables raw, crisp, and cool. No one wants a mushy green bean or a limp carrot. If they're going into a lunchbox, cut veggies up the night before and refrigerate. Experiment with lightly steaming or blanching some veggies, like asparagus, which can taste better slightly cooked. Cooking, especially overcooking, can result in a loss of nutrients, color, and flavor!

WHEN IT'S TIME TO CELEBRATE

Sharing Smart After-School Snacks with Buddies

Older kids who are on their own after school or who are increasingly independent and ready to make their own snacks will have fun making recipes like Whole Wheat Pita Pizzas and Sweet Potato Crunchies, any of our smoothies, or more elaborate foods if they're ready. If your child can operate small appliances like a blender or an air popper for popcorn, or if they've graduated to using the stove and oven, they'll have so much fun feeding their friends healthy foods that their buddies won't even notice that chips and soda are not on this after-school snack lineup! Set some ground rules about kitchen safety (including our "Fight BAC" tips on page 147) as well as cleanup.

One of our HealthBarn USA kids regularly has friends over, and she enjoys feeding them food that she makes herself—all of it healthy, all of it natural. She makes liberal use of ingredients like flaxseed oil and cooks many of our recipes for her friends and family. Snacks like EZ-Make Cookies, Whole Wheat Pita Pizzas, and The Perfect Pop are on the regular rotation. When she first started making snacks (and meals) for her buddies, she reports, one of her best friends wanted to know, "Where's the candy? You guys have weird food in your house!" Now, however, this same friend has gotten hooked on quite a few of our HealthBarn USA recipes and frequently wants to know, "So, what's for dinner tonight? Can I come over?"

From weird to wonderful, one bite at a time!

Make them easy-to-eat. Chop carrots, zucchini, and other long veggies into sticks or circles. Cut broccoli into easy-to-handle florets. Some younger kids have preferences as to shapes and sizes (think of the child who insists that the sandwich always be cut on the diagonal), so let yours have a say in how the celery gets sliced.

Mix and match. Vegetables come in many colors besides green, and mixing them up is one way to offer a child more than one flavor. I love the contrast of cherry tomatoes with broccoli, celery with carrots, and so on. Some kids are purists, though, and don't care for a mix. See if yours have a preference.

Serve them with flavor and flare. We love dipping veggies into our White Bean Dip, Green Edamame Dip, Creamy "Ranch" Dressing, or Creamy Herb Dip. Invest in a small divided container that will hold some dip on one side and vegetables on the other or use bento lunchbox containers.

Grow 'em, don't buy 'em. When I go to work each day at HealthBarn USA, I'm surrounded by living proof that kids are more likely to eat vegetables, salad greens, herbs, and fruit when they grow, harvest, and prepare these foods from nature for themselves. There's just no doubt about it! See the Get Your Hands Dirty features located throughout the book, including "Grow an Organic Garden" in chapter 3 for more information on how to grow food at home in your own organic garden, and "Starting a Schoolyard Garden" in chapter 4 on how to help kids start a garden at school. Don't forget our tips on growing berries and herbs either (in chapter 2 and chapter 7)!

Cook with Veggies. At the barn, we always invite the kids up to the demonstration table to help put the veggies in the cooking pot or pan, and to parents' amazement, we have them eating Quinoa with Kale and Walnuts in no time!

EZ-Make Cookies

We *do* eat cookies at HealthBarn USA! These energy-packed, no-bake tasty treats are made with natural ingredients and are fun to make with friends. (Because no oven is used, EZ Make Cookies is the ideal recipe for kids to prepare without adult supervision.) Make a double batch to prepare for your next snack attack, and keep extras cool in the refrigerator (they taste even better chilled).

ingredients

1½ cups whole-grain cereal (We used Cheerios for the nutrition analysis.)

1 cup natural creamy peanut butter

¼ cup honey

¼ cup plus 2 tablespoons instant nonfat dry milk powder

2 tablespoons semisweet chocolate chips

directions

1. In a bowl, crush the cereal into very small pieces. Add peanut butter, honey, dry milk, and chocolate chips. With your hand or a spoon, mix together to form a ball.

2. Scoop 1 heaping teaspoon of cereal mixture and roll into a 1-inch-round ball. Repeat with remaining cereal mixture. Let set for 10 minutes to firm up. If not eating right away, wrap and refrigerate for up to 1 week.

Makes 18 servings (1 cookie per serving)

Nutrition Facts per serving: 130 calories; 8g fat (1g sat fat, 3g mono, 3g poly, 0g trans fat); 0mg cholesterol; 11g carbohydrate (1g fiber, 6g sugar); 4g protein; 80mg sodium; 2% Daily Value (DV) vitamin A; 2% DV calcium; 4% DV iron

Kids can do everything!

Holy Green Guacamole

Holy guacamole—this is easy to make and features heart-healthy good fat, plus vitamin C. As a bonus, this recipe helps you feel full because it's a good source of fiber, so you won't overdo it. Kids love to mash the avocados, squeeze the limes, and stir—good fun and great taste, all in one bowl!

ingredients

2 ripe avocados (preferably Hass)

1 medium tomato, chopped

Juice of 2 limes

3 tablespoons finely chopped red onion

2 tablespoons chopped fresh cilantro leaves or parsley leaves

¼ teaspoon ground cumin

⅛ teaspoon sea salt

⅛ teaspoon freshly ground black pepper

Corn chips and/or cut-up vegetables

directions

1. Cut each avocado in half lengthwise; discard the pit from each avocado. With a spoon, scoop out avocado flesh and place in a medium bowl. With a fork, mash avocado.

2. Stir in the tomato, lime juice, onion, cilantro, cumin, salt, and pepper.

3. Serve at room temperature, or cover and refrigerate for up to 2 hours. Serve with corn chips or cut-up vegetables.

Makes 10 servings (2 tablespoons per serving)

Nutrition Facts per serving: 70 calories; 6g fat (1g sat fat, 4g mono, 1g poly, 0g trans fat); 0mg cholesterol; 5g carbohydrate (3g fiber, 1g sugar); 1g protein; 10mg sodium; 2% Daily Value (DV) vitamin A; 15% DV vitamin C; 2% DV iron

Kids can mash avocado and stir ingredients.

Spinach and Artichoke Dip

This fabulously flavorful low-fat dip tastes amazing but it's a slimmed-down take on the popular (and very rich) appetizer that tempts many a diner! Our version is a good source of fiber for digestive health and features immune-boosting vitamin A.

ingredients

1 bag (6 ounces) baby spinach leaves

1 can (15 ounces) low-sodium cannellini beans (white kidney beans), drained and rinsed

14 ounces frozen (thawed) artichoke hearts or 1 can (14 ounces) artichoke hearts, drained and rinsed

1 package (3 ounces) reduced-fat cream cheese

1 clove garlic, chopped

¼ cup loosely packed fresh basil leaves

⅛ teaspoon freshly ground black pepper

½ cup (2 ounces) shredded low-moisture, part-skim mozzarella cheese

Pita chips and/or cut-up vegetables

directions

1. Preheat oven to 350°F.

2. In a medium saucepan, heat 4 cups of water to boiling over high heat. Meanwhile, prepare an ice bath in a large bowl; set aside.

3. When water comes to a boil, add spinach in small batches and cook for 30 seconds. With a slotted spoon, transfer each batch to the ice bath to stop the cooking and retain vibrant green color. Squeeze as much liquid out of the spinach as possible. (If you like, squeeze excess liquid into a mug to drink . . . it's full of nutrients!)

4. In a food processor, combine the spinach, beans, artichoke hearts, cream cheese, garlic, basil, and pepper. Pulse until smooth.

5. Transfer mixture to bowl and stir in ¼ cup mozzarella. Spoon into greased shallow baking dish; top with the remaining ¼ cup mozzarella.

6. Bake for 10–15 minutes or until dip is heated through and top is lightly browned and starting to bubble around the edges.

7. Serve with pita chips or cut-up vegetables.

Makes 20 servings (2 tablespoons per serving)

Nutrition Facts per serving: 50 calories; 2g fat (1g sat fat, 1g mono, 0g trans fat); 5mg cholesterol; 6g carbohydrate (3g fiber, 0g sugar); 3g protein; 70mg sodium; 10% Daily Value (DV) vitamin A; 2% DV vitamin C; 4% DV calcium; 8% DV iron

> **Kids can add cooked ingredients to food processor and pulse; and can add mozzarella and spoon the mixture into the baking dish.**

Homemade Vs. Store-Bought: The Facts!

HealthBarn USA's Spinach and Artichoke Dip	TGI Friday's Frozen Spinach & Artichoke Cheese Dip Reference: product package
Ingredients: Spinach, cannellini beans, artichoke hearts, reduced-fat cream cheese, garlic, basil, pepper, part-skim mozzarella cheese	**Ingredients:** Spinach, water, artichoke hearts (water, salt, citric acid), low-moisture part-skim mozzarella cheese (milk, nonfat milk, cultures, salt, enzymes), Parmesan cheese (part-skim milk, cheese cultures, salt, enzymes), whey protein concentrate (milk), roasted garlic (garlic, water, phosphoric acid), Neufchâtel cheese (milk and cream, cheese culture, salt, stabilizers [carob bean, guar, and/or xanthan gum]), cheese powder (whey, sunflower oil, maltodextrin [corn], Parmesan cheese [part-skim milk, cheese culture, salt, enzymes], salt, enzyme-modified Romano cheese [Romano cheese (cow's milk, cultures, salt, enzymes), water, salt], yeast extract, citric acid, lactic acid, sodium phosphate), contains 2% or less of: cream powder (cream, soy lecithin, tocopherols, ascorbyl palmitate), flavor (water, cream, salt, butterfat, natural flavor, propylene glycol, xanthan gum), cheese powder (dehydrated cheese, whey, butter, buttermilk solids, salt, natural flavors, lactic acid, modified cornstarch, sunflower oil, corn maltodextrin, sodium phosphate, calcium phosphate, citric acid, fermented wheat protein, yeast extract, flavor enhancer [disodium inosinate, disodium guanylate]), modified cornstarch, cheese flavor (cheddar cheese flavor [milk, salt, enzymes, cultures], flavors, corn maltodextrin, salt), salt, xanthan gum, canola oil, black pepper
Nutrition Facts (per serving): 50 calories; 2g fat (1g sat fat, 1g mono, 0g trans fat); 5mg cholesterol; 6g carbohydrate (3g fiber, 0g sugar); 3g protein; 70mg sodium; 10% Daily Value (DV) vitamin A; 2% DV vitamin C; 4% DV calcium; 8% DV iron	**Nutrition Facts** (per serving): 30 calories; 1.5g fat (1g sat fat, 0g trans fat); less than 5mg cholesterol; 2g carbohydrate (less than 1g fiber, less than 1g sugar); 2g protein; 100mg sodium; 10% Daily Value (DV) vitamin A; 4% DV vitamin C; 6% DV calcium
OURS: • 8 ingredients	**THEIRS:** • 84 ingredients • contains multiple preservatives and artificial flavor enhancers

Caprese Salad on a Stick

We've given this classic Italian salad a brand new look by skewering the ingredients, but we've kept its mouthwatering combination of creamy mozzarella, sweet cherry tomatoes, and homegrown fresh basil, drizzled with extra-virgin olive oil and a pinch of sea salt. It's a satisfying snack on its own, or pair this delicious mix of calcium and vitamins A and C with your favorite grilled entrée to create a well-balanced dinner.

ingredients

1 bamboo skewer

3 bocconcini (fresh mini mozzarella cheese balls)

3 fresh basil leaves

3 cherry tomatoes

1 teaspoon extra-virgin olive oil

Pinch sea salt (optional)

directions

1. On the skewer, stack 1 cheese ball, 1 basil leaf, and 1 tomato, in order. Repeat until all ingredients are used.

2. Drizzle oil over the assembled skewer and sprinkle with salt, if you like.

Makes 1 serving (1 skewer per serving)

Nutrition Facts per serving: 80 calories; 5g fat (0.5g sat fat, 4g mono, 0.5g poly, 0g trans fat); 5mg cholesterol; 3g carbohydrate (1g fiber, 1g sugar); 8g protein; 140 mg sodium; 15% Daily Value (DV) vitamin A; 10% DV vitamin C; 20% DV calcium; 2% DV iron

Kids can skewer ingredients and drizzle with oil.

Mango and Peach Salsa

If you like salsa, you will love this twist. A different taste from your traditional tomato-based salsa, this recipe provides a sweet alternative. The longer you allow the flavors to blend, the better it tastes. Snack on it with pita chips or whole-grain crackers, and try it as a topping for chicken and fish too.

ingredients

2 ripe mangoes, peeled and coarsely chopped

2 small ripe peaches, coarsely chopped

¼ medium red onion, coarsely chopped

3 tablespoons chopped fresh cilantro leaves or parsley leaves

2 tablespoons coarsely chopped green bell pepper (or 1 jalapeño chile, minced, if you like it spicy)

Juice of 2 limes

⅛ teaspoon sea salt

Pita chips and/or whole wheat crackers

directions

In a medium bowl, stir together all ingredients except the pita chips and whole wheat crackers. Cover and refrigerate for up to 4 days if not serving right away.

Makes 36 servings (2 tablespoons per serving)

Nutrition Facts per serving: 10 calories; 0g fat; 0mg cholesterol; 3g carbohydrate (0g fiber, 1g sugar); 0g protein; 0mg sodium; 4% Daily Value (DV) vitamin A; 4% DV vitamin C.

> Kids can take mango, peach, and pepper slices and chop using a plastic knife with adult supervision; they can also juice the limes.

Pesto-Stuffed Cherry Tomatoes

These red and green delights are a finger food fresh from the garden and bursting with flavor and vitamins A and C. Savor these stuffed tiny tomatoes alone or toss them into a bowl of greens to liven up a salad.

ingredients

30 cherry tomatoes

½ cup plus 2 tablespoons Basil Pesto (page 223)

directions

1. Cut each cherry tomato in half. With the tip of a spoon, scrape out pulp; discard or add to a soup. Place the tomato halves, cut sides down, on a large plate to drain; set aside.

2. Preheat oven to 350°F. Line a baking sheet with foil.

3. Prepare Basil Pesto as recipe directs; reserve ½ cup plus 2 tablespoons.

4. Fill tomato halves with pesto (about ½ teaspoon per half).

5. Place the stuffed tomatoes on prepared baking cookie sheet. Bake for 5–10 minutes or until lightly brown on top. Cool slightly before serving.

Makes 6 servings (10 halves per serving)

Nutrition Facts per serving: 70 calories; 5g fat (1g sat fat, 3g mono, 1g poly, 0g trans fat); 0mg cholesterol; 5g carbohydrate (2g fiber, 2g sugar); 3g protein; 40mg sodium; 35% Daily Value (DV) vitamin A; 25% DV vitamin C; 6% DV calcium; 6% DV iron

Kids can halve tomatoes using a plastic knife with adult supervision; scrape out pulp; and fill tomatoes with pesto.

Pizza Potato Skins

We've taken two of our favorite tastes and found a way to combine them into a crunchy snack you can't resist. We've topped potato skins with tomato sauce, cheese, and fresh herbs from the garden for vitamin C, fiber, calcium, and iron.

ingredients

4 medium baking (russet) potatoes (10 ounces each), scrubbed

⅛ teaspoon sea salt

⅛ teaspoon freshly ground black pepper

1 cup no-salt-added marinara sauce

⅔ cup (2.5 ounces) shredded low-moisture, part-skim mozzarella cheese

¼ cup loosely packed fresh oregano leaves, finely chopped

directions

1. Pierce the potatoes with a fork in several places. Place on a paper towel in the microwave oven. Cook potatoes on high for 15 minutes or until fork-tender, turning potatoes over once halfway through cooking. (Or, preheat oven to 450°F. Pierce potatoes with fork; place on oven rack and bake for 45 minutes or until fork-tender). Remove potatoes from microwave or oven; cool until easy to handle.

2. Preheat oven to 375°F. Cut each potato in half lengthwise. With a spoon, scoop the cooked potato from skins, leaving ¼ inch of potato in the skin. Wrap and refrigerate cooked potato for use in another recipe, like Creamy Broccoli Soup (page 133) or Sweet Potato Gnocchi with Basil Pesto (page 218). Arrange potato skins, skin side down, on a greased baking sheet; sprinkle with salt and pepper. Bake for 10–15 minutes, turning over once halfway through baking, until skins start to crisp.

3. Remove the baking sheet from the oven. Turn oven to broil. Turn the potato skins over, skin side down; top with marinara sauce, mozzarella, and oregano. Broil skins until cheese melts and sauce bubbles.

Makes 8 servings (1 potato skin per serving)

Nutrition Facts per serving: 130 calories; 2.5g fat (1g sat fat, 1g mono, 0g trans fat); 5mg cholesterol; 22g carbohydrate (3g fiber, 2g sugar); 5g protein; 95mg sodium; 4% Daily Value (DV) vitamin A; 20% DV vitamin C; 10% DV calcium; 10% DV iron

---

Kids can take cooked skins and top with marinara sauce, mozzarella, and oregano.

Whole Wheat Pita Pizzas

It's okay to eat *this* pizza between meals. Pita pizzas are simple to assemble, especially if you keep toppings like shredded mozzarella, chopped veggies, and herbs on hand. Pita bread made with natural ingredients is a guilt-free, fiber-rich alternative to a white flour crust. The healthy pizza fixings make this after-school snack a good source of vitamins A and C and bone-building calcium.

ingredients

4 (4-inch) whole wheat pitas

½ cup no-salt-added marinara sauce

⅓ cup (1.5 ounces) shredded low-moisture, part-skim mozzarella cheese

½ cup small broccoli florets

¼ cup sliced mushrooms

¼ cup chopped fresh basil leaves

directions

1. Preheat oven to 375°F.

2. Place pitas on a baking sheet (do not slice open). Spread 2 tablespoons of sauce on each pita. Top with mozzarella, broccoli, and mushrooms. Sprinkle with basil.

3. Bake pitas for 10–15 minutes or until cheese melts and edges are crispy.

Makes 4 servings (1 pita pizza per serving)

Nutrition Facts per serving: 120 calories; 2.5g fat (1g sat fat, 1g mono, 0g trans fat); 5mg cholesterol; 18g carbohydrate (3g fiber, 2g sugar); 6g protein; 200mg sodium; 10% Daily Value (DV) vitamin A; 15% DV vitamin C; 10% DV calcium; 6% DV iron

---

Kids can top pita pizza with sauce, cheese, and veggies before baking.

Pumpkin Pie Dip

We love pumpkin pie, so we decided to create a creamy dip with the same special taste. Serve it as an appetizer or dessert, and dip sliced apples, pears, or salty whole wheat pretzels in it. Low-fat and loaded with vitamin A, this crowd pleaser is a holiday favorite, but you can enjoy it year-round.

ingredients

6 ounces reduced-fat cream cheese, at room temperature

⅓ cup plain nonfat Greek yogurt

1 can (15 ounces) pure pumpkin (not pumpkin pie mix)

2 tablespoons agave nectar

2 tablespoons packed brown sugar

2½ teaspoons ground cinnamon

1 teaspoon ground allspice

¼ teaspoon ground cloves

¼ teaspoon grated nutmeg

⅛ teaspoon sea salt

Sliced fresh fruit and/or salted whole wheat pretzels

directions

1. In a food processor, combine cream cheese and yogurt; blend until smooth. Add pumpkin and remaining ingredients except fruit and pretzels; blend until well mixed.

2. Cover and refrigerate for at least 30 minutes or up to 4 days. Serve dip with sliced fruit or pretzels.

Makes 32 servings (2 tablespoons per serving)

Nutrition Facts per serving: 25 calories; 1.5g fat (1g sat fat, 0.5g mono, 0g trans fat); 5mg cholesterol; 3g carbohydrate (1g fiber, 2g sugar); 1g protein; 25mg sodium; 45% Daily Value (DV) vitamin A; 2% DV vitamin C; 2% DV calcium; 2% DV iron

---

Kids can add ingredients to food processor and pulse.

The Perfect Pop

This truly perfect recipe is an all-time favorite at HealthBarn USA. "It's so good," says one of our taste testers, "that you want to eat it again and again!" The tofu reduces the unhealthy saturated fat you'll find in most frozen dessert bars and makes this a must-have chocolaty after-school snack.

ingredients

3 ounces semisweet chocolate or ½ cup semisweet chocolate chips

½ cup silken light tofu, drained

¼ teaspoon vanilla extract

5 ripe but firm medium bananas

15 wooden ice cream bar sticks

directions

1. Roughly chop chocolate into small pieces.

2. In a metal bowl set over a saucepan of simmering water, heat chocolate until it melts, stirring occasionally. Remove saucepan; cool chocolate slightly.

3. Meanwhile, line a tray with waxed paper; set aside.

4. In a food processor, blend tofu until smooth. Add cooled chocolate and vanilla; blend until well mixed.

5. Peel bananas and cut each crosswise into thirds. Insert an ice cream bar stick, ½ inch deep, in one end of each banana piece.

6. Place the chocolate mixture in a pie plate. Roll each banana piece in chocolate mixture to lightly coat and eat right away. Or, if not serving right away, freeze immediately for at least 1 hour, then place frozen pops in freezer-weight plastic bag and freeze for up to 1 week.

Makes 15 servings (1 pop per serving)

Nutrition Facts per serving: 70 calories; 2g fat (1g sat fat, 0g trans fat); 0mg cholesterol; 13g carbohydrate (1g fiber, 8g sugar); 1g protein; 5mg sodium; 2% Daily Value (DV) vitamin A; 6% DV vitamin C; 2% DV calcium; 8% DV iron

---

Kids can pulse ingredients in a food processor, slice bananas using a plastic knife with adult supervision, insert stick, and roll bananas in chocolate mixture.

Grilled Cheese Stackers

Here's our take on a homemade grilled cheese sandwich, and it's sure to please. We put our HealthBarn USA twist on this sandwich classic, making it with reduced-fat cheddar and adding juicy slices of tomato and some fresh basil, and then stacking it into squares—literally!

ingredients

- ½ cup (2 ounces) shredded 50% reduced-fat cheddar cheese
- 8 slices whole-grain bread
- 4 thick tomato slices
- 8 fresh basil leaves
- 8 bamboo skewers

directions

1. Lightly grease a griddle or skillet; heat over medium heat.
2. Place 2 tablespoons of cheese on each of 4 bread slices; top each with a tomato slice, then remaining bread.
3. Cook sandwiches until golden brown on both sides and cheese melts, 3–5 minutes per side.
4. Cut 1 sandwich into 4 squares or triangles. Stack 2 sandwich pieces on top of each other; top with a basil leaf and "spear" with a skewer.
5. Repeat to make 8 skewers in all.

Makes 8 servings (1 skewer per serving)

Nutrition Facts per serving: 90 calories; 2g fat (1g sat fat, 1g mono, 0g trans fat); 5mg cholesterol; 12g carbohydrate (2g fiber, 2g sugar); 6g protein; 180mg sodium; 4% Daily Value (DV) vitamin A; 2% DV vitamin C; 8% DV calcium; 4% DV iron

Kids can build sandwiches, flip them on the grill with adult supervision, and skewer sandwich quarters.

Jersey-Fresh Bruschetta

HealthBarn USA started in the rolling green farm country of New Jersey, which celebrates its prized Jersey tomatoes. We combined our juicy summer bounty with our favorite fresh Italian herbs, straight from the garden, and concocted this delicious and healthy version of bruschetta. It's a little messy, but it has a lot of flavor, healthy fats, fiber, and iron.

ingredients

1 recipe Sweet Oat Baguette (pages 224–25)

6 medium plum tomatoes, chopped

2 cloves garlic, minced

¼ cup chopped fresh basil leaves

2 teaspoons extra-virgin olive oil

1 teaspoon chopped fresh oregano leaves

½ teaspoon sea salt

¼ teaspoon freshly ground black pepper

directions

1. Prepare Sweet Oat Baguette as recipe directs.

2. Preheat oven to 400°F. Cut baguette diagonally into ¼-inch-thick slices. Place on a baking sheet and toast in the oven for about 10 minutes or until lightly browned. Cool toasts on a wire rack.

3. In a large bowl, stir together tomatoes and remaining ingredients.

4. Place toasts on serving tray. Top each toast with 2 tablespoons of the tomato mixture.

Makes 12 servings (2 toasts per serving)

Nutrition Facts per serving: 260 calories; 9g fat (1g sat fat, 6g mono, 1g poly, 0g trans fat); 15mg cholesterol; 39g carbohydrate (5g fiber, 4g sugar); 8g protein; 75mg sodium; 6% Daily Value (DV) vitamin A; 8% DV vitamin C; 4% DV calcium; 15% DV iron

---

Kids can chop tomatoes, basil, and oregano using a plastic knife with adult supervision; they can also top toasts with the tomato mixture.

Carrot Halwa Dip

Kids are crazy about eating carrots, but usually they eat them with dip and the carrot is the dipper. In this traditional Indian dish (served warm), however, the carrot itself is the dip! Dip celery sticks and sliced bell peppers into this HealthBarn USA favorite, which is loaded with vitamin A and is a good source of calcium.

ingredients

4 cups low-fat (1%) milk

4 cups shredded carrots (10–12 medium carrots)

⅓ cup raisins

¼ cup packed brown sugar

½ teaspoon ground cardamom

2 tablespoons blanched almonds, chopped*

Sliced celery sticks and/or bell peppers

---

* To blanch almonds, heat a small pot of water to boiling over high heat. Add almonds and cook 1 minute. Drain and rinse with cold water. Peel thin brown skin off almonds, but be careful: they're slippery! FYI—blanched almonds are easier for our bodies to digest, which means that we absorb more of the nutrients and protein from these super tree nuts.

directions

1. In a large, deep skillet, heat milk over medium-high heat to boiling, about 5 minutes, stirring occasionally. Add carrots; heat to boiling. Reduce heat to medium and cook, uncovered, for 45 minutes to 1 hour to reduce mixture to about 2½ cups, stirring frequently.

2. Add raisins to carrot mixture while there is still some liquid left and continue to cook until raisins plump, about 5 minutes. Stir in brown sugar and cardamom and cook until mixture is very thick and all milk is absorbed, about 10 minutes longer, stirring occasionally.

3. Spoon the warm dip into a serving bowl and sprinkle with almonds. Serve with celery sticks and/or bell peppers for dipping.

Makes 16 servings (2 tablespoons per serving)

Nutrition Facts per serving: 70 calories; 1.5g fat (0g sat fat, 1g mono, 0.5g poly, 0g trans fat); 5mg cholesterol; 12g carbohydrate (1g fiber, 10g sugar); 3g protein; 55mg sodium; 90% Daily Value (DV) vitamin A; 4% DV vitamin C; 10% DV calcium; 2% DV iron

---

Kids can shred carrots and peel skin off almonds; they can also stir mixture with adult supervision.

Yogurt Sundaes

Move over, neon-pink GoGurt. A healthy day means *white* yogurt with natural toppings! Even our youngest farmers, the Seedlings, have a blast making and eating their very own calcium-loaded sundaes at HealthBarn USA.

ingredients

2 cups vanilla low-fat yogurt

1 cup Crunchy Granola with Walnuts (page 52)

1 cup blueberries (or substitute strawberries or raspberries)

directions

Spoon ¼ cup yogurt into each of 8 sundae dishes or dessert bowls. Top each with 2 tablespoons granola and 2 tablespoons blueberries.

Makes 8 servings (½ cup per serving)

Nutrition Facts per serving: 80 calories; 2.5g fat (0.5g sat fat, 1g poly, 0g trans fat); 5mg cholesterol; 11g carbohydrate (1g fiber, 8g sugar); 3g protein; 40mg sodium; 2% Daily Value (DV) vitamin A; 4% DV vitamin C; 10% DV calcium; 2% DV iron

---

Kids can build their own sundaes!

CHAPTER 6

Come and Get It!
The Family Meal

RECIPES

For many families, dinner is the time when everyone finally comes together at the table. Breakfast may be a quick meal that kids and grown-ups eat at different times; lunch happens at school or at work. But dinner is usually when we have the opportunity to sit down together as a family and focus on each other and on a good meal.

Another of our Seven Healthy Habits is **establishing a family meal**—and usually that happens in the evening, as our healthy day begins to wind down. However, I do like to remind kids and parents that a family meal can happen whenever everyone sits down together—minus the TV, the cell phone, the books or newspapers, and any other distractions. The time of day doesn't matter, nor does the location. (I'll give you tips later in this chapter on how to make dining out a relaxing, fun, and healthy family experience.)

When I was growing up, our family dinner was actually breakfast! My father, who commuted from our suburban home into New York City, often got home too late for us to eat dinner together. One of our HealthBarn USA families regularly treats breakfast like a family meal too. Says the mom, "We have a place to come together to start our day, share our thoughts with each other, try new foods, and organize ourselves before we go our separate ways. It is 'our special time as a family' that I treasure every day."

A growing body of research has shown that a family meal can contribute dramatically to the mental and physical well-being of parents and children alike, though in many American households it happens barely twice a week. Here is some compelling evidence for making family meals a more frequent occurrence, ideally once a day.*

◆ Kids who sit down to family meals on a daily basis are less likely to use drugs, alcohol, and tobacco.

◆ Girls, in particular, are less likely to develop eating disorders like anorexia if they eat regularly with their families.

◆ Parents who do family meals are more in tune with what's happening at a child's school, with their friends, or with whatever may be important to a child.

◆ Adults and children alike generally eat more healthfully at a family meal.

---

* Numerous organizations ranging from the American Academy of Pediatrics to the National Center on Addiction and Substance Abuse (CASA) have published extensive research on the values of a family meal. Laurie David's book, *The Family Dinner: Great Ways to Connect with Your Kids, One Meal at a Time* (New York: Grand Central Life & Style, 2010), is packed with ideas for parents who want to make the most of this time with their children.

Parents often ask me how to make family meals healthier. More vegetables? Leaner protein? Whole grains? Organic ingredients? Yes, good food—the food that makes up a true healthy day—is part of the answer, but it's not just about what's on the plate. It's also what *happens* at the table. When everyone is truly present—when no one is taking a call, texting, or changing the channel—and engaged as a family, wonderful things can take place.

Not long ago, seven-year-old Sarah and her mom came to HealthBarn USA. They seemed to be doing everything right—good, all-natural foods; family meals; kids involved in cooking and preparing foods—and I was curious to see what else we could do to improve the way this family approached eating. One of our HealthBarn  USA activities is "Family Mealtime Rules" (see page 180), where kids get to make up rules that grown-ups have to follow too. Sarah suggested a rule that her mom turn off the TV during dinner. The family had a nightly habit of watching the Food Network while they ate, but Sarah wanted to pull the plug.

About two weeks later, her mother approached me, full of gratitude for what we'd done. I wasn't sure what change we'd affected until she explained. The family decided to follow Sarah's no-TV rule, though at first, this mom didn't see what the big deal was; they were simply watching the cooking shows for fun and entertainment. But suddenly, there was no TV noise—and the family started to talk more. Within days, Sarah—an easygoing child who never gave any hint of trouble at school—explained that she was being teased and bullied by two girls at school who were making her days very difficult. Sarah's parents were able to talk to the school and improve their daughter's situation immediately, and everyone was much happier.

This family got healthier—not just through food, but through action. They came together at the table, they turned off the TV, and they connected through talking, something that the background noise wouldn't let them do until they took action and hit the off button. Remember our motto at HealthBarn USA: "Strong bodies, healthy minds." Eating right takes care of the body, and positive action takes care of the mind. We helped Sarah and her family—not by telling them to exercise more or eat more fruits and vegetables, but by showing them the bigger picture of what healthy means.

Family Mealtime Rules: Follow Ours, and Make Up Your Own!

Sarah put "No TV" at the top of her list of rules, and it's actually the first of three family meal rules we recommend at HealthBarn USA. The others are: (2) No phones, and (3) Have fun!

As a parent, you no doubt have some rules of your own that you expect your children to follow: wash your hands; no talking with your mouth full; don't kick your brother under the table; and so forth. Instead of making all the rules yourself, let your child have a say. Start with our three rules and take it from there. Let your child brainstorm some ideas, add the ones you feel strongly about (hand-washing!) and once you've all agreed on your own family mealtime rules, let her write them up and post them in a place where everyone will see them (perhaps the always-reliable refrigerator door).

For kids, most rules made by adults send a message that says, "Children misbehave, so therefore we have these rules." No running! No talking! No laughing! As an adult, you know that rules are often there to protect a child, enhance an experience, or instill some social proprieties ("no spitting!"). But kids just see rules as all written by adults and all beginning with the word "no," and they tune out. That's why letting them take charge of family mealtime rules is so valuable. When they write these rules, they're invested in making the experience a special one for kids and parents alike.

Finally, remember to observe the rules yourself. No phones means *no phones*. You may think that it's harmless just to check that one email or text, but as the adult, once you cross that line you'll have a hard time convincing your child—particularly when they are teens—not to do the same.

If you or another person in your household are having trouble letting go of the Blackberry, consider using this idea that some kids at HealthBarn USA came up with. The children wanted to enforce the "no electronic devices rule" and came up with a plan to designate a special box where family members deposit all their beeping gadgets and ringing gizmos—similar to the bins used by airport security for passengers with laptops and other hardware that will set off the metal detectors. Before entering the kitchen or dining room for a family meal, everyone places their turned-off phone, DS, iPad, or other electronic device into "the box." After eating as a family, adults and kids can reclaim their property. The kids tried it at home and got great results!

Still Eating in Front of the TV?
Cancel <u>That</u> Show

Kids who eat meals in front of the television are more likely to consume higher levels of calories and can be more prone to weight gain. Researchers at Baylor College of Medicine found that over the course of one week, overweight children ate at least 50 percent of their meals in front of the TV, compared to kids with normal body weights, who ate 35 percent or fewer of their meals while watching. Overall, children who ate at the table with their families drank fewer high-calorie sodas and ate more veggies than their TV-watching peers.[*]

Many studies have found a link between eating in front of the TV (or computer screen) and overeating. But there are other reasons this behavior gets in the way of a healthy day. You already know TV gets in the way of conversation. It also stops us from tasting and enjoying good food. If you want your family to savor delicious foods from nature, and to eat that way for life, then they need to **eat mindfully and taste their food.** Kids also need to learn to pay attention to when they feel full and don't need to eat more food or drink more milk. That's unlikely to happen if they're more concerned about what Sponge Bob and Patrick are about to do to Squidward. (Note: I'm focusing on kids' TV-watching habits here—but the fact is that many grown-ups get home from work and automatically flip on the flat-screen to watch the news or carry their meal away from the table to go watch the game. It's an easy habit to get into and a hard one to break, but it's important to do so for your family and your health.)

Also, all that television comes with a whole lot of advertising—particularly on channels geared to kids. Fast-food restaurants, snack food manufactures, and makers of soda and other sugary beverages are major advertisers on these channels. Studies have shown that kids are more likely to ask for these unhealthy foods if they are exposed to commercials touting these products.

Dinner is one thing, you may be thinking, but what's the harm in just snacking in front of the TV? It's the same problem—we don't taste our food, and we don't pay attention to how much of it we're eating. Didn't you ever go to the movies, order a large popcorn, and suddenly find yourself wondering where it went? You ate it all while you were watching that car chase! When we get caught up in what's on the screen, we don't pay much attention to what (and how much) we're eating—whether it's candy or carrots.

Don't let your kids get into the habit of chewing and changing the channel (or sitting at the computer) at the same time. It may not seem as risky to their health as texting while driving, but over the long term, it's right up there.

---

[*] Nanci Hellmich, "Many Kids Are Eating (Too Much) in Front of TV," *USA Today*, February 14, 2001. From a study conducted by researchers at the Children's Nutrition Research Center (Baylor College of Medicine), which surveyed 287 fourth-, fifth-, and sixth-graders and their dinner habits for seven days.

Kid Food: It's Time to Get It Off the Menu

If breakfast involves quick eating and simple food, and lunch is the meal over which parents have the least control, then dinner is when many of us try to make up for it all. You want a peaceful meal with foods that will please both adults and kids. You don't want whining or home-cooked food greeted with, "What is *that*?" You want meaningful conversation, not arguments over how many mouthfuls of peas are being eaten. You are tired after a long day of school and work and don't want a food fight. Enter the processed chicken nugget, the "kids menu" at even the nicest of restaurants, or bland versions of "adult" food, stripped of all seasonings and supposedly appealing to young taste buds.

Marketers of prepared foods smartly target working parents—in particular, moms—with "easy" solutions for weeknight dinners. In the 1970s, when mothers were surging into the workforce, Hamburger Helper was introduced along with ever-expanding aisles of convenience foods in the local supermarket. The boxes, pouches, and cans have multiplied, joined by even more products like frozen dinners aimed straight at youngsters. ConAgra's "Kid Cuisine" is built around entrées like microwavable corn dogs and pizza.

Eating establishments, from quality restaurants known for their high-end cuisine to fast-food chains, pacify parents and children alike with separate children's menus. At the better places, ocean-fresh seafood, organic poultry, and grass-fed beef may be on the menu, but so are fish sticks, chicken nuggets, and burgers. As for the fast-food chains, they've been making happy profits from Happy Meals for decades.

Perhaps worst of all, too many families have embraced the "kids' menu" philosophy in their own kitchens. Mom and Dad are having grilled salmon, but the kids want burgers. The grown-ups have oven-roasted potatoes with rosemary; the kids want their potatoes fried or mashed. Sometimes the meals bear no resemblance to each other, with entirely different food being served; other times, the children's meals are bland shadows of what the parents eat. Pasta with arugula, shrimp, and tomatoes for the adults; pasta with butter for the kids.

How to "Fix" Dinner, Once and for All

Besides the "kid food" trap, I've observed many parents feeding their children in an almost retro fashion, as if they were trained in a 1940s home economics class: the meat, the vegetable, the starch, all on the same plate but never cooked together or integrated in any way, as if the food were served on a divided plate. Here is the skinless, barely seasoned chicken breast; here is the plain rice; here is the limp broccoli; and never shall they touch. The result is a no-fun, no-flavor presentation of food—healthy, perhaps, but it's this kind of dull dining that turns "healthy" into "boring."

Remember the story of the parent who swore that her child would never, *ever* eat Swiss chard on pizza, only to watch her son happily munch away? It's that same assumption—a hard-to-shift stance that says "but he won't eat it!"—that causes parents to stress out over a family dinner and choose some version of the "kids' menu" or serve boring fare. But kids deserve to enjoy delicious-tasting, healthy food, and treating their meals separately—separate from what the adults eat, and separated into boring components on the plate—does not encourage adventurous, nutritious eating.

If you are ready to clear the table of kid food in time for your next family meal, the recipes from HealthBarn USA are the perfect place to start. Those at the end of this chapter, in particular, are designed for family meals, but virtually every recipe in the book can be served up family style. Here are some more tips to help you put some flavor (and fun) into family dining:

✦ *Don't push vegetables to the side.* A parent told me that his son always eats his vegetables last, and that it's pure agony watching this child take tiny bites of his now-cold spinach and chew every mouthful slowly. When he wanted to know how to get his child to like his veggies more (and eat them at a normal pace), I gave him this advice: *make vegetables part of the meal.* Instead of a separate serving of spinach, how about our Spinach Pesto Pasta? My young niece Georgia didn't like eating veggies—until my sister made her a batch of our Sweet Potato Pancakes. Now they are her favorite breakfast and my sister loves them too.

  Many of our recipes incorporate fresh vegetables, like the cauliflower in Mike's Sicilian Stew, or bell peppers in the Veggie Stir-Fry with Soba Noodles, or zucchini in Yum! Yum! Dumplings. (We don't "sneak" these veggies in as a puree, either! As I already mentioned, I don't believe in hiding what is healthy. Kids deserve to know what they're eating.)

✦ *Serve a side salad.* When I was growing up, my parents always had a salad on the table at dinnertime. I grew up assuming that was just what you did as a family, and it was a very healthy habit. We kids liked salad a lot, and I realize that it was because we watched our parents eating it. They loved salads and ate them with enthusiasm as if they were eating chocolate cake, so of course we wanted to join in. Toss up our Mixed Greens with Flaxseed Oil Dressing or the Mighty Beet Salad. As with all new foods you're trying to introduce to your kids—*you have to put it out there to find out if they like it, and you have to eat it too.*

REAL-LIFE RESULTS:
Family Finally Enjoys Dinner Together!

Do you need a dinner makeover in your house? Good, healthy food is on the table, but do you want to hide under it, rather than sit at it with your kids? Such was the case for one HealthBarn USA mom who described her family meals as stress-packed free-for-alls. Her three children—including a set of twins—would argue nonstop at the table, chew some food, fight more, chew some more food, fight to get in the last word, and flee. Dinner was a quick-and-dirty deal, and it was creating a lot of anxiety (and actual heartburn) for this parent. As it turns out, the kids weren't having such a great time either. They weren't unusually difficult children, but they just rubbed each other the wrong way when they sat down at the table for a meal.

I talked to her about the family mealtime rules and how to best help these children set aside their disagreements during dinner. My advice? You don't just set the table—you have to set the mood! In this case, relaxing music, nice dishes, and candles (kids love candles) went a long way toward defusing the tense situation. It was as if the kids' behavior fell into place to reflect the calmer, more peaceful atmosphere their mother created. "I almost didn't recognize my family," she said. She told her children that if they continued to behave this well she would treat them to a nice dinner at a favorite restaurant—they did and she did.

You don't need to break out Grandma's china on a nightly basis or create place settings worthy of Buckingham Palace, but take a closer look at what your table looks like. Is it a welcoming place? Are the older kids still eating on their preschool dishes on top of worn-out kiddie placemats? Is the table cluttered with the remains of the day? Dining room tables are notorious repositories for old math homework, broken crayons, unread newspapers, and the mail. If your table looks like a rummage sale, it's time to set up some ground rules for what goes where. One mom has a system with small tote bags for each family member. If something stays on the table for more than a day, it goes into the bag. The bag must be gone through by its owner at least once a week, or the contents are recycled, put in the giveaway bag, or tossed. The kids have learned to stop leaving stuff on the table that they need for school or play (but Dad has a way to go).

Make it easy for your kids to clear the table off before mealtime and set it up for breakfast, lunch, or dinner. Keep the "good candles" and nice dishes in an accessible location—and use them! Let children pick quiet music that won't interfere with family conversation and set the table (but don't worry if the forks are on the wrong side). When it's time to call everyone to the table, let one child do the job (without hollering) of gathering the others. The food—and now the mood—is just right, so sit down, enjoy your meal, and enjoy your family.

◆ *If they won't eat it tonight, that doesn't mean they won't eat it tomorrow.* See above—it might be salad, it might be turkey burgers, it might be soy milk. If your child has never eaten this way before, you have to start somewhere, and you can't give up. Start slowly with familiar foods such as our Homemade Chicken Nuggets or the Garden-Fresh Pasta. On average, it takes kids about ten to thirteen exposures to get accustomed to a new food. Don't pull it off the menu permanently after just one try.

◆ *Let them into the kitchen.* As with other meals and snacks, let your children have some say in what they eat, and let them help to prepare it as well. It may be more challenging on busy weeknights to let young kids into the kitchen, but don't discourage their efforts at contributing to a healthy day. Even small children can sort and wash produce, use a plastic knife to slice soft fruits, measure, pour, stir, set a timer, get out ingredients, and more. (The recipes for Sweet Potato Gnocchi with Basil Pesto and our Cheesy Lasagna Rolls, in particular, offer many ways for kids of all ages to assist in the kitchen, and they are favorites at the barn.) If they're helping to put the food on the table, they're more likely to eat it.

◆ *Don't use dessert as a means to an end.* You've heard it, and perhaps you've even said it yourself: "Finish your vegetables if you want dessert." But using an unhealthy food to motivate kids to finish a healthy one is a no-win situation. It reinforces the idea of healthy food as being about as much fun as medicine. Special occasions are an exception, but day-to-day meals don't require dessert. We do enjoy dessert at HealthBarn USA and love recipes like our Raspberry Crumble, our Chocolate Banana Crepes, and Sweet Fruit Pancake Tacos—but these aren't daily treats. (Offering fresh fruit and nuts is also an appealing and effortless way to conclude a meal—and one that you *can* do every day.)

◆ *Show the way, and then step out of the way.* Modeling healthy behavior—whether it's through good food, physical activity, or actions like turning off your cell phone at dinner—is important. *But you also need to give your child a chance to adopt these behaviors for herself.* Be patient—at first your healthy day may only last until morning snack time, but that doesn't mean you won't make it all the way through to bedtime at some point soon. If you find yourself thinking things like, "She won't eat salad so I'm not going to serve her any," or "She won't want to go for a bike ride so I'm not going to ask," or "She'll be so upset if I turn off the TV so I'll let her watch more," consider that you (or your partner in parenting) may be the one putting up a roadblock to healthy change.

Serving Size Surprise

Most kids like fiddling with scales, measuring cups, and spoons, but it's unrealistic to think that they'll weigh and measure their food on a regular basis. But your child already possesses a visual reminder to help her with serving sizes—one that she can always keep with her, and that is highly practical and literally handy. It's a fist.

At HealthBarn USA, we tell kids that **one fist generally represents one kid-size serving of food.** So, if she's about to eat a cookie and it's three times the size of her fist, then she needs to find two friends to share it with! How big is that piece of chicken? Bigger than Dad's fist? Then give some to Dad! How about that scoop of mashed potatoes? If it's the size of her fist then it's just right. (Note: for veggies and fruits, one cup is generally one serving.)

hands-on family fun

If you do own a kitchen scale, let your kids weigh and measure different foods, like a bagel, for example. A single serving of bread is one ounce, but how much does that bagel weigh? If it looks like some of the supersize bagels I've encountered at my local deli, I bet it's three times that amount.

Unfortunately, we often just eat what's put in front of us (or we take more than we need) without considering whether or not the amount is more than one serving. Playing around with a food scale, measuring cups, and measuring spoons will increase your child's serving size savvy—and yours too. (Looking at serving size info on packages helps too—more on that opposite). How about a typical serving of rice? Let her measure out a half cup of cooked rice into a measuring cup and then pour it onto a plate. That's one serving—not half a plate full!

If you would like to learn more as a family about appropriate serving sizes, visit www.choosemyplate.gov. You'll find more detailed information there on what constitutes one serving of a particular food.[*]

---

[*] For information on "portion distortion," and to play a game that links calories and exercise, visit http://hp2010.nhlbihin.net/portion, a family-friendly website sponsored by the U.S. Department of Health and Human Services and the National Institutes of Health.

Ultimately, though, do what we do at the barn: keep it simple and use that mighty fist.

How to Resize a Supersize Meal

It's really easy to overeat when you're eating prepared foods from restaurants and other sources. Is there too much food on that plate for one person? If so, here are some solutions the kids at HealthBarn USA suggest:

- Share your order with a friend.

- Eat half of it and save the rest for a meal tomorrow.

- It's okay to leave leftovers if you're full.

- Order a smaller serving.

- Make your own food and eat at home!

Research suggests that it's also possible to overeat at home if we get too used to the oversize portions we regularly encounter in restaurant settings. Even though we think of supersize portions in relation to food we're served by restaurants, we can sometimes fall into the trap of supersizing our otherwise healthy home-cooked foods, if we don't remain aware of what normal serving sizes actually are. (Note that our recipes always indicate the amount for a single serving.)

Throughout this book, I've mentioned the importance of the ingredients labels on packages, which can be more revealing about the healthiness of a food than the nutrition facts labels. However, it **is** important to look at the nutrition facts to note what makes up a single serving. If we don't pay attention, it's easy to overeat—even healthy foods.

Get your children involved in figuring out how many servings are in a single package, especially if they're learning multiplication and division. They can use their math skills to become even sharper supermarket spy kids!

Healthy Food, Healthy Portions: You Can't Have One Without the Other

Congratulations on making it this far into our healthy day! Your kids are choosing foods from nature and perhaps growing some of it themselves. They are trying new foods—and giving them a thumbs up! They're in the kitchen helping or cooking up a storm on their own. Your supermarket spy kid has helped you cut your grocery-shopping time in half, and everyone is feeling pretty good about breakfast, lunch, dinner, and everything in between.

But then one day, your healthy kid says to you, "So if organic butter, locally grown walnuts, and fair-trade dark chocolate are all really good foods from nature, then why can't I eat another brownie?" "Since this low-fat milk is a good choice, why can't I have a bigger glass (to go with my extra brownie)?" "Wow, this fresh spinach pesto is so good that I don't just want seconds—I want thirds. Fourths. Can I have fifths?" Perhaps you just have a major growth spurt on your hands, but at some point, a conversation about portion control is a valuable one to have with your children. All the recipes in this book give specific information defining a single serving for kids, and a single serving is generally what we recommend. Seconds or

pantry pick

Fish There's nothing fishy about the benefits of the omega-3 fatty acids found in fish and fish oil, including DHA. According to some studies, kids who consume omega-3s found in fish—like our simple but delicious Steamed Salmon Pouches—can reap the benefits of these "healthy fats," including better cognitive function. (For adults, other benefits of omega-3s include improved cardiovascular health and lower risks of diseases ranging from rheumatoid arthritis to depression.)

Fatty fish (unsaturated "good" fat, that is) like salmon and sardines offer the most omega-3s, but this brain-building nutrient is also found in many other varieties of seafood, like shrimp, and to a lesser extent in freshwater fish. In addition to being a good source of omega-3s, fish is a terrific and versatile lean protein source. Check out our fantastic fish recipes, including Brown Rice Risotto with Shrimp, Citrus and Herb Shrimp Kebabs, and Coconut Shrimp with Pineapple Herb Dipping Sauce.

thirds of some foods may be appropriate for your child (and if they want more veggies, I always oblige!), but obviously for treats and snack foods it's important to be aware of how much is being consumed.

You can oversee portion sizes in your own home when you and your family prepare your own food, but once you opt for takeout or enter a restaurant—whether it's a fast-food joint or a little corner bistro—the notion of serving size seems to drop away. We live in a supersize world, where the average bagel could feed three people and restaurants serve cuts of meat that can't even fit on a normal plate. Perhaps you've done what we do at HealthBarn USA and talked to your kids about eating all things—including healthy, natural foods—in moderation, but nothing brings that lesson to life like allowing kids to weigh and measure foods.

WHEN IT'S TIME TO CELEBRATE

Friday Night Pizza Party

Ahh, Fridays! It's the end of the work week and the school week, and time to relax and usher in the weekend. If the kids are clamoring for pizza and you're feeling like ordering one, consider ending your healthy day—and your healthy week—with a family pizza party (friends are welcome too!) and making your own. Because everyone gets to make their own mini pizza, all you have to do is provide the dough and the toppings (see our recipe for Whole Wheat Pizza Dough).

At HealthBarn USA, we do the "Pizza Challenge." We start with our Whole Wheat Pizza Dough as the base along with low-sodium marinara sauce and low-moisture, part-skim mozzarella, placed in separate bowls. We challenge the HealthBarn USA kids to go to the garden and harvest seasonal vegetables to create their own edible masterpieces.

If you don't have a garden, don't despair. Just chop up colorful bell peppers, spinach, mushrooms, and herbs and place in separate bowls. Be adventurous and include a dish of our Basil Pesto (one of our campers pulled leftover pesto from the refrigerator for his secret ingredient—and it was delicious!), as well as capers and olives in separate bowls.

At the barn, the categories in our delectable competition are Best Tasting, Most Creative, Most Colorful (that is, most veggies), and Best Teamwork. Everyone wins this challenge by loading up on vegetables, good food, and a lot of fun.

Happy Friday!

Stacey's Tips

When Your Family Meal Is a Restaurant Meal

Family meals don't always happen at home. Many families love eating out, and it can certainly be a satisfying (and healthy) treat—and a nice break from cooking—when done right! Make your next restaurant meal fit into a healthy day of eating by trying the following:

Let kids look closely at the menu and see if they can spot natural and organic ingredients, including seasonal fruits and veggies. Locally grown is even better!

- For beverages, avoid soda but choose fizzy seltzer with lemon or lime. Older kids might go for unsweetened, freshly brewed iced tea.

- Let your kids "spy" for these words on the menu: *grilled, baked, braised, broiled, roasted, steamed,* and *stir-fried*. These cooking techniques use less fat than frying and sautéing. Can they find the whole grains on the menu? Ask them to spy for *bulgur wheat, quinoa,* and *brown rice*.

- Looking to eat less? Order children's portions; make a meal out of two appetizers; share entrées and order more sides of baked or steamed veggies; ask for the bread basket to be brought with the meal (and let your kids dip their bread in olive oil instead of using butter); order soup—it's filling—and take into account that cream-based soups can have more fat and calories than broth-based; control sauces and dressings by asking for them on the side, and use a fork to toss your salad to make a small amount of dressing go further.

- Your family is now serving-size savvy. Take home the extras or leave a little behind on the plate.

- And for dessert, fresh fruit and sorbet are excellent choices, or order a single yummy dessert—and lots of spoons for sharing!

- For easy-to-make, healthy versions of popular restaurant dishes, see our recipes for Chinese Chicken Rice Bowl, Veggie Pad Thai, Yum! Yum! Dumplings, Indian Veggie Medley, Shabu-Shabu HealthBarn USA, and Eggplant Parmesan Towers.

- Finally—and this applies to all meals, whether eaten at home or out—share this HealthBarn USA rule with your kids: *Don't yuck my yum!*

As you know, the number one rule when it comes to trying new foods at HealthBarn USA is "No yucks allowed!" Instead we express our opinions with thumbs up, thumbs down, or thumbs to the side. Still, the occasional "yuck!" does slip out, and when this happens, the kids who are enjoying the food in question all look at the offender and say, "Don't yuck my yum!" It's a fun and catchy way of reminding children (and adults!) to respect the tastes of all eaters.*

---

* Parents can be guilty of yucking the yum too! If the responsibilities of planning and preparing meals fall on one parent, the less-involved parent may sometimes be a little too freewheeling with voicing negative opinions about the food in front of impressionable kids. One parent saying "yuck" can undo another parent's hard work.

Compost!

If you don't compost your kitchen scraps, it's time to start—and it's so much easier than you think. This is a terrific activity for children. The "gross" factor that puts off so many adults is exactly what attracts so many kids. Saving their "trash" and mixing it all together . . . watching earthworms . . . stirring up the "black gold" . . . they love it!

Kids seem to understand right away that the foods that make the best compost are pure foods from nature. The more natural ingredients we eat, the more scraps from compost we collect and the more rich soil for our plants we create. Doritos and Lunchables? Junky foods make for junky compost!

The main rule about composting your kitchen scraps is what **not** to put in the pile (besides processed and artificial foods that won't break down well), and it's a pretty short list: meat, poultry, fish, or dairy items. Otherwise, you can enlist your family to help you save the following items:

get your hands dirty

- Fruit and vegetable trimmings, peels, pits, rinds, etc.
- Bread, grains (moldy and stale is fine)
- Coffee grounds and paper filters, tea bags (paper)
- Egg shells
- Nonfood items that you may add include grass clippings, fall leaves, newspapers, sawdust, and wood shavings

To begin composting you can go low-tech and simply toss scraps as you collect them into a covered crock or small pail on the kitchen counter, dumping them into a larger plastic or metal receptacle outside and letting time and nature do their work. At HealthBarn USA, we don't even use a container—we put scraps straight into our compost pile in the ground, and regularly turn the compost with a pitchfork or shovel.

If that's too labor-intensive or if you don't have the space or desire for a pile, there are compost bins available for purchase at many garden stores. The basic design is usually a plastic, animal-proof bin with some form of ventilation, sometimes with a crank that turns and "cooks" the compost. Scraps go into a secured opening on top, and an opening at the bottom of the bin allows you to remove the rich compost once it is ready and use it throughout your lawn and garden. Visit www.howtocompost.org for detailed information on this easy-to-do activity that will benefit the earth. It's a hands-on lesson for kids of all ages, and it's one more way to make each day a healthy day.

Homemade Chicken Nuggets

If you're looking for a healthy chicken nugget recipe that your kids will love, you have found it. For a natural and savory coating, we mixed panko bread crumbs with a variety of seasonings that will appeal to the whole family. High in protein and a good source of iron, these cooked nuggets freeze very well. Make extras so that they can be served in a pinch!

ingredients

⅓ cup whole wheat flour

1 teaspoon garlic powder

1 teaspoon onion powder

½ teaspoon sea salt

½ teaspoon paprika

2 large egg whites

4½ teaspoons honey

1 tablespoon tomato paste

1 cup panko bread crumbs

1 pound skinless, boneless chicken breasts, cut into fifteen 1-inch chunks

directions

1. Preheat oven to 450°F. Grease a baking sheet.

2. In a large bowl, mix together flour, garlic powder, onion powder, salt, and paprika. In a pie plate, whisk together egg whites, honey, and tomato paste. Place panko in a medium bowl.

3. One at a time, coat chicken chunks with flour mixture, shaking off any excess; then dip in egg-white mixture, allowing excess to drip off. Finally, toss in panko, pressing crumbs onto chicken if necessary to coat evenly.

4. Place chicken chunks on prepared baking sheet and spread out to allow for even cooking.

5. Bake the chicken for 12–15 minutes or until crust is golden brown and crisp and chicken reaches an internal temperature of 165°F.*

Makes 5 servings (3 nuggets per serving)

Nutrition Facts per serving: 210 calories; 2g fat (0g sat fat, 1g mono, 0g trans fat); 55mg cholesterol; 23g carbohydrate (2g fiber, 6g sugar); 25g protein; 170mg sodium; 4% Daily Value (DV) vitamin A; 4% DV vitamin C; 2% DV calcium; 10% DV iron

Kids can place chicken chunks in flour, egg mixture, and panko to coat; and they can place them on the baking sheet. (Make sure hands are thoroughly washed after handling raw poultry.)

* To freeze chicken nuggets: Prepare recipe as above, then cool nuggets. Arrange in a single layer on a baking sheet and freeze until frozen. Transfer to freezer-weight plastic bag and freeze for up to 6 months. To reheat, place frozen nuggets on a baking sheet and bake in 450°F oven for 10–12 minutes or until crisp and heated through.

Homemade Vs. Store-Bought: The Facts!

HealthBarn USA's Homemade Chicken Nuggets	**Banquet Chicken Nuggets** Reference: product package
Ingredients: Whole wheat flour, garlic powder, onion powder, sea salt, paprika, egg whites, honey, tomato paste, panko bread crumbs, skinless chicken breast	**Ingredients:** Chicken breast with rib meat, water, breader (bleached wheat flour, salt, dextrose, yeast, soybean oil, spice extractives of paprika), batter (water, yellow corn flour, cornstarch, spices, salt, sugar, autolyzed yeast extract, guar gum, leavening [sodium acid pyrophosphate, sodium bicarbonate, monocalcium phosphate], garlic powder), textured soy flour, soy flour, contains 2% or less of: modified food starch, salt, autolyzed yeast extract, sodium tripolyphosphate, flavoring, spice; fried in vegetable oil with BHT
Nutrition Facts (per serving): 210 calories; 2g fat (0g sat fat, 1g mono, 0g trans fat); 55mg cholesterol; 23g carbohydrate (2g fiber, 6g sugar); 25g protein; 170mg sodium; 4% Daily Value (DV) vitamin A; 4% DV vitamin C; 2% DV calcium; 10% DV iron	**Nutrition Facts** (per serving): 210 calories; 11g fat (2g sat fat, 0g trans fat); 15mg cholesterol; 17g carbohydrate (3g fiber, less than 1g sugar); 11g protein; 400mg sodium; 2% Daily Value (DV) calcium; 6% DV iron
OURS: • 10 ingredients • baked	**THEIRS:** • 26 ingredients • multiple preservatives added • fried

Brown Rice Risotto with Shrimp

This hearty and healthy whole-grain risotto, made with brown rice instead of the traditional arborio, has even gotten the thumbs up from some Italian grandparents of our HealthBarn USA kids—they've made the switch! Like you, they love the fact that it's high in calcium and protein, and is a good source of fiber, vitamin C, and iron. Like the kids, they love that it tastes delicious.

ingredients

1 teaspoon olive oil

1 medium onion, chopped

1 clove garlic, minced

1 cup short-grain brown rice

2½ cups reduced-sodium vegetable broth

3 tablespoons minced fresh parsley leaves

1 teaspoon minced fresh rosemary leaves

¼ teaspoon saffron threads

12 medium shrimp, shelled and deveined

3 tablespoons freshly grated Parmesan cheese

Pure saffron is made up of tiny, bright red threads. The redder the saffron, the higher the quality. The tips of the threads should be a slightly lighter orange-red color. This will show that it is not cheap saffron that has been tinted red to look expensive.

directions

1. In a large nonstick saucepan, heat oil over medium heat. Add onion and cook until tender, about 10 minutes, stirring occasionally. Stir in garlic; cook for 30 seconds. Add rice and cook for 2 minutes, stirring constantly.

2. Stir broth, parsley, rosemary, and saffron into the rice mixture; heat to boiling over high heat. Reduce heat to low; cover and simmer until rice is tender and liquid is absorbed, about 45 minutes.

3. Meanwhile, in a medium saucepan, heat 1 quart of water to boiling over high heat. Add shrimp and cook until opaque throughout, about 2 minutes. Drain shrimp; keep warm.

4. When rice is done, remove saucepan from heat; stir in Parmesan. Add shrimp to rice mixture and toss until mixed. Serve warm.

Makes 4 servings (1 cup per serving)

Nutrition Facts per serving: 260 calories; 4g fat (1g sat fat, 1g mono, 1g poly, 0g trans fat); 35mg cholesterol; 43g carbohydrate (3g fiber, 2g sugar); 11g protein; 220mg sodium; 6% Daily Value (DV) vitamin A; 10% DV vitamin C; 15% DV calcium; 10% DV iron

Kids can mince herbs using a plastic knife with adult supervision.

BBQ Turkey Pizza

This pizza is made using our homemade grilled Whole Wheat Pizza Dough. Topped with lean turkey flavored by an irresistible mix of our special sauce, herbs, and veggies, plus mozzarella, it's a good source of protein and iron, and it's high in vitamin C. This recipe works well as a group activity because everyone can have a task in the kitchen, and each diner can make a personal pizza.

ingredients

1 recipe Whole Wheat Pizza Dough (page 196)

¾ cup ketchup

1 tablespoon cider vinegar

1½ teaspoons low-sodium soy sauce

⅛ teaspoon ground cumin

⅛ teaspoon ground nutmeg

Juice of ½ lemon

1 tablespoon olive oil

2 medium sweet onions, such as Vidalia, thinly sliced

2 yellow bell peppers, chopped

⅛ teaspoon freshly ground black pepper

1 pound ground turkey (99% lean)

¼ cup loosely packed fresh basil leaves, chopped

¼ cup loosely packed fresh oregano leaves, chopped

⅔ cup (2.5 ounces) shredded low-moisture, part-skim mozzarella cheese

---

Nutrition Facts per serving: 170 calories; 3.5g fat (1g sat fat, 2g mono, 0g trans fat); 10mg cholesterol; 24g carbohydrate (2g fiber, 5g sugar); 10g protein; 200mg sodium; 4% Daily Value (DV) vitamin A; 45% DV vitamin C; 6% DV calcium; 10% DV iron

directions

1. Prepare Whole Wheat Pizza Dough as recipe directs.

2. In a medium saucepan, combine ketchup, vinegar, soy sauce, cumin, nutmeg, and lemon juice; heat to boiling over medium heat. Reduce heat to low and simmer, uncovered, for about 15–20 minutes or until sauce thickens and is reduced to ⅔ cup, stirring occasionally.

3. In a large nonstick skillet, heat oil over medium heat. Add onions, yellow peppers, and black pepper. Reduce heat to low and cook until onions caramelize, about 20 minutes, stirring occasionally.

4. Transfer onion mixture to a bowl. In the same skillet, over medium-high heat, cook turkey until browned, 15–20 minutes, stirring frequently. Add basil and oregano to turkey as it cooks. Add turkey to onion mixture.

5. Grease a large ridged grill pan and heat over medium heat until hot.

6. Place dough rounds on a hot grill pan and cook until underside of dough turns golden and grill marks appear, about 4 minutes. With tongs, turn crusts over. Brush crusts with sauce, dividing evenly among pizzas. Then top crusts with turkey mixture and mozzarella. Cook pizzas until cheese begins to melt, about 4 minutes longer.

7. Transfer pizzas to a cutting board; let cool a few minutes. Cut each pizza into quarters to serve.

Makes 20 servings (½ pizza per serving)

Kids can roll out dough, grill dough with adult supervision, and top pizzas with prepared ingredients.

Whole Wheat Pizza Dough

Use this recipe whenever you have pizza night in your house; and make and freeze extra dough balls for pizza emergencies. Finding premade pizza dough is a tough challenge because most store-bought offerings are high in sodium and may contain extra ingredients you don't want or need. We went back to basics and made our own low-fat, low-sodium, whole-grain dough that we top with loads of fresh veggies and garden-fresh herbs. For extra-crunchy creations, we prefer to grill our pizzas instead of baking them in the oven. You can grill inside on your stovetop using a ridged grill pan, or on an outdoor grill.

ingredients

2 cups whole wheat flour

1½ cups unbleached all-purpose flour, plus extra for dusting

2 teaspoons baking powder

1½ cups water

2 tablespoons extra-virgin olive oil

1 tablespoon honey

Nutrition Facts per serving: 100 calories; 2g fat (0g sat fat, 1g mono, 0g trans fat); 0mg cholesterol; 18g carbohydrate (2g fiber, 1g sugar); 3g protein; 55mg sodium; 2% Daily Value (DV) calcium; 4% DV iron

---

directions

1. In a large bowl, combine flours and baking powder. Make a well in the center of the dry ingredients and add water, oil, and honey. With a large spoon, stir ingredients together until dough comes away from side of bowl easily, making sure that no flour remains on the sides of the bowl.

2. On a surface lightly dusted with all-purpose flour, knead the dough for 5–10 minutes or until pliable, adding flour as needed to keep the dough from sticking to your hands and the work surface.

3. Shape dough into a ball and wrap tightly in plastic wrap. Refrigerate at least 30 minutes or until easy to roll.

4. On a floured surface, cut the dough ball into 10 equal pieces. With a floured rolling pin, roll each piece into a 5-inch round, about ½-inch thick (it doesn't have to be perfect!). Stack the rounds on a greased baking sheet as they are rolled, with a sheet of plastic wrap between each layer; cover loosely with plastic wrap until ready to cook.

5. *To grill dough on the stovetop:* Grease a large ridged grill pan and heat over medium heat until hot. Place dough rounds on hot grill pan and cook until underside of dough turns golden and grill marks appear, about 4 minutes. With tongs, turn crusts over and grill for another 4 minutes. (Add toppings once pizza dough is grilled or as indicated in individual recipes.)

Makes 20 servings (½ crust per serving)

Kids can measure and mix ingredients.

Homemade Vs. Store-Bought: The Facts!

HealthBarn USA's Whole Wheat Pizza Dough	Boboli Original Pizza Crust Reference: www.boboli.com
Ingredients: Whole wheat flour, unbleached all-purpose flour, baking powder, water, extra virgin olive oil, honey	**Ingredients:** Unbleached enriched wheat flour (flour, malted barley flour, reduced iron, niacin, thiamine mononitrate [vitamin B1], riboflavin [vitamin B2], folic acid), water, palm oil, yeast, salt, milk casein, sugar, mozzarella cheese (milk, cheese cultures, salt, enzymes), preservatives (calcium propionate, sorbic acid), fumaric acid, modified food starch, sodium phosphate, whey, monoglycerides, lactic acid, natural flavor, garlic, artificial color
Nutrition Facts (per serving): 100 calories; 2g fat (0g sat fat, 1g mono, 0g trans fat); 0mg cholesterol; 18g carbohydrate (2g fiber, 1g sugar); 3g protein; 55mg sodium; 2% Daily Value (DV) calcium; 4% DV iron	**Nutrition Facts** (per serving): 180 calories; 3g fat (1.5g sat fat, 0g trans fat); 0mg cholesterol; 32g carbohydrate (1g fiber, 1g sugar); 6g protein; 350 mg sodium; 6% Daily Value (DV) calcium; 10% DV iron
OURS: • 6 ingredients	**THEIRS:** • 28 ingredients • contains palm oil, which is a source of saturated fat • preservatives and artificial color added

Spinach Salad with Raspberry Vinaigrette

Kids know that locally grown produce (especially spinach) tastes fresh and delicious, but locally harvested honey is good for you too! Add local honey to foods, beverages, and salad dressings especially when allergy season is in full bloom—it's a natural way to relieve seasonal allergy symptoms. This salad is an excellent source of antioxidant vitamins A and C that help protect your immune system. "Bee" smart and go local!

ingredients

2 large eggs

¼ cup flaxseed oil

¼ cup cider vinegar

¼ cup fresh or frozen (thawed) raspberries

2 tablespoons honey

1 tablespoon Dijon mustard

1 tablespoon fresh peppermint leaves

⅛ teaspoon sea salt

⅛ teaspoon freshly ground black pepper

1 clove garlic, coarsely chopped

½ cup (¼-inch dice) red bell pepper

½ cup raisins or dried cranberries

8 cups (8 ounces) baby spinach leaves

directions

1. Hard-cook the eggs: In a medium saucepan, place eggs and enough cold water to cover eggs by at least 1 inch; heat to boiling over high heat. Immediately remove saucepan from heat and cover tightly; let stand 15 minutes. Pour off hot water and run cold water over eggs to cool.

2. Meanwhile, in a blender, combine the oil, vinegar, raspberries, honey, Dijon, mint, salt, black pepper, and garlic; blend until smooth. If mixture is too thick, add water, 1 teaspoon at a time, to reach desired consistency.

3. Remove shells from eggs. Cut eggs into a ¼-inch dice.

4. Place eggs, red pepper, and raisins in separate bowls with spoons to make a salad bar.

5. To create a salad: Place 1 cup spinach leaves in serving bowl; top with 1 tablespoon eggs, 1 tablespoon red pepper, and 1 tablespoon raisins. Spoon 2 tablespoons raspberry vinaigrette on top.

6. Repeat to make 8 salads in all.

Makes 8 servings (1 cup per serving)

Nutrition Facts per serving: 150 calories; 8g fat (1g sat fat, 2g mono, 5g poly, 0g trans fat); 45mg cholesterol; 16g carbohydrate (2g fiber, 12g sugar); 3g protein; 115mg sodium; 25% Daily Value (DV) vitamin A; 30% DV vitamin C; 4% DV calcium; 8% DV iron

Kids can add dressing ingredients to blender and blend; they can make their own salad.

Mike's Sicilian Stew

The kids at HealthBarn USA think our friend Mike makes the best pizza in New York City, but he also has another gift: he can make cauliflower taste better than pasta! The lowly cauliflower isn't too popular because so many people don't know how to cook it properly, but Mike's here to help. His super stew will satisfy, plus it uses an underrated but amazing veggie that offers riboflavin, niacin, magnesium and phosphorous, fiber, vitamins C and K, vitamin B6, folate, potassium, manganese, and pantothenic acid (phew!).

ingredients

1 tablespoon olive oil

2 sweet onions, such as Vidalia, cut into ¼-inch dice (about 2 cups)

2 cloves garlic, minced

1 can (14.5 ounces) crushed tomatoes

1 cup water

1 large head cauliflower (2½ pounds), broken into 1½-inch florets

1 pound lean ground beef (93% lean)

1 tablespoon minced fresh thyme leaves

1 tablespoon minced fresh basil leaves

2 tablespoons freshly grated Parmesan cheese

directions

1. In a large saucepot or Dutch oven, heat oil over medium heat. Add onions and cook until tender, about 10 minutes, stirring occasionally. Add garlic and cook 30 seconds, stirring.

2. Stir in tomatoes, water, and cauliflower; heat to boiling. Reduce heat to low and simmer, covered, for 25 minutes or until cauliflower is fork-tender.

3. Meanwhile, in a large skillet, over medium-high heat, cook ground beef until browned, stirring occasionally. Drain off fat.

4. When cauliflower is done, stir in browned beef and herbs and simmer, covered, for 15 minutes to blend flavors.

5. Spoon into 8 individual bowls and sprinkle with Parmesan, divided evenly among the bowls.

Makes 8 servings (1 cup per serving)

Nutrition Facts per serving: 150 calories; 5g fat (1g sat fat, 3g mono, 1g poly, 0g trans fat); 30mg cholesterol; 14g carbohydrate (3g fiber, 6g sugar); 15g protein; 150mg sodium; 8% Daily Value (DV) vitamin A; 90% DV vitamin C; 6% DV calcium; 10% DV iron

---

Kids can break cauliflower into florets using their hands.

Cheesy Lasagna Rolls

This recipe is a really fun twist (literally!) on traditional lasagna. We add
silken tofu to this three-cheese pasta dish to boost the protein and calcium.
At HealthBarn USA, we've discovered that the kids really have fun with
this recipe as a group activity. Get ready to dig into this muscle and bone-
boosting dish, with its smart combination of protein, iron, and calcium.

ingredients

10 whole wheat lasagna noodles (or
other lasagna noodles)

2 cups low-sodium marinara sauce

1 cup silken light tofu

2 tablespoons part-skim ricotta
cheese

2 tablespoons freshly grated
Parmesan cheese

⅛ teaspoon freshly ground black
pepper

2 cups baby spinach leaves, coarsely
chopped

½ cup loosely packed fresh basil
leaves, chopped

3 tablespoons shredded low-
moisture, part-skim mozzarella
cheese

directions

1. Heat a large pot of water to boiling over high heat. Add
lasagna noodles and cook until al dente, about 9 minutes.

2. Drain noodles; rinse with cold running water. Place noodles
on a clean, flat work surface.

3. Preheat oven to 400°F. Into each of 10 muffin cups, spoon
1 teaspoon marinara sauce; set aside.

4. Place the tofu between several layers of paper towels and
squeeze out excess liquid. In a small bowl, stir together tofu,
ricotta, Parmesan, and pepper.

5. Spoon 2 tablespoons of the cheese mixture onto each noodle
and spread to make a thin layer. Then, spread 2 tablespoons of
marinara sauce over cheese layer on each noodle. Top with
spinach and basil, divided evenly among the 10 noodles.

6. Roll each noodle tightly, in jelly-roll fashion. Place 1 lasagna
roll in each muffin cup; top with remaining marinara sauce
and sprinkle with mozzarella.

7. Bake lasagna rolls for 10 minutes or until heated through and
cheese melts.

Makes 5 servings (2 lasagna rolls per serving)

Nutrition Facts per serving: 250 calories; 4g fat (1g sat fat, 1g mono,
1g poly, 0g trans fat); 5mg cholesterol; 41g carbohydrate (9g fiber, 6g
sugar); 15g protein; 180mg sodium; 35% Daily Value (DV) vitamin A;
10% DV vitamin C; 25% DV calcium; 60% DV iron

**Kids can layer the noodles with filling,
roll them, and place them in muffin cups.**

Yum! Yum! Dumplings

We call these Yum! Yum! Dumplings because that was our reaction after the first bite! This authentic Korean family recipe is chock-full of healthy fats and protein. Make sure to mince as directed and to drain all the liquid from the tofu and shredded zucchini so that your final product will not be soggy.

ingredients

Dumplings

1 package (14 ounces) firm tofu, drained

1 medium zucchini (10 ounces)

4 scallions, minced

2 cloves garlic, minced

1 teaspoon Asian sesame oil

½ teaspoon freshly ground black pepper

1 package (16 ounces) egg roll wrappers

5 tablespoons olive oil

Dipping Sauce

¼ cup low-sodium soy sauce

2 tablespoons unseasoned rice vinegar

1 teaspoon Asian sesame oil

Juice of 1 lime

Nutrition Facts per serving: 160 calories; 7g fat (1g sat fat, 4g mono, 2g poly, 0g trans fat); 5mg cholesterol; 18g carbohydrate (1g fiber, 1g sugar); 6g protein; 290mg sodium; 2% Daily Value (DV) vitamin A; 8% DV vitamin C; 6% DV calcium; 8% DV iron

---

directions

1. Prepare Dumplings: Place tofu between several layers of paper towels and squeeze out excess liquid. Place tofu in a large bowl and mash it with a fork until it resembles scrambled eggs; set aside.

2. Shred zucchini. With your hands, squeeze out the excess liquid. Place zucchini in the bowl with the tofu.

3. Add scallions, garlic, sesame oil, and pepper to the bowl and mix by hand until well blended.

4. Cut egg roll wrappers into quarters to make 4 squares each. Place ¼ cup water in small bowl to use as "dumpling glue."

5. Place 1 wrapper square in your hand and coat 2 adjacent edges with water, using your finger as a brush. Place 1 heaping teaspoon dumpling mixture in center of wrapper, then bring 2 opposite corners of wrapper together over filling to make a triangle. Pinch and pleat edges together to seal in filling. Repeat the process with the remaining wrappers and mixture.

6. In a large skillet, heat 1 tablespoon of oil over medium heat, making sure to coat the skillet bottom completely. Place enough dumplings in skillet, in one layer, to cover bottom of skillet. Cook for 2–3 minutes or until browned on the bottom. Turn dumplings over; cover and cook 2–3 minutes to brown other side. Transfer dumplings to a serving plate; keep warm. Repeat with remaining oil and dumplings.

7. While the dumplings are cooking, prepare Dipping Sauce: In a small bowl, stir together soy sauce, vinegar, sesame oil, and lime juice.

8. Serve the dumplings with the dipping sauce.

   Makes 15 servings (5 dumplings per serving)

Kids can stuff, seal, and pinch the dumplings, as well as cook with adult supervision.

Quinoa with Kale and Walnuts

Our favorite whole grain is quinoa because it smells so good when it's cooking and because it's full of great stuff. It's a complete protein (it contains lysine, an amino acid missing in most grains), and is a good source of riboflavin, vitamin E, iron, magnesium, potassium, zinc, and fiber. We added fresh kale because it's the super leafy green loaded with vitamins A and C, and the walnuts offer healthy fats, including omega-3 fatty acids. Move over rice—we're all about quinoa.

ingredients

- 1 cup quinoa
- 1 tablespoon olive oil
- 1 clove garlic, minced
- 2 cups water
- 4 ounces kale, chopped
- 1 cup grape tomatoes, halved
- 2 tablespoons freshly grated Parmesan cheese
- 3 tablespoons walnuts, finely chopped
- Torn fresh basil leaves for garnish

directions

1. Rinse quinoa with cold running water and drain.

2. In a medium saucepan, heat oil over medium heat. Add quinoa and cook until toasted, about 10 minutes, stirring constantly. Add garlic and cook 1 minute, stirring. Add water; heat to boiling. Reduce heat to low; cover and simmer for 12–15 minutes or until water is absorbed.

3. When quinoa is cooked, add kale and tomatoes to quinoa in saucepan. Cook over low heat until kale begins to wilt and tomatoes are warm, about 1 minute, stirring. Stir in Parmesan and walnuts. Garnish with basil leaves. Sprinkle with additional Parmesan, if you like.

Makes 5 servings (1 cup per serving)

Nutrition Facts per serving: 210 calories; 8g fat (1g sat fat, 3g mono, 4g poly, 0g trans fat); 0mg cholesterol; 28g carbohydrate (3g fiber, 1g sugar); 7g protein; 55mg sodium; 70% Daily Value (DV) vitamin A; 50% DV vitamin C; 8% DV calcium; 20% DV iron

---

Kids can measure ingredients and add Parmesan.

Chicken Fiesta Fajitas

We use a cinnamon "dry rub" to season this chicken instead of a vegetable oil marinade, to keep saturated fat low and keep the chicken tasty and tender. Cinnamon is a natural insulin sensitizer, meaning that it helps to keep your blood sugar stable. We use traditional corn tortillas, which are a good source of fiber. Serve this dish that's loaded with vitamin C with Holy Green Guacamole (page 163), and hasta luego . . . we're off to the fiesta!

ingredients

1 tablespoon ground cinnamon

¼ teaspoon sea salt

¼ teaspoon freshly ground black pepper

1½ pounds skinless, boneless chicken breasts

1 medium green bell pepper

1 medium red bell pepper

1 large sweet onion, such as Vidalia

2 tablespoons canola oil

1 clove garlic, minced

Juice of 2 limes

12 (6-inch) corn tortillas, warmed

directions

1. Preheat oven to 400°F. Grease a baking sheet.

2. In a bowl, combine cinnamon, salt, and black pepper. Add chicken to bowl with seasonings and toss to coat evenly.

3. Place chicken on the prepared baking sheet. Bake for 25–30 minutes or until it reaches an internal temperature of 165°F. Cool slightly, then pull into shreds with 2 forks.

4. Meanwhile, slice the green and red peppers lengthwise into thin slices. Cut onion in half, then cut each half into thin slices. In a large skillet, heat oil over medium heat. Add the peppers and onions and cook for 7–10 minutes or until tender-crisp, stirring occasionally. Stir in garlic; cook 30 seconds more.

5. Add chicken and lime juice to skillet with peppers; heat through.

6. Spoon chicken mixture into serving bowl. Place tortillas on plates. Let everyone make his or her own fajitas.

Makes 12 servings (1 fajita per serving)

Nutrition Facts per serving: 310 calories; 6g fat (0g sat fat, 2g mono, 3g poly, 0g trans fat); 35mg cholesterol; 46g carbohydrate (4g fiber, 2g sugar); 17g protein; 160mg sodium; 8% Daily Value (DV) vitamin A; 40% DV vitamin C; 2% DV calcium; 6% DV iron

---

Kids can chop peppers using a plastic knife with adult supervision, and can stuff tortillas with prepared ingredients.

Coconut Shrimp with Pineapple Herb Dipping Sauce

Tired of the same old appetizers? We were too, which is why we were inspired to create these coconut shrimp starters. These tasty bites offer a good balance of protein, healthy fats, and carbohydrates. The sweet and tangy dipping sauce brings out the fabulous flavor of the shrimp.

ingredients

Coconut Shrimp

½ cup unsweetened shredded coconut

¼ cup whole wheat flour

2 large egg whites

1 tablespoon water

½ cup panko bread crumbs

18 large shrimp, shelled and deveined with tail part of shell left on

1 tablespoon low-sodium soy sauce

⅛ teaspoon freshly ground black pepper

Pineapple Herb Dipping Sauce

½ (8-ounce) can pineapple chunks in juice

½ cup loosely packed fresh herbs (basil, rosemary, parsley)

Juice of ½ lime

Nutrition Facts per serving:
45 calories; 1.5g fat (1g sat fat, 0.5g mono, 0g trans fat); 10mg cholesterol; 5g carbohydrate (1g fiber, 2g sugar); 3g protein; 45mg sodium; 2% Daily Value (DV) vitamin A; 2% DV vitamin C; 2% DV iron

---

directions

1. Prepare the Coconut Shrimp: Preheat oven to 350°F. Spread coconut on an ungreased baking sheet. Toast in the oven for 3–5 minutes or until golden brown, stirring frequently to ensure even cooking. Transfer coconut to a pie plate; cool.

2. Turn oven temperature up to 425°F. Grease the same baking sheet. Place flour in a small bowl. In another small bowl, whisk egg whites with water until foamy. Stir panko into the coconut in the pie plate. In a large bowl, toss shrimp with soy sauce and pepper.

3. One at a time, hold shrimp by tail and coat with flour, shaking off excess; then dip in egg white mixture. Finally, roll in coconut mixture to coat well.

4. Place shrimp on the prepared baking sheet. Bake for 10–12 minutes or until shrimp are opaque throughout and coating is crisp.

5. Meanwhile, prepare the Pineapple Herb Dipping Sauce: Drain pineapple, reserving ¼ cup juice. In a food processor, pulse pineapple, reserved pineapple juice, herbs, and lime juice until blended.

6. Serve coconut shrimp with dipping sauce.

Makes 18 servings (1 shrimp per serving)

Kids can crack, separate, and whisk eggs; coat shrimp with different mixtures; and place on baking sheet.

Chinese Chicken Rice Bowl

We created these Chinese Chicken Rice Bowls to satisfy the urge for Chinese takeout, but to keep things healthier with brown rice and lean chicken. Nutty-tasting brown rice is a whole grain that pairs beautifully with this vitamin C–packed chicken preparation, and the shiitake mushrooms make it extra special. Serve orange wedges for a refreshing dessert.

ingredients

2 cups water

1 cup short-grain brown rice

1 pound shiitake mushrooms

1½ pounds skinless, boneless thin-cut chicken breasts or chicken tenders

2 tablespoons canola oil

½ red or green bell pepper, cut into ¼-inch dice

1 can (6 to 8 ounces) sliced water chestnuts, drained and chopped

2 cloves garlic, chopped

¼ cup loosely packed fresh chives, chopped

1 tablespoon grated peeled fresh ginger

1 tablespoon grated fresh orange peel

3 tablespoons low-sodium soy sauce

directions

1. Cook rice in a rice cooker as manufacturer directs. Or, in a medium saucepan, heat water and rice to boiling over high heat. Reduce heat to low; cover and simmer for 40–50 minutes or until rice is tender and liquid is absorbed. Set rice aside in a bowl.

2. Meanwhile, remove the tough stems from the mushrooms and discard. With a damp towel, wipe mushroom caps clean. Slice mushrooms. Cut chicken into 1-inch chunks.

3. In a large skillet or wok, heat oil over high heat. Add chicken and cook, stirring constantly (stir-frying), for 2–3 minutes or until chicken reaches an internal temperature of 165°F. Add mushrooms, pepper, and water chestnuts and cook for 2–3 minutes longer.

4. Add garlic, chives, ginger, and orange peel; stir-fry 1 minute longer. Add soy sauce and toss to coat mixture evenly.

5. Transfer chicken mixture to platter. Spoon rice into 10 individual serving bowls and top with chicken mixture.

Makes 10 servings (1 cup per serving)

Nutrition Facts per serving: 200 calories; 4g fat (0g sat fat, 2g mono, 1g poly, 0g trans fat); 40mg cholesterol; 20g carbohydrate (2g fiber, 1g sugar); 19g protein; 170mg sodium; 6% Daily Value (DV) vitamin A; 20% DV vitamin C; 2% DV calcium; 6% DV iron

---

Kids can spoon rice into bowls and top with mixture.

Citrus and Herb Shrimp Kebabs

Summer means grilling, and grilling means kebabs. Bright citrus flavors and fresh herbs make these shrimp kebabs a warm-weather classic that you'll be sure to make year after year. The natural citrus juices are loaded with vitamins A and C to keep your immune system in tip-top shape.

ingredients

8 bamboo skewers

1½ cups water

1 cup jasmine rice

2 medium (10 ounces each) zucchini

2 medium yellow bell peppers

2 tablespoons olive oil, divided

¼ teaspoon sea salt, divided

¼ teaspoon freshly ground black pepper, divided

½ cup loosely packed fresh mint leaves, chopped

⅓ cup loosely packed fresh basil leaves, chopped

1 tablespoon chopped chives

Juice and grated peel of 1 orange, 1 lemon, and 1 lime

1 tablespoon grated, peeled fresh ginger

2 cloves garlic, coarsely chopped

⅓ cup plain low-fat yogurt

1 pound large shrimp (about 24), shelled and deveined with tail part of shells left on

¼ cup loosely packed fresh Italian parsley leaves, chopped

directions

1. Soak skewers in water for 20 minutes to help prevent burning. In a medium saucepan, heat 1½ cups water and rice to boiling over high heat. Reduce heat to low; cover and simmer for 15–20 minutes or until rice is tender and liquid is absorbed. (Or cook in a rice cooker as the manufacturer directs.) Remove from heat and fluff with a fork.

2. Meanwhile, cut each zucchini in half lengthwise, then crosswise into ½-inch-thick half moons. Cut peppers into 1-inch pieces. In a medium bowl, toss vegetables with 1 tablespoon oil and ⅛ teaspoon each of salt and black pepper; set aside.

3. In a small bowl, mix together mint, basil, and chives. In a food processor, blend citrus juices and peel, ginger, garlic, half of herb mixture, and remaining 1 tablespoon oil until pureed. Transfer 2 tablespoons citrus mixture to a small serving bowl. Stir in yogurt and set aside.

4. Into a medium bowl, pour the remaining citrus mixture; stir in ⅛ teaspoon each salt and black pepper. Add shrimp and toss to coat well.

5. Prepare outdoor grill for grilling over medium-high heat. Grease grill grate.

6. Thread the shrimp on 4 skewers (discard citrus mixture) and vegetables on remaining skewers, alternating zucchini and yellow peppers.

7. Grill the shrimp for about 4–5 minutes, turning once or until opaque, and grill the vegetables for about 10 minutes or until tender-crisp, turning skewers occasionally. Remove shrimp and vegetables from skewers and place on a platter.

8. Stir parsley and remaining herb mixture into rice. Spoon rice onto 8 plates; top with shrimp and vegetables. Drizzle with yogurt sauce.

Makes 8 servings (½ cup rice, ½ vegetable skewer, and 3 shrimp per serving)

Nutrition Facts per serving: 130 calories; 4g fat (0.5g sat fat, 3g mono, 0.5g poly, 0g trans fat); 35mg cholesterol; 17g carbohydrate (2g fiber, 3g sugar); 7g protein; 65mg sodium; 10% Daily Value (DV) vitamin A; 130% DV vitamin C; 6% DV calcium; 8% DV iron

---

Kids can skewer shrimp and vegetables.

Eggplant Parmesan Towers

This recipe "stacks up" better than the traditional eggplant parm you'll find on the menu at your favorite Italian restaurant. With eggplant abundant in our garden, we wanted to lighten up the old-school version, which can be very heavy and high in calories. We started by baking instead of frying the eggplant, which reduced the extra calories and saturated fat, but we still kept the crunchy texture by using panko bread crumbs. The result is a protein- and fiber-packed side dish or main course, if you serve it with a mixed green salad. They can be a little messy, but that also makes them really fun to eat!

ingredients

Olive oil in spray bottle

1 cup panko bread crumbs

1 tablespoon freshly grated
   Parmesan cheese

¼ teaspoon sea salt

⅛ teaspoon freshly ground
   black pepper

2 large egg whites

1 tablespoon water

½ large eggplant, cut
   crosswise into fifteen
   ¼-inch thick slices

5 tablespoons low-sodium
   marinara sauce

5 tablespoons shredded
   low-moisture, part-skim
   mozzarella cheese

directions

1. Preheat oven to 400°F. Spray a baking sheet with oil.

2. Place panko in a pie plate; stir in Parmesan, salt, and pepper. In another pie plate, whisk the egg whites with water until foamy.

3. Dip each eggplant slice into the egg mixture, making sure to coat both sides, then dip into panko mixture to coat both sides. Place on prepared baking sheet.

4. Spray the tops of the eggplant slices with oil. Bake for 20–25 minutes or until tender and lightly browned, carefully turning slices over halfway through cooking. Remove the pan with eggplant from the oven. Do not turn off oven.

5. Place 1 teaspoon of marinara sauce and 1 teaspoon mozzarella on each of the 5 largest eggplant slices. Top each with another eggplant slice. Repeat with remaining sauce, mozzarella, and eggplant to make stacks or "towers," each with 3 slices of eggplant.

6. Return the pan with eggplant towers to the oven and bake about 5 minutes longer or until cheese melts.

Makes 5 servings (1 tower per serving)

Nutrition Facts per serving: 110 calories; 2g fat (1g sat fat, 1g mono, 0g trans fat); 5mg cholesterol; 17g carbohydrate (4g fiber, 4g sugar); 6g protein; 150mg sodium; 2% Daily Value (DV) vitamin A; 6% DV vitamin C; 8% DV calcium; 6% DV iron

Kids can crack, separate, and whisk egg whites; dip sliced eggplant in egg and panko mixtures; and create towers by layering ingredients.

Garden-Fresh Pasta

We know your time is precious, so we created this easy-to-make dish that only requires one pot—no need to cook the pasta separately. This is a family favorite because you can get it onto the table quickly and cleanup is a snap. Best of all, it's extremely nutritious with its combo of vitamin C, fiber, calcium, and iron. Cooking tomatoes increases the lycopene, a nutrient that protects your immune system.

ingredients

1 tablespoon olive oil

2 cloves garlic, minced

6 ripe tomatoes (about 3 pounds), each cut into eighths

¼ cup loosely packed fresh basil leaves, chopped (also try a mixture of oregano, basil, chives, and/or parsley)

1 package (13.25 ounces) whole wheat penne or rotelle pasta

¼ cup freshly grated Parmesan cheese

directions

1. In a large saucepan, heat oil over medium heat. Add garlic and cook for 30 seconds. Add tomatoes and basil. Cover and cook for 10 minutes or until tomatoes are soft and a broth forms. Depending on juiciness of tomatoes, you may need to add ¼ –½ cup of water to have about 2½ cups of broth.

2. When the broth is boiling, add pasta; cover and cook for 15–18 minutes, stirring occasionally, until pasta is al dente. Remove from heat and stir in Parmesan.

Makes 7 servings (1 cup per serving)

Nutrition Facts per serving: 270 calories; 5g fat (1g sat fat, 2g mono, 1g poly, 0g trans fat); 5mg cholesterol; 47g carbohydrate (6g fiber, 5g sugar); 9g protein; 85mg sodium; 4% Daily Value (DV) vitamin A; 35% DV vitamin C; 10% DV calcium; 10% DV iron

---

Kids can cut tomatoes using a plastic knife with adult supervision.

Homemade Chicken Penicillin Soup

This immune-boosting soup is the best natural "medicine" for staying strong during flu season because it's loaded with the antioxidant vitamins A and C. We have been told that a bowl of this soup looks like we went down to the garden, picked a lot of vegetables, and threw them all in a pot. That's pretty close to how we actually make it! We also use skinless chicken breasts, low in fat and high in protein, but made flavorful and succulent by the variety of veggies that give this soup a big boost of flavor. The whole wheat spaghetti adds fiber.

ingredients

2 tablespoons olive oil

2 cloves garlic, chopped

2 pounds skinless, boneless chicken breasts

5 stalks celery, chopped (about 1½ cups)

4 carrots, chopped (about 1 cup)

3 parsnips, chopped (about 1½ cups)

3 tomatoes (1½ pounds), cut into quarters

¼ cup loosely packed fresh parsley leaves, chopped

3 quarts water

¼ teaspoon sea salt

¼ teaspoon freshly ground black pepper

4 ounces whole wheat spaghetti

Freshly grated Parmesan cheese (optional)

Nutrition Facts per serving: 170 calories; 4g fat (1g sat fat, 2g mono, 1g poly, 0g trans fat); 45mg cholesterol; 15g carbohydrate (3g fiber, 4g sugar); 20g protein; 110mg sodium; 70% Daily Value (DV) vitamin A; 25% DV vitamin C; 4% DV calcium; 8% DV iron

directions

1. In a large saucepot, heat oil over medium heat. Add garlic and cook 30 seconds or until it just starts to turn brown, stirring constantly.

2. Add the chicken breasts to the pot and cook until they reach an internal temperature of 165°F, about 10 minutes. Add celery, carrots, parsnips, tomatoes, and parsley. Add 3 quarts water or enough to cover ingredients. Heat to boiling over high heat. Reduce heat to very low and simmer, uncovered, for 2 hours.

3. Remove chicken from the saucepot; cut into bite-size chunks and set aside.

4. Remove pot from heat. Pour ⅓ of mixture into a blender; cover, with center part of blender cover removed to let steam escape, and blend until pureed. (Or, use an immersion blender and puree in saucepot.)

5. Pour the pureed soup into a bowl and repeat in batches with remaining mixture. Return all soup to the saucepot; add chicken and stir in salt and pepper. Return the soup to boiling.

6. Once the soup is boiling, break spaghetti in half and add to saucepot. Boil for 7–8 minutes or until pasta is al dente.

7. To serve, ladle 1 cup of soup into each of 12 bowls. Sprinkle with Parmesan, if you like.

Makes 12 servings (1 cup per serving)

Kids can chop veggies using a plastic knife with adult supervision and break spaghetti in half using their hands.

Homemade Vs. Store-Bought: The Facts!

HealthBarn USA's Homemade Chicken Penicillin Soup	Campbell's Chicken Noodle Soup Reference: product package
Ingredients: Olive oil, garlic, skinless chicken breast, celery, carrots, parsnips, tomatoes, parsley, water, sea salt, pepper, whole wheat spaghetti	**Ingredients:** Chicken stock, enriched egg noodles (wheat flour, eggs, niacin, ferrous sulfate, thiamine mononitrate, riboflavin, folic acid), chicken meat, water, contains less than 2% of: salt, chicken fat, cornstarch, monosodium glutamate, mechanically separated chicken, modified food starch, yeast extract, flavoring, sodium phosphate, sodium protein isolate, beta-carotene, dehydrated chicken
Nutrition Facts (per serving): 170 calories; 4g fat (1g sat fat, 2g mono, 1g poly, 0g trans fat); 45mg cholesterol; 15g carbohydrate (3g fiber, 4g sugar); 20g protein; 110mg sodium; 70% Daily Value (DV) vitamin A; 25% DV vitamin C; 4% DV calcium; 8% DV iron	**Nutrition Facts** (per serving): 60 calories, 2g fat (0.5g sat fat, 0.5g mono, 0g trans fat); 15mg cholesterol; 8g carbo-hydrate (1g fiber, 1g sugar); 3g protein; 890mg sodium; 4% Daily Value (DV) vita-min A; 2% DV iron
OURS: • 12 ingredients	**THEIRS:** • 22 ingredients • contains monosodium glutamate (MSG)

Moo Shu Chicken

When ordering Chinese food, the healthy choice on the menu is usually the moo shu pancake meal, with its emphasis on lots of veggies for an appropriate serving size. We've made it even healthier in our home-cooked version, which uses our Simply Crepes recipe (page 58) for the pancake. The result is protein packed and high in the antioxidant vitamins A and C—and it's fun to make for a family dinner or party.

Ingredients

1 recipe Simply Crepes (page 58)

3 teaspoons canola oil

3 teaspoons Asian sesame oil

4 large egg whites

1 pound skinless, boneless chicken breasts, thinly sliced lengthwise into 1-inch strips

1 tablespoon grated, peeled fresh ginger

2 cloves garlic, minced

2 cups thinly sliced napa cabbage

1 cup shredded carrots (2 carrots)

1 cup (3 ounces) fresh bean sprouts, drained and rinsed

3 scallions, thinly sliced

1 medium red bell pepper, thinly sliced

2 tablespoons low-sodium soy sauce

2 tablespoons unseasoned rice vinegar

2 tablespoons agave nectar

directions

1. Prepare Simply Crepes as recipe directs.

2. In a large skillet or wok, heat 1 teaspoon of canola oil and 1 teaspoon of sesame oil over medium heat. In a small bowl, whisk egg whites. Add beaten eggs to skillet and cook, stirring, until scrambled. Transfer eggs to a plate.

3. In the same skillet, heat the remaining 2 teaspoons of canola and 2 teaspoons of sesame oil over medium-high heat. Add chicken and cook until it reaches an internal temperature of 165°F, 3–5 minutes, stirring quickly and frequently (stir-frying). Stir in ginger and garlic; cook 1 minute. Add cabbage, carrots, bean sprouts, scallions, and pepper and stir-fry for 3 minutes or until vegetables are tender-crisp.

4. In a cup, stir soy sauce, vinegar, and agave nectar; add to chicken mixture and cook 1 minute longer to blend flavors. Remove skillet from heat; stir in cooked egg.

5. Divide the chicken mixture among 12 crepes; roll up to enclose mixture.

Makes 12 servings (1 pancake per serving)

Nutrition Facts per serving: 160 calories; 3.5g fat (0.5g sat fat, 2g mono, 1g poly, 0g trans fat); 40mg cholesterol; 15g carbohydrate (2g fiber, 6g sugar); 15g protein; 170mg sodium; 45% Daily Value (DV) vitamin A; 30% DV vitamin C; 6% DV calcium; 6% DV iron

---

Kids can fill the crepes with prepared ingredients and fold to serve.

Steamed Salmon Pouches

We went fishing for brain food at HealthBarn USA and came up with this recipe. Because we steam the salmon, it doesn't taste or smell fishy (this is why some kids won't go for fish). With that problem solved, young eaters will be willing to try this high-protein dish that's loaded with brain-building omega-3 fatty acids and is a good source of vitamin C. Serve this dish with the Mixed Greens with Flaxseed Oil Dressing (page 226) for even more healthy fat.

ingredients

4 squares (12 inches each) parchment paper or foil

2 teaspoons extra-virgin olive oil

12 ounces wild salmon fillet, cut into 4 pieces

1 lemon, cut into quarters

½ teaspoon sea salt

directions

1. Preheat oven to 400°F.

2. On half of each parchment square, place ½ teaspoon oil; top with a piece of salmon, flesh side up.

3. Squeeze juice from a lemon quarter onto each salmon piece; sprinkle with salt. Fold unfilled half of parchment over salmon. Seal packets, beginning at one corner, crimping edge all around.

4. Place packets in a rimmed baking sheet. Bake for 15 minutes (packets will puff up and brown).

5. When salmon is cooked, carefully cut packets open to serve (be careful, there will be a lot of steam). Salmon should flake easily when tested with a fork.

Makes 4 servings (1 piece salmon per serving)

Nutrition Facts per serving: 150 calories; 8g fat (1g sat fat, 4g mono, 3g poly, 0g trans fat); 45mg cholesterol; 1g carbohydrate (1g fiber, 1g sugar); 17g protein; 100mg sodium; 10% Daily Value (DV) vitamin C; 2% DV calcium; 8% DV iron

---

Kids can squeeze lemon, sprinkle sea salt, and fold parchment paper before baking.

Quinoa-Stuffed Peppers

All carbohydrates are not created equal! In fact, complex carbohydrates, such as whole grains, contribute significant amounts of protein, fiber, antioxidants, vitamin E, the B vitamins, and trace minerals to our diets to make us strong. This quinoa recipe is so popular at HealthBarn USA that we have to grow more bell pepper plants in the garden to keep up with the demand from our hungry young diners. The high levels of vitamin C in this meal ensure that our bodies will absorb the iron it also contains.

ingredients

6 red, yellow, and/or orange bell peppers

1 cup quinoa

1¼ cups low-sodium vegetable broth

2 tablespoons olive oil

1 sweet onion, such as Vidalia, coarsely chopped

1 clove garlic, minced

3 medium tomatoes (1½ pounds), chopped

1 medium zucchini (10 ounces), chopped

1 medium yellow squash (10 ounces), chopped

1 tablespoon chopped chives

1 tablespoon chopped fresh basil leaves

1 tablespoon chopped fresh oregano leaves

¼ teaspoon sea salt

¼ teaspoon freshly ground black pepper

¼ cup freshly grated Parmesan cheese

directions

1. Blanch the peppers in a large pot of boiling water for 5 minutes. Drain; cool.

2. Rinse quinoa with cold water and drain. In a medium saucepan, heat broth to boiling over high heat. Stir in quinoa. Reduce heat to low; cover and simmer for 12–15 minutes or until quinoa is tender and liquid is absorbed. Uncover; fluff with a fork.

3. In a large skillet, heat oil over medium heat. Add onion and cook until tender, about 10 minutes, stirring occasionally. Stir in garlic; cook for 30 seconds. Add tomatoes, zucchini, yellow squash, herbs, salt, and black pepper and cook until vegetables are soft, 10–15 minutes, stirring occasionally.

4. Remove skillet from heat; stir in quinoa. Preheat oven to 350°F.

5. Cut each pepper in half; discard seeds and membranes. Spoon the quinoa mixture into the pepper halves. Place the stuffed peppers in an 18 x 12-inch glass baking dish; sprinkle with Parmesan, divided evenly among peppers. Bake for 10–15 minutes or until cheese is slightly brown and mixture is heated through.

Makes 12 servings (½ pepper per serving)

Nutrition Facts per serving: 120 calories; 4g fat (1g sat fat, 2g mono, 1g poly, 0g trans fat); 0mg cholesterol; 19g carbohydrate (3g fiber, 6g sugar); 4g protein; 60mg sodium; 40% Daily Value (DV) vitamin A; 150% DV vitamin C; 6% DV calcium; 10% DV iron

Kids can chop veggies using a plastic knife, with adult supervision, and spoon mixture into pepper halves.

Shabu-Shabu HealthBarn USA

Shabu-shabu translates to "swish swish" in Japanese, and that is what you do when cooking this dish. You take these natural ingredients, "swish" them in the vegetable broth, and watch them cook right in front of your eyes! This low-fat meal is high in vitamins A and C, is an excellent source of fiber, and is a fun one for families to make together. For an alternate protein source instead of the shrimp, hard-cook some eggs in the broth.

ingredients

1 quart low-sodium vegetable broth

4 scallions, thinly sliced

12 large shrimp, shelled and deveined with tail part of shell left on

2 cups (2-inch pieces) napa cabbage

2 cups small broccoli florets

2 cups thin diagonally sliced carrots (4 carrots)

4 fondue forks

Low-sodium soy sauce for dipping (optional)

directions

1. In a fondue pot or casserole that's top-of-range safe, heat broth and scallions to boiling over high heat. Place the pot on an electric burner or other heat source, over medium heat, in the middle of the table.

2. Place 3 shrimp, one-fourth of vegetables, and a fondue fork on each of 4 plates.

3. Let each person pick up shrimp and vegetables with fork and "swish" (shabu) them back and forth in broth or rest fork on the side of the pot until the food is cooked, 3–5 minutes for vegetables, 5–7 minutes for shrimp.

4. Eat as food is cooked. Serve with soy sauce for dipping, if you like.

5. When all food has been cooked, drink the broth too.

Makes 4 servings (1 cup broth with vegetables and 3 shrimp per serving)

Nutrition Facts per serving: 90 calories; 1g fat (0g sat fat, 0g trans fat); 30mg cholesterol; 13g carbohydrate (5g fiber, 6g sugar); 7g protein; 230mg sodium; 250% Daily Value (DV) vitamin A; 80% DV vitamin C; 10% DV calcium; 8% DV iron

Kids (and adults) can cook their own food in the broth.

Turkey Burgers with Sweet Oat Rolls

These turkey burgers pack more than just protein; they are loaded with nutrient-packed spinach! We wanted to "green" the turkey burger and came up with this great-tasting recipe that nourishes and satisfies. They taste great on our freshly baked, high-fiber Sweet Oat Rolls (page 224). Round out this healthy burger for lunch or dinner with a side order of our Zucchini Sticks (page 140).

ingredients

10 Sweet Oat Rolls (page 224)

1 teaspoon olive oil

1 small sweet onion, such as Vidalia, very finely chopped

1 clove garlic, coarsely chopped

1 bag (9 ounces) spinach

½ cup loosely packed fresh basil leaves

1 pound ground turkey (99% lean)

1 large egg white

¼ cup (1 ounce) reduced-fat feta cheese or goat cheese

2 tablespoons low-sodium soy sauce

Lettuce leaves and sliced tomatoes (optional)

Nutrition Facts per serving: 300 calories; 8g fat (1g sat fat, 5g mono, 1g poly, 0g trans fat); 30mg cholesterol; 38g carbohydrate (6g fiber, 4g sugar); 20g protein; 240mg sodium; 20% Daily Value (DV) vitamin A; 10% DV vitamin C; 6% DV calcium; 20% DV iron

directions

1. Prepare Sweet Oat Rolls as recipe directs.

2. In a large saucepan, heat 4 cups of water to boiling over high heat. Meanwhile, prepare an ice bath in a large bowl; set aside.

3. In a medium nonstick skillet, heat oil over medium heat. Add onion and cook until tender, about 10 minutes, stirring occasionally. Add garlic and cook for 30 seconds, stirring. Set aside to cool.

4. When water comes to a boil, add spinach and basil, in batches, and blanch for 30 seconds. With a slotted spoon, transfer each batch to the ice bath to stop cooking and retain bright green color. Squeeze as much liquid out of the leaves as possible. (If you like, squeeze excess liquid into a mug to drink; it is full of nutrients.) Place spinach mixture on paper towels to drain; pat dry if necessary. Coarsely chop leaves, then squeeze out any remaining liquid.

5. Prepare an outdoor grill for grilling over medium-high heat. Grease grill grate.

6. In a large bowl, stir ground turkey, egg white, spinach mixture, onion mixture, feta, and soy sauce just until blended, but do not overmix. Shape mixture into ten 3-inch round patties.

7. Grill turkey burgers for 10–12 minutes or until cooked through, turning over once.

8. Slice the 10 oat rolls open and place a turkey burger inside each roll. Add lettuce and tomato, if you like.

Makes 10 servings (1 burger per serving)

Kids can shape rolls and turkey burgers and fill their rolls with burgers.

Tomato Dumpling Soup

This tomato dumpling soup took the top prize at the Suffern, New York, Farmers' Market Tomato Fest recipe contest, and once you taste it, you'll know why. It's high in vitamin C and lycopene, both of which protect your immune system. It's the perfect soup to serve with our Grilled Cheese Stackers (for a compliment of calcium)!

ingredients

Dumplings

½ cup unbleached all-purpose flour

¼ cup whole wheat flour

⅛ teaspoon sea salt

⅛ teaspoon freshly ground black pepper

¼ cup trans-fat-free natural buttery spread

¼ cup ice water

½ cup loosely packed fresh herb blend (basil, rosemary, thyme, oregano), chopped

Tomato Broth

2 teaspoons olive oil

1 large onion, coarsely chopped

2½ cups water or low-sodium vegetable broth

3½ pounds tomatoes, chopped

⅛ teaspoon sea salt

⅛ teaspoon freshly ground black pepper

Nutrition Facts per serving: 100 calories; 5g fat (1g sat fat, 2g mono, 1g poly, 0g trans fat); 0mg cholesterol; 13g carbohydrate (2g fiber, 4g sugar); 2g protein; 50mg sodium; 4% Daily Value (DV) vitamin A; 40% DV vitamin C; 2% DV calcium; 6% DV iron

---

directions

1. Prepare Dumplings: In a medium bowl, stir together the flours, salt, and pepper. Add buttery spread and stir with fork until the mixture resembles the size of peas. Gradually add ice water, kneading the mixture in the bowl, with floured hands, until dough forms. Knead herbs into dough. Wrap dough tightly with plastic wrap and refrigerate for 30 minutes or until easy to handle.

2. Prepare the Tomato Broth: In a large saucepot, heat oil over medium heat. Add onion and cook 5 minutes. Add water or broth, tomatoes with their juice, salt, and black pepper; heat to boiling over high heat. Boil for 10 minutes. Remove saucepot from heat.

3. Pour about ⅓ of soup into blender; cover, with center part of cover removed to let steam escape, and blend until pureed. (Or, use an immersion blender and puree in saucepot.)

4. Pour blended soup into a large bowl and repeat in batches with remaining mixture. Return all soup to saucepot and return to boiling.

5. On a floured surface, with a floured rolling pin, roll dumpling dough out ¼ inch thick. With a floured knife, cut the dough into ½-inch square dumplings; pinch dumplings with your fingers to plump. Drop all dumplings into boiling tomato broth; cook for 10–15 minutes or until cooked through and floating to the surface.

Makes 12 servings (1 cup per serving)

Kids can roll out dough and pinch dumplings.

Sweet Potato Gnocchi with Basil Pesto

Gnocchi (pronounced *knee-oh-key*) is a fun word to say but it's even more fun to eat! We added sweet potatoes to this classic Italian pasta to give it a big boost of vitamins and minerals—including an amazing boost of vitamin A. The sweet taste of the gnocchi in contrast with cool, refreshing pesto has kids (and grown-ups) asking for seconds of this high-fiber, super dish.

ingredients

½ cup Basil Pesto (page 223)

Gnocchi

2 small sweet potatoes
   (8 ounces each)

1 medium baking (russet) potato
   (8 ounces)

⅛ teaspoon sea salt

⅛ teaspoon freshly ground black
   pepper

1½ cups unbleached all-purpose
   flour

1 cup quinoa flour (or whole
   wheat flour)

directions

1. Prepare Basil Pesto as recipe directs. Set aside ½ cup and cover.

2. Prepare Gnocchi: Pierce potatoes with a fork in several places. Place potatoes on a paper towel in the microwave oven. Cook on high for 10–12 minutes or until fork-tender, turning over once halfway through cooking. (Or, preheat oven to 450°F. Pierce potatoes with a fork; place on oven rack and bake for 45 minutes or until fork-tender.) Remove potatoes from microwave or oven; cool until easy to handle.

3. Heat a large saucepan of water to boiling over high heat to cook gnocchi.

4. When potatoes are cool enough to handle, peel potatoes. Press the warm potatoes through a food mill or ricer into a large bowl. (Or, mash with a potato masher until no lumps remain.) Stir in salt and pepper. With your hands, knead the flours into the mashed potatoes (about ½ cup at a time) until a dough forms. (Amount of flour may vary. You want to use as little flour as possible to achieve a dough consistency.)

5. Once you've got a workable dough, pinch off a small piece and drop into boiling water to test readiness. Within a few minutes the dough should rise to the top and retain its shape. If it does not rise, you may need to add more flour to the dough.

6. Divide the dough into 6 equal pieces. On a lightly floured surface, with floured hands, roll 1 piece of dough at a time into a ½-inch diameter rope. Cut rope into ½-inch lengths, reshaping if necessary into square pillow shapes. Transfer to a rimmed baking sheet. Repeat rolling and cutting with remaining dough. (Gnocchi can be made up to 4 hours before cooking; cover and refrigerate.)

7. Drop gnocchi, in batches, into boiling water and cook until they float to the surface. With a slotted spoon, transfer gnocchi to a serving bowl.

8. To serve, toss warm gnocchi with pesto to coat evenly.

Makes 5 servings (1 cup per serving)

Nutrition Facts per serving: 410 calories; 8g fat (1g sat fat, 4g mono, 3g poly, 0g trans fat); 0mg cholesterol; 74g carbohydrate (9g fiber, 8g sugar); 12g protein; 105mg sodium; 370% Daily Value (DV) vitamin A; 45% DV vitamin C; 10% DV calcium; 30% DV iron

---

Kids can place ingredients for pesto into food processor and blend; roll out dough and shape gnocchi; and cook gnocchi using a slotted spoon with adult supervision.

Veggie Stir-Fry with Soba Noodles

If you like spaghetti, you'll love buckwheat soba noodles, a good source of protein. This savory stir-fry looks like a work of art when it's done because the variety of veggies adds so much brightness and color—plus loads of nutrition. Get chopping!

ingredients

10 ounces buckwheat soba noodles

1 teaspoon canola oil

2 red, orange, and/or yellow bell peppers, chopped

2 cloves garlic, minced

1 medium zucchini (10 ounces), cut into ¼-inch dice

4 scallions, sliced

1½ cups packed spinach leaves, coarsely chopped

1 tablespoon sesame seeds

1 tablespoon low-sodium soy sauce

2 teaspoons Asian sesame oil

directions

1. In a large pot of boiling water, cook soba noodles as label directs. Drain; set aside.

2. In a medium saucepan, heat oil over medium-high heat. Add peppers and cook until tender-crisp, about 5–7 minutes, stirring frequently. Add garlic and cook 1 minute.

3. Add zucchini and scallions and cook 3 minutes more. Add spinach; cook until wilted.

4. To the vegetables in the saucepan, add soba noodles, sesame seeds, soy sauce, and sesame oil; cook 2 minutes longer to blend flavors.

Makes 7 servings (1 cup per serving)

Nutrition Facts per serving: 190 calories; 3g fat (0g sat fat, 1g mono, 1g poly, 0g trans fat); 0mg cholesterol; 36g carbohydrate (3g fiber, 3g sugar); 6g protein; 75mg sodium; 8% Daily Value (DV) vitamin A; 120% DV vitamin C; 4% DV calcium; 8% DV iron

Kids can chop vegetables using a plastic knife with adult supervision.

Crunchy Tuna Burgers

Take a heart-healthy break from the same old burger with this fresh new taste. Our protein-packed tuna burger, filled with vegetables rich in vitamins A and C, has a crunchy secret ingredient: panko bread crumbs. Serve them on a whole-grain bun, like our Sweet Oat Rolls (page 224), or on top of a leafy green salad.

ingredients

2 tablespoons olive oil

1 carrot, shredded (½ cup)

½ medium red onion, finely chopped (½ cup)

½ red bell pepper, finely chopped (½ cup)

3 (5-ounce) cans water-packed chunk light tuna

Juice of 1 lemon

1½ teaspoons Dijon mustard

½ teaspoon freshly ground black pepper

½ teaspoon sea salt

¾ cup panko bread crumbs

¼ cup chopped fresh parsley leaves

3 large egg whites, beaten

Whole-grain buns or garden salad (optional)

directions

1. In a large nonstick skillet, heat 1 tablespoon of oil over medium heat. Add carrot, onion, and red pepper and cook until tender, 4–6 minutes, stirring occasionally. Remove skillet from heat.

2. Drain tuna; place in a large bowl and flake with a fork. Stir in cooked vegetables, lemon juice, Dijon, black pepper, and salt. Add panko, parsley, and egg whites and mix thoroughly.

3. Shape tuna mixture into ten 1-inch-thick patties.

4. In the same skillet, heat 1 teaspoon oil over medium heat. Add 4 patties and cook until heated through and golden brown on both sides, 5–10 minutes, turning over once.

5. Repeat with remaining oil and patties. Serve hot.

6. If you like, serve burgers on buns or add to a salad.

Makes 10 servings (1 burger per serving)

Nutrition Facts per serving: 100 calories; 4g fat (1g sat fat, 2g mono, 0g trans fat); 15 mg cholesterol; 6g carbohydrate (1g fiber, 1g sugar); 13g protein; 210mg sodium; 25% Daily Value (DV) vitamin A; 25% DV vitamin C; 2% DV calcium; 6% DV iron

---

Kids can shape tuna burgers and grill with adult supervision.

Veggie Pad Thai

We've used multigrain angel hair pasta as the "noodle" in our take on pad thai, one of the most popular Asian takeout dishes of all time. But who needs takeout when it's so easy to make your own? The tofu adds protein, the pasta boosts the fiber, and the delicious cashews contribute to the healthy fat. The veggies add a bounty of nutrients and lots of color, and we lowered the sodium without losing the flavor.

ingredients

½ pound multigrain angel hair pasta (or rice stick noodles)

1 package (14 ounces) firm tofu, drained

2 tablespoons no-salt-added tomato sauce

2 tablespoons water

1 tablespoon unseasoned rice vinegar

1 tablespoon brown sugar

2 teaspoons low-sodium soy sauce

2 tablespoons canola oil, divided

4 large egg whites, beaten

2 cloves garlic, minced

1 cup shredded carrots (2 carrots)

2 cups (6 ounces) fresh bean sprouts, drained and rinsed

2 scallions, thinly sliced

¼ cup (1 ounce) raw cashews, chopped

2 tablespoons chopped fresh parsley or cilantro leaves

2 limes, cut into 8 total wedges

directions

1. In a large saucepot of boiling water, prepare pasta as label directs. Drain and set aside.

2. Place tofu between several layers of paper towels and press to extract as much liquid as possible. Cut into ¼-inch pieces.

3. In a small bowl, stir together the tomato sauce, water, vinegar, brown sugar, and soy sauce; set aside.

4. In a large skillet or wok, heat 1 tablespoon of the oil over high heat. Add tofu and cook, stirring quickly and frequently (stir-frying) for about 3 minutes or until lightly browned on all sides. With a slotted spoon, transfer tofu to a plate.

5. Wipe skillet clean. In the same skillet, heat the remaining 1 tablespoon oil over high heat. Add egg whites, stirring until scrambled. Add garlic; cook 15 seconds, stirring.

6. Add the sauce mixture, carrots, and pasta, and cook over medium heat for 3–4 minutes or until mixture is dry. Add the bean sprouts and tofu; toss to mix.

7. Transfer pasta mixture to a platter and top with scallions, cashews, and parsley. Serve with lime wedges to squeeze over individual servings.

Makes 8 servings (1 cup per serving)

Nutrition Facts per serving: 240 calories; 9g fat (1g sat fat, 3g mono, 3g poly, 0g trans fat); 0mg cholesterol; 31g carbohydrate (4g fiber, 5g sugar); 12g protein; 80mg sodium; 50% Daily Value (DV) vitamin A; 20% DV vitamin C; 10% DV calcium; 10% DV iron

---

Kids can measure ingredients before cooking.

Basil Pesto

Basil is one of our favorite herbs to grow in the HealthBarn USA garden because it smells so good when we pick it for our favorite savory topping—pesto! This recipe is one of our most popular, and it's also an excellent source of vitamin A. Serve this delicious pesto with pasta, use it as a spread instead of mayo on a sandwich or wrap, or use it as a topping for our Whole Wheat Pizza Dough (page 196).

ingredients

4 cups loosely packed fresh basil leaves

¼ cup hulled raw sunflower seeds

2 cloves garlic

½ teaspoon sea salt

¼ teaspoon freshly ground black pepper

5 tablespoons low-sodium vegetable broth (or water)

2 tablespoons extra-virgin olive oil

¼ cup freshly grated Parmesan cheese

directions

1. In a food processor or blender, pulse basil leaves, sunflower seeds, garlic, salt, and pepper until finely chopped.

2. With food processor still running, *gradually* add broth and oil through feed tube to form a smooth, thick consistency.

3. Transfer pesto to a medium bowl and fold in Parmesan.

4. Cover and refrigerate. Can be made up to 2 days ahead.

Makes 8 servings (2 tablespoons per serving)

Nutrition Facts per serving: 70 calories; 6g fat (1g sat fat, 3g mono, 1g poly, 0g trans fat); 0mg cholesterol; 2g carbohydrate (1g fiber, 0g sugar); 2g protein; 45mg sodium; 25% Daily Value (DV) vitamin A; 6% DV vitamin C; 6% DV calcium; 6% DV iron

Kids can place ingredients in food processor and blend.

Sweet Oat Rolls

We love the fabulous taste of home-baked bread, and it smells so good! These rolls are easy to make, even for non–bread bakers, and this recipe makes a great family project. With its back-to-basics ingredients list, these naturally nutritious whole-grain rolls (and the baguette variation) are superior to what you'll find on the store shelves.

ingredients

1¾ cups warm water (105°–115°F), divided

1 envelope active dry yeast (2¼ teaspoons)

2 tablespoons agave nectar

2½ cups whole wheat flour

1 cup old-fashioned oats

1 teaspoon sea salt

1 large egg, beaten

¼ cup plus 1 tablespoon extra-virgin olive oil

1 cup unbleached all-purpose flour (used to knead dough)

directions

1. In a large bowl, combine ¼ cup of the warm water with yeast and agave nectar; stir until yeast dissolves. Let stand until foamy, about 5 minutes.

2. With a wooden spoon, stir in whole wheat flour, oats, salt, egg, ¼ cup oil, and remaining 1½ cups warm water until blended and a soft dough forms.

3. Scrape the dough onto a surface lightly coated with all-purpose flour. With well-floured hands, knead dough for 5–6 minutes or until smooth, adding more flour as needed to keep dough from sticking to surface and hands (but make sure not to over-flour).

4. When the dough is pliable and springy (it should be hard to pull apart), divide it into 14 equal pieces. Shape each into a ball.

5. Drizzle remaining 1 tablespoon of oil over balls; with hands, lightly coat entire surface of each ball.

6. Place balls, about 1 inch apart, on a large baking sheet. Cover with paper towels and let rise in a warm place (80°–85°F) until doubled in size, about 1 hour.

7. Preheat oven to 350°F. Bake rolls for 15–20 minutes or until golden brown. Cool on a wire rack.

Makes 14 servings (1 roll per serving)

Nutrition Facts per serving: 210 calories; 7g fat (1g sat fat, 4g mono, 1g poly, 0g trans fat); 15mg cholesterol; 32g carbohydrate (4g fiber, 2g sugar); 6g protein; 45mg sodium; 2% Daily Value (DV) calcium; 10% DV iron

To Make a Sweet Oat Baguette

Prepare as in the Sweet Oat Rolls recipe steps 1–3, but in step 4, instead of making rolls, shape the dough into a long loaf by rolling dough back and forth with hands on floured surface until it is about 16 inches long and 4 inches wide. Drizzle and coat loaf with oil as above in step 5. Let rise on a baking sheet as in step 6. Bake loaf for 30–35 minutes or until golden brown. Cool.

Kids can shape rolls.

Homemade Vs. Store-Bought: The Facts!

HealthBarn USA's Sweet Oat Rolls	Pepperidge Farm Classic Hamburger Buns Reference: product package
Ingredients: Water, yeast, agave nectar, whole wheat flour, old-fashioned oats, sea salt, egg, olive oil, unbleached all-purpose flour	**Ingredients:** Unbromated unbleached enriched wheat flour (flour, niacin, reduced iron, thiamine mononitrate [vitamin B1], riboflavin [vitamin B2], folic acid), water, yeast, high-fructose corn syrup, wheat gluten, soybean oil, contains 2% or less of: sugar, datem (dough conditioner), lower sodium natural sea salt, salt, calcium propionate and sorbic acid to retard spoilage, mono- and diglycerides, nonfat milk, malted barley flour, enzymes
Nutrition Facts (per serving): 210 calories; 7g fat (1g sat fat, 4g mono, 1g poly, 0g trans fat); 15mg cholesterol; 32g carbohydrate (4g fiber, 2g sugar); 6g protein; 45mg sodium; 2% Daily Value (DV) calcium; 10% DV iron	**Nutrition Facts** (per serving): 120 calories; 2g fat (0.5g sat fat, 0.5g mono, 1g poly, 0g trans fat); 0mg cholesterol; 22g carbohydrate (1g fiber, 3g sugar); 5g protein; 150mg sodium; 2% Daily Value (DV) calcium; 6% DV iron
OURS: • 9 ingredients	**THEIRS:** • 22 ingredients • contains high-fructose corn syrup • multiple preservatives added

Mixed Greens with Flaxseed Oil Dressing

This salad is bursting with flavor and nutrition, including antioxidants and omega-3 fatty acids. You can make this flaxseed oil salad dressing directly in the bowl with the mixed greens. Kids like this because they can use their hands to mix the salad—just make sure those hands are super clean!

ingredients

5 cups chopped Romaine lettuce

5 cups chopped mixed greens such as butter and leaf lettuce

¼ cup flaxseed oil

Juice of 1 lemon

2 tablespoons low-sodium soy sauce

1 tablespoon pure maple syrup

¼ teaspoon sea salt

¼ teaspoon freshly ground black pepper

directions

1. In a large salad bowl, place chopped greens. Evenly drizzle oil over greens.

2. Squeeze juice from lemon over greens. Add soy sauce, maple syrup, salt, and pepper.

3. With clean hands, toss salad to evenly distribute dressing.

Makes 10 servings (1 cup per serving)

Nutrition Facts per serving: 60 calories; 6g fat (1g sat fat, 1g mono, 4g poly, 0g trans fat); 0mg cholesterol; 3g carbohydrate (1g fiber, 2g sugar); 1g protein; 95mg sodium; 50% Daily Value (DV) vitamin A; 15% DV vitamin C; 2% DV calcium; 4% DV iron

---

Kids can juice lemons, add ingredients, and toss salad using their hands.

The Beet Cake

This cascading layer "cake" of fresh beet slices and spreadable goat cheese topped with fresh herbs and walnuts gets a double thumbs up (a very special honor) from the kids at HealthBarn USA. Fresh beets are full of nutrients including folate (a B vitamin), manganese (a trace mineral), and betacyanin (an antioxidant) to keep your body strong. Kids will eat beets when they're served up like this (and they love to assemble this tower of nutrient power).

ingredients

1 medium beet

1 tablespoon semi-soft goat cheese

1 tablespoon fresh orange juice

1 teaspoon chopped fresh herbs (any combination)

1 walnut half, broken into pieces

directions

1. In a small saucepan, combine beet and enough water to cover; heat to boiling over high heat. Reduce heat to low; cover and simmer for 20–30 minutes or until fork-tender. Drain beet; set aside to cool.

2. When cool enough to handle, peel beet under warm running water. Cut into 3 round slices.

3. To assemble the "cake," place 1 beet slice on a plate; spread with ½ tablespoon goat cheese. Repeat layering, ending with beet slice. Drizzle with orange juice; top with herbs and walnut.

Makes 1 serving (1 "cake" per serving)

Nutrition Facts per serving: 70 calories; 3g fat (1g sat fat, 1g mono, 1g poly, 0g trans fat); 5mg cholesterol; 10g carbohydrate (3g fiber, 7g sugar); 3g protein; 90mg sodium; 4% Daily Value (DV) vitamin A; 20% DV vitamin C; 2% DV calcium; 6% DV iron

Kids can layer beets with filling.

No-Bake White Mac and Cheese

If you like macaroni and cheese but don't want the artificial orange-colored instant stuff from the box, you're going to love our easy-to-make version. This mac and cheese is creamy white—the way cow's milk cheese looks before it gets tinted with added coloring. This side dish is also a good source of protein and calcium. The ground flaxseeds add omega-3 fatty acids, making this classic comfort food side dish healthier than ever.

ingredients

- 1 package (13.25 ounces) whole wheat elbow pasta
- 2 tablespoons olive oil
- ¼ cup whole wheat flour
- 2 cups water
- 1 cup low-fat (1%) milk
- ¼ teaspoon grated nutmeg
- 1½ cups (6 ounces) shredded 50% reduced-fat white cheddar cheese
- 1½ cups fresh or frozen (thawed) shelled edamame (soy beans)
- ¼ cup freshly grated Parmesan cheese
- 1 tablespoon ground flaxseeds
- ¼ teaspoon freshly ground black pepper
- ⅓ cup panko bread crumbs

directions

1. In a large pot of boiling water, cook pasta as label directs. Drain and set aside.

2. In a large saucepan, heat oil over medium heat. Whisk in flour; cook for 1 minute, whisking constantly. Gradually whisk in water and milk, then nutmeg. Cook, whisking constantly, until mixture boils and is thick enough to coat the back of a spoon, 2–3 minutes.

3. Stir in cheddar until melted. Add pasta, edamame, Parmesan, flaxseeds, and pepper to cheese mixture and stir to combine. Remove saucepan from heat.

4. In a small ungreased skillet over medium heat, cook panko until toasted, about 5 minutes, stirring frequently. Sprinkle panko on top of pasta mixture before serving.

Makes 22 servings (½ cup per serving)

Nutrition Facts per serving: 130 calories; 4g fat (1g sat fat, 1g mono, 1g poly, 0g trans fat); 5mg cholesterol; 16g carbohydrate (2g fiber, 1g sugar); 7g protein; 80mg sodium; 4% Daily Value (DV) vitamin A; 2% DV vitamin C; 10% DV calcium; 4% DV iron

---

Kids can measure ingredients before cooking.

Homemade Vs. Store-Bought: The Facts!

HealthBarn USA's No-Bake White Mac and Cheese	Kraft Macaroni and Cheese (Original) Reference: product package
Ingredients: Whole wheat elbow pasta, olive oil, wheat flour, water, low-fat milk, nutmeg, 50% reduced-fat white cheddar cheese, edamame, Parmesan cheese, flaxseeds, pepper, panko bread crumbs	**Ingredients:** Enriched macaroni product (wheat flour, niacin, ferrous sulfate [iron], thiamine mononitrate [vitamin B1], riboflavin [vitamin B2], folic acid); cheese sauce mix (whey, milk fat, milk protein concentrate, salt, sodium tripolyphosphate, contains less than 2%: of citric acid, lactic acid, sodium phosphate, calcium phosphate, yellow 5, yellow 6, enzymes, cheese culture)
Nutrition Facts (per serving): 130 calories; 4g fat (1g sat fat, 1g mono, 1g poly, 0g trans fat); 5mg cholesterol; 16g carbohydrate (2g fiber, 1g sugar); 7g protein; 80mg sodium; 4% Daily Value (DV) vitamin A; 2% DV vitamin C; 10% DV calcium; 4% DV iron	**Nutrition Facts** (per serving): 400 calories; 19g fat (4.5g sat fat, 4g trans fat); 15mg cholesterol; 49g carbohydrate (1g fiber, 7g sugar); 10g protein; 710mg sodium; 15% Daily Value (DV) vitamin A; 15% DV calcium; 10% DV iron
OURS: • 12 ingredients	**THEIRS:** • 19 ingredients • contains preservatives and food dyes

Veggie Pancakes

Pancakes for dinner? Why not? Our savory version delivers plenty of vitamins A and C from the veggies and protein from the eggs. Serve as a light dinner with soup or a salad.

ingredients

3 medium carrots, peeled and cut into 1-inch chunks

3 medium parsnips, peeled and cut into 1-inch chunks

1 medium zucchini, cut into 1-inch chunks

1 medium onion, cut into 1-inch chunks

¾ cup panko bread crumbs

½ cup freshly grated Parmesan cheese

½ teaspoon sea salt

½ teaspoon freshly ground black pepper

6 large egg whites

2 large eggs, beaten

directions

1. In a food processor, pulse carrots, parsnips, zucchini, and onion until mixture resembles coarse crumbs. Transfer vegetables to a large bowl and squeeze excess liquid from vegetable mixture.

2. Add panko, Parmesan, salt, pepper, egg whites, and eggs to vegetables; mix thoroughly.

3. Heat a large, greased nonstick skillet over medium heat. Drop vegetable mixture by ¼ cup into the skillet, making 4 pancakes at a time. With the back of a spatula, flatten the vegetable mixture to make pancakes ½ inch thick.

4. Cook pancakes until underside is golden brown and crisp, about 4–6 minutes. With a spatula, turn pancakes over and cook for 3–5 minutes longer or until second side is brown and crisp. Transfer pancakes to a plate; keep warm.

5. Repeat with remaining vegetable mixture. Serve hot.

Makes 9 servings (2 pancakes per serving)

Nutrition Facts per serving: 100 calories; 2.5g fat (1g sat fat, 1g mono, 0g trans fat); 45mg cholesterol; 12g carbohydrate (2g fiber, 4g sugar); 7g protein; 180mg sodium; 70% Daily Value (DV) vitamin A; 15% DV vitamin C; 8% DV calcium; 6% DV iron

---

Kids can crack eggs and separate egg whites; mix ingredients; and flip pancakes with adult supervision.

Mighty Beet Salad

Beets, both red and yellow, are a favorite root vegetable that we grow and harvest throughout the fall at HealthBarn USA. They are sweet and a natural source of iron. We added oranges to this salad because their vitamin C helps our bodies absorb the iron in beets. You'll feel mighty strong when you eat this mighty beet salad!

ingredients

1 pound red and/or yellow beets (about 3 medium)

2 navel oranges

3 tablespoons cider vinegar

¼ teaspoon freshly ground black pepper

⅛ teaspoon sea salt

3 tablespoons extra-virgin olive oil or walnut oil

5 cups packed mixed salad greens

¼ cup chopped walnuts, toasted

1 tablespoon goat cheese, crumbled

directions

1. In a medium saucepan, combine beets and enough water to cover; heat to boiling over high heat. Reduce heat to low; cover and simmer for 20–30 minutes or until fork-tender. Drain beets; set aside to cool.

2. When beets are cool enough to handle, peel under warm running water. Cut beets into ¼-inch wedges and place in a bowl.

3. From 1 orange, grate 1¼ teaspoons peel and squeeze ¼ cup juice. Peel remaining orange and separate into segments; set aside.

4. In a large bowl, whisk together orange juice, orange peel, vinegar, pepper, and salt. Gradually whisk in oil until blended. Add beets and orange segments to citrus dressing.

5. Divide the salad greens among 8 bowls; top with beets and orange mixture. Sprinkle with walnuts and goat cheese.

Makes 8 servings (1 cup per serving)

Nutrition Facts per serving: 110 calories; 8g fat (1g sat fat, 5g mono, 2g poly, 0g trans fat); 0mg cholesterol; 8g carbohydrate (2g fiber, 5g sugar); 2g protein; 40mg sodium; 30% Daily Value (DV) vitamin A; 40% DV vitamin C; 4% DV calcium; 4% DV iron

Kids can chop beets using a plastic knife with adult supervision and can toss the salad.

Indian Veggie Medley

One fun way to introduce new veggies is to put them into dishes from different cultures. We took cauliflower, combined it with peas, and accented it with some magical spices from India. The new flavors got a big thumbs up from our taste testers. Besides the vitamin C and iron in this recipe, you get a dose of powerful antioxidants from the turmeric.

ingredients

2 tablespoons canola oil

6 bay leaves

½ teaspoon cumin seeds

1 large head cauliflower (2½ pounds), cut into florets

1 teaspoon peeled, finely chopped fresh ginger

½ teaspoon turmeric

1 cup water

1 cup fresh or frozen (thawed) peas

½ cup fresh cilantro or parsley leaves, chopped

2 tablespoons plain nonfat Greek yogurt

¼ teaspoon sea salt

directions

1. In a wok or large saucepan, heat oil over high heat. Add bay leaves and cumin seeds and cook for 2 minutes, stirring until seeds crackle and are fragrant.

2. Add cauliflower and cook until lightly browned, about 5–7 minutes, stirring frequently. Add ginger and turmeric and stir until cauliflower is evenly coated. Stir in water; heat to boiling. Reduce heat to medium; cover and cook for 10 minutes. Stir in peas and cook, uncovered, until most of liquid evaporates and cauliflower is fork-tender, about 5–7 minutes longer. Transfer vegetable mixture to a large serving bowl and discard bay leaves; drain any excess liquid.

3. Add cilantro, yogurt, and salt to vegetable mixture and toss to coat evenly.

Makes 5 servings (1 cup per serving)

Nutrition Facts per serving: 120 calories; 6g fat (0g sat fat, 3g mono, 2g poly, 0g trans fat); 0mg cholesterol; 14g carbohydrate (6g fiber, 4g sugar); 5g protein; 80mg sodium; 6% Daily Value (DV) vitamin A; 130% DV vitamin C; 6% DV calcium; 10% DV iron

---

Kids can break cauliflower into florets using their hands.

Italian-Style Lentil Soup

Lentil soup is the ultimate comfort food during the chilly winter season. This heart-healthy and delicious soup, from the creator of Mike's Sicilian Stew, boasts vitamin A, iron, protein, and fiber. One bowl will warm you up and keep you healthy on the inside, no matter how cold it gets outside!

ingredients

3 tablespoons olive oil, divided

6 stalks celery, finely chopped (1½ cups)

5 carrots, finely chopped (1¼ cups)

1 medium onion, finely chopped

1 clove garlic, sliced

8 cups water

2 cups lentils (French green lentils or other variety of your choice), rinsed and picked over

1 can (14.5 ounces) no-salt-added whole peeled tomatoes

1 teaspoon sea salt

½ teaspoon chopped fresh oregano leaves

directions

1. In a large saucepan, heat 2 tablespoons of oil over medium heat. Add celery, carrots, onion, and garlic and cook for 10–15 minutes or until tender and lightly browned.

2. Add water, lentils, tomatoes with their juice, salt, and oregano; heat to boiling over high heat. Reduce heat to low; cover and simmer for 45–60 minutes or until lentils are tender, stirring soup occasionally.

3. Ladle soup into bowls and drizzle with remaining 1 tablespoon oil divided evenly among the bowls.

Makes 14 servings (1 cup per serving)

Nutrition Facts per serving: 130 calories; 3.5g fat (0g sat fat, 2g mono, 1g poly, 0g trans fat); 0mg cholesterol; 19g carbohydrate (5g fiber, 3g sugar); 6g protein; 85mg sodium; 40% Daily Value (DV) vitamin A; 6% DV vitamin C; 2% DV calcium; 15% DV iron

Kids can chop vegetables using a plastic knife with adult supervision.

Turkey and Acorn Squash Stuffing

Acorn squash is an all-time autumn favorite, but after you eat this dish, you won't want to wait till Thanksgiving. This veggie is packed with nutrients, but it also has a naturally sweet flavor that works perfectly in this recipe. Use it as a traditional turkey stuffing, or serve it as a side dish. Either way the leftovers are amazingly good!

ingredients

2 small acorn squash (about 1 pound each), halved and seeded

2 cups water

¾ cup bulgur wheat

½ teaspoon sea salt, divided

2 teaspoons olive oil

½ pound ground turkey (99% lean)

⅛ teaspoon ground cinnamon

⅛ teaspoon grated nutmeg

2 stalks celery, finely chopped

1 small onion, finely chopped

3 cloves garlic, finely chopped

¼ cup golden raisins

¼ cup chopped fresh parsley leaves

2 tablespoons hulled pumpkin seeds, toasted (optional)

Nutrition Facts per serving: 200 calories; 2.5g fat (0g sat fat, 1g mono, 0.5g poly, 0g trans fat); 15mg cholesterol; 36g carbohydrate (6g fiber, 9g sugar); 13g protein; 100mg sodium; 15% Daily Value (DV) vitamin A; 35% DV vitamin C; 8% DV calcium; 15% DV iron

directions

1. Preheat oven to 400°F. Grease a rimmed baking sheet. Place squash, cut sides down, on baking sheet. Roast squash until fork-tender, about 35 minutes. Set aside to cool.

2. In a small saucepan, heat water to boiling over high heat. Add bulgur and ¼ teaspoon of the salt. Reduce heat to low; cover and simmer for 15 minutes. Remove saucepan from heat; let stand 5 minutes. Then fluff with a fork.

3. While bulgur is cooking, in a medium skillet, heat oil over medium heat. Add ground turkey, cinnamon, nutmeg, and remaining ¼ teaspoon salt. Cook turkey until browned and cooked through, stirring occasionally. With a slotted spoon, transfer turkey mixture to a bowl, leaving any liquid in the skillet.

4. To the liquid in the skillet, add celery and onion and cook over medium heat for 8–10 minutes or until tender, stirring occasionally. Add garlic and cook for 30 seconds, stirring. Remove skillet from heat; stir in turkey mixture.

5. With a spoon, scoop out the squash from shells. Add squash to turkey mixture. Then, add bulgur, raisins, parsley, and pumpkin seeds, if using. Toss to mix.

6. If serving stuffing as side dish, heat over medium heat until hot. Or, if you like, set aside to use as stuffing for turkey.

Makes 6 servings (1 cup per serving)

Kids can measure ingredients before cooking.

Sweet Potato Crunchies

These irresistible "crunchies" disappear as soon as we make them so prepare to double the recipe for this popular appetizer. They're loaded with good stuff, especially vitamin A, fiber, and iron. This recipe works well as a fun group activity, especially during the holiday season.

ingredients

4 medium sweet potatoes
(12–14 ounces each)

2 cups whole-grain cereal, crushed
(We used Cheerios for the
nutrition analysis.)

2 tablespoons extra-virgin olive oil

1 tablespoon honey

¼ teaspoon grated nutmeg

¼ teaspoon ground cinnamon

⅛ teaspoon sea salt

⅛ teaspoon freshly ground black
pepper

80 whole cloves (optional)

½ teaspoon Hungarian sweet
paprika

Nutrition Facts per serving: 120 calories; 4g fat (0.5g sat fat, 3mg mono, 0.5g poly, 0g trans fat); 0g cholesterol; 21g carbohydrate (3g fiber, 5g sugar); 2g protein; 95mg sodium; 190% Daily Value (DV) vitamin A; 6% DV vitamin C; 4% DV calcium; 15% DV iron

directions

1. Pierce sweet potatoes with fork in several places. Place potatoes on a paper towel in the microwave oven. Cook potatoes on high for 12–15 minutes or until fork-tender, turning potatoes over once halfway through cooking. (Or, preheat oven to 450°F. Pierce potatoes with fork; place on oven rack and bake for 45 minutes or until fork-tender.)

2. Cool potatoes until easy to handle. When cool enough to handle, peel potatoes. Press the warm potatoes through a food mill or ricer into a large bowl. (Or, mash potatoes with potato masher until smooth.)

3. Preheat oven to 350°F. Grease a large baking sheet.

4. Add cereal, oil, honey, nutmeg, cinnamon, salt, and pepper to the potatoes and mix thoroughly. With the palms of your hands, shape 1 tablespoon of the sweet potato mixture at a time into a ball; place on the prepared baking sheet. Repeat until all of the mixture is used.

5. Insert 2 cloves in each ball, if using (for baking only); sprinkle with paprika.

6. Bake the sweet potato balls for 35 minutes or until a toothpick inserted in the center of the balls comes out clean. Transfer to wire racks to cool. When cool, remove cloves (if using).

Makes 8 servings (5 crunchies per serving)

Kids can roll balls; they can also add and remove cloves.

Raspberry Crumble

This delicious baked dessert tastes so indulgent that parents and kids say it's too good to be healthy! But it contains heart-healthy fats, so we can have it for dessert or as an after-school snack served with some yogurt.

ingredients

1½ cups Crunchy Granola with Walnuts (page 52)

1 large egg white

¼ cup unsweetened applesauce

¼ cup canola oil

½ cup whole wheat flour

½ cup unbleached all-purpose flour

1 teaspoon baking powder

½ teaspoon baking soda

1 cup seedless raspberry fruit spread

directions

1. Prepare Crunchy Granola with Walnuts as recipe directs and reserve 1½ cups in a medium bowl.

2. Preheat oven to 350°F. Grease an 8-inch square metal baking pan.

3. In another medium bowl, whisk together egg white, applesauce, and oil.

4. To the bowl with granola, add flours, baking powder, and baking soda, and stir to combine.

5. Add the wet ingredients to the dry ingredients and mix just until blended.

6. Press ⅔ of dough into the prepared pan. Spread fruit spread over dough, leaving a ½-inch border on all sides. Crumble the remaining dough over the top.

7. Bake for 18–20 minutes or until golden brown on top. Cool on a wire rack for at least 30 minutes or until fruit spread is no longer runny. Cut into 2-inch squares to serve.

Makes 16 servings (1 square per serving)

Nutrition Facts per serving: 140 calories; 5g fat (0g sat fat, 2g mono, 2g poly, 0g trans fat); 0mg cholesterol; 23g carbohydrate (1g fiber, 14g sugar); 2g protein; 80mg sodium; 2% Daily Value (DV) calcium; 2% DV iron

Kids can crack, separate, and whisk eggs; spread fruit spread over dough; and crumble topping.

Apple Crisp

There are a zillion varieties of apples—from Granny Smith to Braeburn to Gala. Whether you like them tart or sweet, you'll love them in this recipe. Choose whatever variety appeals to you to make this treat. We've topped each serving with our Crunchy Granola and Walnuts recipe (page 52); because the apples are slightly warm after cooking, the result tastes just like an old-fashioned apple crisp—except now it has whole grains, fiber, and no saturated fat. The agave nectar adds extra sweetness in a natural way.

ingredients

8 small apples

½ cup water

1 tablespoon agave nectar

½ teaspoon ground cinnamon

1 cup Crunchy Granola with Walnuts (page 52)

directions

1. Peel, core, and cut apples into 1-inch chunks.

2. In a large saucepan, stir together the water and agave nectar; heat to boiling over medium heat. Add apples and cinnamon; cover and cook until liquid evaporates and apples are soft, 15–20 minutes, stirring occasionally.

3. Remove saucepan from heat. With a potato masher, mash apples until slightly chunky.

4. To serve, spoon ½ cup of the apple mixture into each of 8 dessert bowls; top each with 2 tablespoons of granola.

Makes 8 servings (½ cup per serving)

Nutrition Facts per serving: 100 calories; 1.5g fat (0g sat fat, 1g poly, 0g trans fat); 0mg cholesterol; 22g carbohydrate (3g fiber, 15g sugar); 1g protein; 0mg sodium; 2% Daily Value (DV) vitamin A; 8% DV vitamin C; 2% DV calcium; 2% DV iron

---

Kids can chop apples using a plastic knife with adult supervision and top their apple mixture with granola.

Grilled Peach Sensation

There is more than one way to eat a fresh peach, and our recipe involves firing up the grill for this unbelievably delicious snack or dessert. We've mixed low-fat vanilla yogurt and cinnamon—what a perfect complement to sweet, warm, vitamin-packed peaches! It takes just a few minutes to prepare and looks impressive too.

ingredients

6 firm but ripe small peaches

1 teaspoon canola oil

½ cup vanilla low-fat yogurt

¼ teaspoon ground cinnamon

directions

1. Cut each peach into quarters; discard pits.
2. Place a ridged grill pan over medium heat and brush with oil.
3. Place peaches on the grill pan and cook for 4–6 minutes until there are grill marks on both sides and peaches are soft and heated through, turning over once. (For the best grill marks, do not move peaches around on pan other than to turn over.)
4. Meanwhile, in a small bowl, stir together the yogurt and cinnamon.
5. As peaches are done cooking, place 1 peach (4 quarters) on each plate; drizzle with yogurt mixture evenly divided among the plates.

Makes 6 servings (1 peach per serving)

Nutrition Facts per serving: 50 calories; 1g fat (0g sat fat, 1g mono, 0g trans fat); 0mg cholesterol; 9g carbohydrate (1g fiber, 8g sugar); 2g protein; 15mg sodium; 6% Daily Value (DV) vitamin A; 10% DV vitamin C; 4% DV calcium; 2% DV iron

Kids can chop peaches using a plastic knife and grill them with adult supervision; they can also stir yogurt and drizzle cinnamon over peaches.

Chocolate Banana Crepes

Our Simply Crepes recipe (page 58) works for breakfast, lunch, and dinner—as well as in this low-fat but yummy dessert. The chocolate and banana combination is one sweet taste we can't get enough of, but it's okay to indulge in this healthy treat!

ingredients

1 recipe Simply Crepes (page 58)

6 bananas

¼ cup semisweet chocolate chips

directions

1. Prepare Simply Crepes as recipe directs.

2. Cut each banana in half. Slice each half into thin slices, keeping slices from each half banana separate.

3. In a medium skillet over medium heat, place 1 crepe. Top half of crepe with slices from half a banana and 10–12 chocolate chips. When chocolate starts to melt, fold unfilled side of crepe over banana, then fold over again, making a triangle. Turn crepe over to heat through, about 1 minute.

4. Repeat with remaining crepes, bananas, and chocolate chips. Serve warm.

Makes 12 servings (1 crepe per serving)

Nutrition Facts per serving: 130 calories; 2g fat (1g sat fat, 1g mono, 0g trans fat); 15mg cholesterol; 25g carbohydrate (2g fiber, 10g sugar); 5g protein; 55mg sodium; 2% Daily Value (DV) vitamin A; 8% DV vitamin C; 4% DV calcium; 4% DV iron

---

Kids can fill and fold crepes and grill with adult supervision.

Blueberry Rice Pudding

We used brown rice and blueberries for added fiber in this pleasing pudding recipe, and the soy and coconut milks add taste and creaminess. Top with fresh blueberries for an antioxidant boost! Make up a batch and spoon into small bowls to keep on hand in the refrigerator for a quick after-school snack or dessert.

ingredients

5½ cups vanilla soy milk

½ cup light coconut milk (not cream of coconut)

1 cup short-grain brown rice

½ teaspoon sea salt

2 tablespoons brown sugar

2 teaspoons ground cinnamon

1 tablespoon vanilla extract

1 pint blueberries

directions

1. In a large saucepan, combine soy milk, coconut milk, rice, and salt; heat to boiling over medium heat, stirring occasionally. Reduce heat to low; partially cover and simmer until rice is very tender and mixture is thick, about 1 hour, stirring occasionally.

2. Meanwhile, in a small bowl, stir together brown sugar and cinnamon. Set cinnamon sugar aside.

3. Remove the saucepan from heat; stir in vanilla. Cool pudding slightly. Spoon pudding into 10 dessert bowls; top with blueberries and sprinkle with cinnamon sugar.

Makes 10 servings (½ cup per serving)

Nutrition Facts per serving: 190 calories; 3g fat (1g sat fat, 1g poly, 0g trans fat); 0mg cholesterol; 36g carbohydrate (2g fiber, 14g sugar); 6g protein; 75mg sodium; 6% Daily Value (DV) vitamin C; 6% DV calcium; 8% DV iron

---

Kids can measure ingredients before cooking and create sugar mixture.

Sweet Fruit Pancake Tacos

We love to get creative and come up with new ways to eat naturally nutritious foods. That's why we turned pancakes into "tacos" and filled them with a variety of grilled fruit topped with a creamy sauce. You can eat these vitamin-packed treats for dessert or as a snack. Break out the napkins because they're messy to eat, but oh-so-worth-it!

ingredients

2 bananas

2 peaches

2 plums

1 cup plain nonfat Greek yogurt

1 teaspoon grated fresh lemon peel

¼ teaspoon grated nutmeg

¼ teaspoon ground cinnamon

1 tablespoon agave nectar

1 cup buckwheat flour or whole wheat flour

1 cup unbleached all-purpose flour

2 teaspoons baking powder

⅛ teaspoon sea salt

2 large eggs

1½ cups low-fat buttermilk (or buttermilk alternative)

¾ cup water

Nutrition Facts per serving: 210 calories; 2.5g fat (0.5g sat fat, 1g mono, 1g poly, 0g trans fat); 50mg cholesterol; 38g carbohydrate (4g fiber, 15g sugar); 10g protein; 230mg sodium; 4% Daily Value (DV) vitamin A; 10% DV vitamin C; 10% DV calcium; 10% DV iron

directions

1. Grease a ridged grill pan; heat over medium-high heat.

2. Meanwhile, cut each banana in half crosswise, then cut each half lengthwise into quarters. Cut peaches and plums, with skin on, into ¼-inch wedges.

3. Grill fruit for 1–2 minutes, turning over once, until grill marks appear on both sides. (Bananas will cook fastest so be careful not to overcook them or they will turn to mush.) Transfer fruit to a plate; set aside.

4. In a small bowl, stir together yogurt, lemon peel, nutmeg, cinnamon, and agave nectar; set this yogurt sauce aside.

5. In a medium bowl, stir together flours, baking powder, and salt. In another bowl, whisk eggs, buttermilk, and water. Stir wet ingredients into dry ingredients until combined. The batter will have a gluey texture.

6. Heat a nonstick griddle or large nonstick skillet over medium heat. Ladle batter by ½ cup onto the griddle; use back of ladle to spread batter evenly into 6-inch rounds.

7. Cook pancakes until bubbles form on top, about 2 minutes. Turn pancakes over and cook a few minutes longer or until underside is golden. Transfer pancakes to a plate. Repeat with remaining batter.

8. To serve, top each pancake with some grilled fruit and 2 tablespoons of the yogurt sauce. Fold pancake like a taco and eat with your hands.

Makes 8 pancakes (1 pancake per serving)

Kids can fill tacos with prepared ingredients.

Banana Cream Smoothie

We're bananas for this luscious but low–saturated fat smoothie, made with ingredients that combine calcium and fiber. It's a favorite at HealthBarn USA because it's creamy *and* crunchy all at once.

ingredients

8 ice cubes

2 bananas, halved

1 cup vanilla low-fat yogurt

1 cup low-fat (1%) milk

2 tablespoons ground flaxseeds

1 tablespoon instant nonfat dry milk powder

2 teaspoons vanilla extract

¼ teaspoon ground cinnamon

¼ cup whole-grain cereal, crushed (We used Cheerios for the nutrition analysis.)

directions

1. In a blender, crush ice cubes.

2. Add bananas and remaining ingredients, except cereal; blend until smooth.

3. Pour the smoothie into 4 glasses; sprinkle each with 1 tablespoon of the crushed cereal and extra cinnamon, if you like.

Makes 4 servings (1 cup per serving)

Nutrition Facts per serving: 150 calories; 4g fat (1g sat fat, 1g mono, 1g poly, 0g trans fat); 10mg cholesterol; 24g carbohydrate (3g fiber, 15g sugar); 7g protein; 95mg sodium; 6% Daily Value (DV) vitamin A; 10% DV vitamin C; 20% DV calcium; 6% DV iron

Kids can add ingredients to blender and blend, and can crush cereal and top smoothie.

CHAPTER 7

Hitting the Hay: Turning Bedtime into the Best Time

A true healthy day isn't over with the last bite of dinner. Instead, it ends—and begins anew—with a restful and relaxing bedtime routine, followed by sufficient sleep to recharge a growing soul. By now you know that helping your child become "healthy" isn't just about getting him to eat broccoli or her to play basketball. Living the HealthBarn USA way is about reaching the whole child, body and mind; and helping a child to **get a good night's sleep**—one of the last and most important of our Seven Healthy Habits—is an essential part of that process.

Few of us get enough sleep. We are all different but most people function best on six to nine hours a night. Still, according to the Centers for Disease Control and Prevention, up to seventy million Americans are sleep deprived, with an increasing percentage of adults reporting less than six hours of sleep per night. Nodding off during a meeting with colleagues is bad enough, but sleep deprivation has been linked to everything from falling asleep at the wheel to obesity, stress, a variety of illnesses, and premature death.

But sleep deprivation isn't just a problem that adults face. Many children aren't getting enough shut-eye—or else they're in their beds but not sleeping (for reasons we'll explore below). As I've already mentioned, many parents come to me worrying about the fact that their kids aren't eating their vegetables—as if eating spinach was the one thing standing between a child and a lifetime of good health. But when I ask children at our HealthBarn USA school assemblies—from kindergartners to adolescents—"What is keeping you from being healthier?" they almost always say that they don't get enough sleep! The reasons vary—bad dreams, a chatterbox sibling, a late bedtime, too much TV, and more—but the negative consequences for all these kids are the same. Besides having low energy, general crankiness, and a lack of focus or poor performance at school, kids can also suffer from a weakened immune system and slow physical growth and mental development due to not getting enough sleep. In teens, sleep deprivation is linked to stress and serious depression.

All children are different, of course, but generally, pediatricians recommend that school-age children get about ten to twelve hours of sleep a night. Some may get by on less; the average amount of sleep for school-age kids up to age twelve is about 9.5 hours. You know your child best and can probably tell when she's not getting the sleep she needs. It's normal for a child to resist bedtime, and even the most compliant kids will put up a fight from time to time. But sleep is when their bodies and brains recharge. (And yours do too!)

Building a Better Bedtime Routine

Depending on the age of your child or children, you probably have a mental checklist of what needs to happen before you get to the "restful and relaxing" part of a bedtime routine: finish up the last of the homework, squeeze in a favorite TV show or some computer time, ready the backpack and the lunch planning for tomorrow, bathe and brush teeth, and read a bedtime story or two.

It's a fairly unvarying routine from night to night for most families, but as with all things related to children, it will evolve as the years go by (and it's probably different on the weekends—though you should not let your child's sleep routine change too drastically with late nights and sleeping in, or else they'll be off schedule come Monday). As your kids grow increasingly independent, you can count on them to do more to get themselves ready for bed and for the next school day— though hopefully they'll still want you around for some version of the bedtime story! Still, bedtime in a busy household can be anything but relaxing.

If you don't have a consistent bedtime routine in place, or the one you have isn't working, it's time to fix it. Without a good routine, there is no time to wind down— and it's that critical hour or so before bed that really helps kids get into the sleep groove. Here are some tips for catching some ZZZs, HealthBarn USA style:

Give it an hour. If you want your child to go to bed at 9:00, start her moving in that direction at around 8:00. Compressing that bedtime to-do list into twenty minutes or less makes it stressful and rushed. If you have older kids who can get themselves ready, respect their independence but make it clear that you expect them to be in bed by a certain time.

Create some bedtime rituals. Besides the usual bathing, putting on PJs, and brushing teeth, build in pleasurable activities and relaxation time that you and your child can share. Here are some of our favorite ideas:

✦ *Read together.* Little children love being read to—but so do many older children. Hang on to the bedtime story ritual as long as you can, even after they've moved on to reading to themselves. Books also have a way of sparking conversations and encouraging children to talk about their feelings or the events of the day.*

✦ *Sip something soothing.* About an hour before bed, share a cup of herbal tea with your child (see the Stacey's Tips section "A Cup of Calm" below), or try the "chicken soup" of bedtime drinks—warm milk with a touch of honey.

✦ *Hit the right note.* Play relaxing music. Your child may be too old for the nursery tunes CD he fell asleep to when he was an infant, but soothing music still has a

---

* A favorite book we keep in our HealthBarn USA library is Cynthia Brian's *Be the Star You Are!: 99 Gifts for Living, Loving, Laughing, and Learning to Make a Difference* (Berkeley, CA: Celestial Arts, 2001). This book had a huge impact on one child, a boy who kept to himself and didn't make friends easily. He gravitated to this book, and it touched him so deeply that he proudly read it out loud to his family. It was a major breakthrough for this misunderstood child!

calming effect. At the barn, we enjoy Native-American instrumental music and nature sounds. Your child might prefer smooth jazz—whatever works! HealthBarn USA kids who are budding musicians also like to quietly play their instruments in the hour prior to sleep (*quietly* is the key—this may not work if she plays the electric bass).

◆ *Stretch it out.* Relax with your child by doing some basic yoga stretches or other gentle moves to release the day's tension. Do this to music, in silence to encourage relaxation, or while you talk quietly about the day.

◆ *Color your world.* The kids at HealthBarn USA relax by getting out the crayons or markers and coloring in mandalas, symmetrical designs usually in the form of a circle that are tools for meditation in many cultures. As they work quietly and their minds wander, the children seem to let go of their cares. If you are a knitter or have another hobby that takes away stress, you know that feeling of going into "the zone." It's a pretty good place to get to before bedtime! At the barn, we use the *Mandalas Stained Glass Coloring Book* (published by Dover Coloring Books) for translucent mandalas that can be placed in the window when they are completed. Or, visit www.milliande.smugmug.com/Art/Mandala-Coloring-Pages to download free coloring pages.

If they're afraid of the dark, light the way. "There's something under my bed! Did you check the closet? I swear I heard something!" Instead of brushing off children's fears, acknowledge them and offer some reassurances, in whatever way feels most natural to you.

When I was little, my sister Elyse was convinced that there was a cat in our room—not a sweet kitty cat but a scary cat that she feared, and because of this fear she kept us both up at night. Night after night, she worried aloud and my parents told her some variation of, "Don't be silly! Just go to bed!" Finally, my exhausted but creative father came into our room, began making shooing motions with his hands and saying, "Go away kitty! Get out of here now!" He threw open the bedroom window motioning for the "cat" to come, and with one final "Shoo!" and then a dramatic slamming shut of the window, he declared the pesky feline gone. She never complained about that evil kitty again!

Children want their fears—as far-fetched as they may seem to adults—to be acknowledged in some way by someone who cares about them and who can protect them. Fear, after all, is simply an emotion created by the mind that they can't control, but you can help them manage it—and get to sleep.

Stacey's Tips

A Cup of Calm, from Mother Nature

I like drinking herbal teas in the evening to wind down, especially mint for digestion and chamomile flowers for relaxation before going to sleep. At HealthBarn USA, when we talk to the kids about the role of sleep in a healthy lifestyle, we always end our conversations with an infusion of mint or chamomile flowers—herbs we have grown and picked in our own garden. If your family is growing herbs (see the Get Your Hands Dirty tip "Growing Herbs" below), consider adding those two to the mix, and put your child in charge of harvesting and preparing them for evening tea.

Pick chamomile flowers (for tea use the blossoms only) and mint leaves; punch some holes in a brown paper bag and place the fresh herbs inside to dry; close the bag up with a twist tie and let the contents dry thoroughly (approximately two to four weeks). Use about 1 tablespoon of dried herbs per cup of tea in a mesh tea ball.* If you're in search of a stomach-calming remedy for your child (or yourself), try shaving a few pieces of raw ginger root into a cup and steeping in hot water for a few minutes. (Let hot tea and milk cool down sufficiently before your child handles them, or add ice cubes to speed up the process.)

Yogi brand teas (available nationwide or online at www.yogiproducts.com) make two varieties that are especially appropriate for the end of a day: Bedtime and Calming. There are other "sleep" teas on the market, but I've found Yogi, which uses organically grown herbs, to have the most satisfying flavor and restful effect.

---

* Chamomile flowers should always be dried for using as tea; fresh flowers make a bitter brew. Mint, however, can be used fresh. Pour boiling water over just-picked mint leaves for a classic herbal infusion.

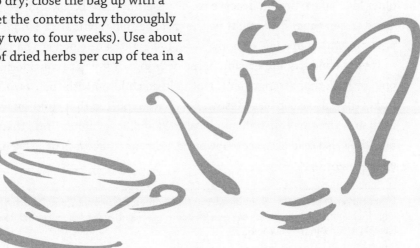

pantry pick

Epsom Salts Forget Mr. Bubble and consider using common Epsom salts at bath time. These natural bath salts are rich in magnesium sulfate and are known for their sedative effect on the nervous system and muscles, their ability to draw toxins from the body, their positive effects on easing digestion, and their moisturizing effects on skin, among other properties.

Use one to two cups of Epsom salts in a bathtub full of warm—not hot—water and let your child luxuriate with a fifteen-minute soak before bedtime, while you supervise. If there is a powdery residue on the skin afterward, it's harmless and can be rinsed off (the residue is simply dried salts that did not dissolve in the water). You can find Epsom salts in most grocery and drug stores. Buy the original Epsom salts, not the ones with lavender added—it's a better value and you can always add a few drops of lavender oil into the bath, which has more of an aroma than the lavender Epsom salts.

Avoid activities that wind them up. Television is a stimulant. So is the computer. So is the cell phone (teens who text before bed get significantly less sleep than those who don't, according to one study). Internet usage and computer games rile kids up—especially war games or those with violence. Some adults feel that older kids, in particular, deserve to give their brains a break and "veg out" with some screen time. That might be the case, perhaps right after school or after powering through a pile of homework, but right before bed is a bad idea.

If your child has a television in his bedroom or if you're considering allowing one, rethink that arrangement. Not only do children with their own TVs watch more; they also sleep less! Researchers have reported that children with televisions in their bedrooms consume more calories and have higher BMIs than those who do not; they also read less, score lower on tests, and have less positive parental engagement.[*]

---

[*] Tara Parker-Pope, "A One-Eyed Invader in the Bedroom," *New York Times,* March 4, 2008. Parker-Pope highlights a growing body of research about the negative consequences of allowing children to have televisions in the bedroom.

Finally, avoid vigorous exercise (commonly known as "horseplay") right before bed. It takes a while to calm down after that tickle contest, so make sure it happens well before bedtime!

Don't be a dripping faucet. Are *you* the reason your child can't fall asleep? One child I worked with had serious sleep issues, though he went to bed at a proper time. It turns out that his bedroom was adjacent to his dad's brightly lit and very loud home office, and his father was up until all hours tapping on his computer, making calls, and going in and out of the room. Then when the father finally did go to bed, he snored! Even with the door closed, this boy couldn't sleep.

Do a quick check to make sure that your child's bedroom is quiet, cool, and dark enough for sleep. Do you leave the door open for his comfort, but then go watch TV at a volume that he can hear? It's not just the monster under the bed that keeps a child awake; it's loud conversation, street noise, a barking dog, a ticking clock, a bright flood light in the backyard. There are many ways to tackle these sleep distractions, like soft music or white noise machines (a fan will do), blackout shades or curtains, or just lowering your *own* volume.

REAL-LIFE RESULTS:
Tooth Fairy Urges Kids to Brush and Floss Daily!

I'll leave it for you to decide if you want to use the Tooth Fairy as the on-the-record source for this newsflash, but if you still have a "believer" in your midst, a plea from the Tooth Fairy can often get kids to brush and floss quicker than Mom or Dad!

Daily brushing and flossing is one of our Seven Healthy Habits. You may be thinking that you don't need a reminder—but kids sure do! Unless you're a dentist, you'd be shocked at how many kids (even the otherwise healthy ones who eat right) do not take care of

 their teeth because they actually don't like it! During the school assemblies I give throughout the year, I present HealthBarn USA's Seven Healthy Habits (listed on page 13 and set in boldface throughout the book). I ask the kids why they wash their hands, and their immediate response is to get rid of germs that will make us sick. Then I tell them that there are more germs living in their mouths than on their hands and that's why it's important to keep your mouth clean every day—and they really get

that message! And if you're paying the price as an adult for not taking proper care of your teeth when you were young, you certainly want to spare your child that dental fate, not to mention the expense, of crowns, bridges, and implants.

When children are very small, it's easy to stand over them until they get the job done, but when they're more independent in their hygiene routines and brush without your supervision, they may not always do it with high dental standards in mind. (Some kids get really good at brushing just long enough to pass the parental breath-sniff test!) Tweens or teens will look forward to brushing about as much as they look forward to an actual trip to the dentist, but they'll often respond to the gross-out factor if you tell them that stinky bacteria will grow in their mouths if they don't brush at least twice a day (preferably after every meal), and floss nightly. (The fear of bad breath usually works on self-conscious adolescents!)

You can also point out the very real risk of a cavity. Remind them that it's a lot less painful to brush and floss than it is to get a filling. The American Academy of Pediatrics and the American Dental Association recommend that children go for a first dental visit at around age two and a half (or when all baby teeth are present) and continue thereafter with regular visits, where a dentist can help you to reinforce the importance of flossing and brushing.

Try some of these activities to help your child grasp that taking good care of our teeth is as much a part of a healthy day as eating right, getting enough exercise, and sleeping properly. Most of these activities are geared for young kids, but older ones will probably like the eye-opening results of the first one.

Egg them on. Boil a few eggs with some black tea bags until the egg is hard-cooked. The shell will be brownish. After the eggs are cooled, let your child "brush" the stain off the eggs with a toothbrush and toothpaste, explaining that we have enamel on our teeth that can get stained with food and drink, just like the eggshell, and that regular brushing will keep teeth clean. (And if the egg is thoroughly cooked, yes, it can be eaten!) Kids will be amazed to watch the eggshell turn from brown to white.

Let them chew it over. Share with your kids the facts about good tooth foods—like calcium-rich foods and crunchy fruits and veggies—and bad tooth foods—like sugary candy or fake "fruit snacks." Foods from nature benefit our teeth, but artificial foods will make them weak and can cause cavities.

Make magic. Young children can cut out pictures of good tooth foods from magazines or grocery-store circulars and decorate paper towel rolls to make "magic wands." Let them bring their wands to the grocery store or into the kitchen and wave them over good tooth foods. (Warning: some may want to accessorize this look with a tiara and tutu!)

Growing Herbs

"This one smells like pizza!" That was the verdict of a boy who roamed through his family's tiny herb patch in summer, rubbing his fingers on an oregano plant and connecting the smell to the taste of one of his favorite foods.

Kids love the surprising variety of scents from different herbs and love making the connection between smell and taste. Children familiar with culinary herbs don't balk at eating foods like pesto (it's no longer mysterious "green stuff" but basil). Junior chefs who are getting hooked on cooking learn to use herbs to make foods taste even better. It's easy to introduce children to herbs at home because they are perhaps the easiest and most satisfying edible plants to grow.

get your hands dirty

At HealthBarn USA, we are crazy about our ever-growing herb garden, which thrives and throws off its amazing scents right smack in the middle of all our vegetables. Even after the last of the summer tomatoes are gone, and well before our spring blossoms debut, we can always find something happening in our herb patch. We grow a combination of culinary and medicinal herbs. The kids seem to appreciate the practical purposes of some herbs, though we grow many plants simply for their beauty and their unmistakable and unique scents.

Basil is a priority for us because we make and eat so much pesto! Some of our other favorites and their traditional uses include: **rue,** a natural insect repellent; **lavender,** for its soothing scent and its reliable flowers that we harvest and dry or infuse in sunflower oil to make our own homemade body oil; **patchouli,** known for its relaxing and exotic scent, which is fun to smell in the garden; **stevia,** a natural sweetener with leaves so sweet that the kids nibble them like candy (they actually chew on this poor plant so much that they're more damaging than marauding deer); **calendula,** for tea—treat it like chamomile and use the dried blossoms—or infused in sunflower oil like lavender, for a super-effective dry-skin moisturizer; **parcel,** which looks like parsley but tastes like celery; **senna,** a natural laxative; **quinine,** at one time, the only cure for malaria; and **arnica,** known for its ability to relieve muscle aches.

Herbs can thrive in a windowsill or have their own plot in your family garden. Encourage your child to rub the leaves of fresh herbs with her fingers and then smell her fingers to enjoy the scents of these magical plants. The general gardening guidelines mentioned earlier still apply—choose healthy plants from a reputable source or grow from seed, and fertilize organically. Here are some additional tips for adding more flavor to your family's healthy day:

Pick a tasty theme. What sorts of foods does your family enjoy? If everyone loves Italian flavors, go for the classics: basil, rosemary, oregano, parsley, sage, and any others that appeal. For a French twist, add some thyme and tarragon. Mexican or Asian? Consider cilantro (coriander), mint, and chives. And don't forget the garlic!

Or grow with the flow. Because herb plants are so hardy and (generally) forgiving, experiment as you wish and let your children pick plants they like. Give them a little backstory on which herbs do what jobs best—whether culinary or medicinal. I'm reminded of a lesson I was giving the kids about mint, where I showed them its many varieties and explained that it was an active ingredient in many commercial breath mints. One boy began to regularly visit the mint and take a few leaves to chew on the spot. I also noticed him stuffing his pockets full of leaves from time to time. "Hey, you must really like that plant," I said. "I sure do! Now that I chew on these leaves no one teases me about my breath anymore!"

Location, location, location. Where you grow your herbs—indoors or out, in containers or in the ground—may influence which ones you grow. Most herbs are compact, though some, like mint or lemon balm, are notorious for invading other parts of the garden! If you want them in your outdoor landscape, you can literally contain them by planting in a plastic pot buried in the ground (make sure you punch some additional drainage holes in the bottom) to contain their aggressive roots.

Follow the sun. Most herbs need at least six hours of sunlight a day. One advantage to containers, if they are not too large, is that they can be moved around from spot to sunny spot, if you don't have a place that gets steady light. And, you can take them indoors during your cold season too!

WHEN IT'S TIME TO CELEBRATE

Sleepover Party!

Sleepovers either end delightfully or disastrously—kids eat junk with abandon, watch TV until all hours, keep each other awake, and undeniably forget to brush and floss! Sure, it's fun while they're in the thick of it, but many a child has returned from a sleepover feeling hungover from bad food, sugary drinks, and no sleep.

It's time to give the sleepover a makeover. The next time your child begs for a sleepover, say yes but implement these ideas from HealthBarn USA. Keep the fun, but lose the junk—and make brushing of teeth nonnegotiable! (The other parents will thank you.)

1. Replace the junk food with real food: Start out with appetizers like any of our dips, and then make a dinner out of our BBQ Turkey Pizza, Homemade Chicken Nuggets, Yum! Yum! Dumplings, Shabu-Shabu HealthBarn USA, or any other festive favorite that can easily turn into a fun group activity. If the kids are old enough, make cooking your own dinner (and helping with cleanup!) part of the evening.

2. Put on some music and let them dance away their dinner. Keep them moving! (Physical activity will help them sleep—but don't do it too close to bedtime.)

3. If movie-viewing is on the schedule, make it special with a batch of Popcorn with Brain Butter during intermission, or offer our Perfect Pop.

4. For girls who want a bit of a spa treatment, let them make up a batch of our beautifying (and edible) Peach and Honey Mask (recipe below). This homemade beauty treatment smells so good that they'll want to eat the leftovers—and they can!

5. Wind things down with cups of herbal tea (or milk and honey) for everyone. Let them listen to music during lights out. You can't stop them from whispering and laughing in the dark, but you can help them relax and get ready for sleep.

6. Rise and shine the next morning with a batch of Rainbow Swirly Smoothies and Chocolate Zucchini Cupcakes.

7. Collapse as soon as the last child is picked up!

Peach and Honey Mask

Our all-natural fruit mask does more than most spa treatments. The peach enzymes stimulate the skin—the largest organ of the body—while the honey naturally moisturizes it at the same time. And you get to eat what's left in the bowl! Girls love this at sleepovers and birthday parties—they feel beautiful inside and out.

ingredients

1 ripe small peach or nectarine, peeled and pitted

1 teaspoon honey

2 tablespoons plain low-fat yogurt

directions for Beauty Mask

1. In a bowl, mash the peach and honey together; add yogurt and continue mashing until you have a workable paste.

2. Pat peach mixture evenly over face and neck and around eyes. Lie back and relax for 10 minutes.

3. Rinse off with warm water.

directions for Breakfast or Snack

1. In a bowl, stir together the honey and yogurt.

2. Cut the peach into ½-inch slices and fold into yogurt mixture.

Makes 1 facial mask or 1 serving (1 cup serving)

Nutrition Facts per serving: 70 calories; 0.5g fat (0g sat fat, 0g trans fat); 5mg cholesterol; 15g carbohydrate (1g fiber, 14g sugar); 2g protein; 20mg sodium; 6% Daily Value (DV) vitamin A; 10% DV vitamin C; 6% DV calcium; 2% DV iron

---

Stacey's Pantry List

If you were ever to visit HealthBarn USA and snoop in our cabinets, you'd most likely find the following items in our kitchen. Try keeping some or all of our recommended staples on hand, which will make cooking with our recipes even easier. In some cases I've included brand names that I prefer—for taste, performance in our recipes, and overall quality (minimally processed, pure ingredients). Most of these brands are widely available, or you can find them online.

Pasta, Rice, Grains, and Flours

Barilla Plus pastas

Ronzoni Healthy Harvest whole-grain, heart-healthy lasagna or Hodgson Mill lasagna

Ancient Harvest Quinoa pasta, gluten-free elbows
(we always keep a box in the barn for our gluten-free kids)

Soba noodles

Bob's Red Mill brown rice

Bob's Red Mill quinoa

Bob's Red Mill hard red spring wheat berries

Organic corn kernels

Oats

Bob's Red Mill whole wheat flour

Bob's Red Mill white flour (King Arthur Flour brand is also good)

Hodgson Mill buckwheat flour

Condiments, Sweeteners, and Oils

Simply Heinz ketchup

Bragg Liquid Aminos (a healthy substitute for soy sauce)

Madhava agave nectar

Cinnamon

Honey

Blackstrap or Grandma's molasses (unsulfured)

Olive oil (use pure olive oil for cooking and
extra-virgin olive oil for dressings and as a finishing oil)

Canola oil

Barlean's flaxseed oil

Nut Butters and Fruit Spreads

Polaner All Fruit with Fiber spreads

Bionaturæ organic fruit spreads

Smucker's natural peanut butter
(we also like Once Again peanut or almond butter, but it's harder to find)

SunButter (an acceptable alternative to peanut or tree nut butters)

Dairy and Dairy Alternatives

Stonyfield low-fat yogurt and milk

Rice Dream rice milk (original enriched, vanilla)

Parmesan cheese

Mozzarella cheese (low-moisture, part-skim)

Pasteurized liquid egg whites (for recipes that call for egg whites only)

Frozen and Refrigerated Items

Frozen strawberries

Frozen mangoes

Frozen edamame

Tropicana calcium-fortified orange juice

Miscellaneous

Instant dry milk powder (organic or store brand)

Ian's panko bread crumbs

Hershey's cocoa

Nestle Toll House semisweet morsels

Raisins (not golden raisins because they are sulfured)

Raw sunflower seeds

Raw almonds and raw walnuts

Erewhon 100% whole-grain cereals

Pacific Natural Foods organic, free-range, low-sodium chicken broth
and low-sodium vegetable broth

Wellsley Farms or Rozzano low-sodium marinara sauce (available at BJ's Wholesale Club)

Nasoya tofu and wonton wrappers

Whole Foods Market's 365 Everyday Value® products are high quality and reasonably priced

Supermarket Spy Kids Worksheet

Use this sheet when playing Supermarket Spy Kids!
Instructions are found on page 69.

List the natural foods you found today!

1) _____

2) _____

3) _____

4) _____

5) _____

What natural foods will you be taking home to try this week?
(for example: strawberries on yogurt for breakfast!)

1) _____

2) _____

3) _____

4) _____

5) _____

Weekly Menu Planners

	Monday	Tuesday	Wednesday	Thursday	Friday	Saturday	Sunday
Breakfast	Farm-Fresh Omelet	Whole-Grain Breakfast Cookie	Creamy Berry Crepes	Yogurt Sundaes	Rainbow Swirly Smoothie	Chocolate Zucchini Cupcakes	Sweet Potato Pancakes
A.M. Snack	The Barn Bar	Homemade Chocolate Milk with Fresh Fruit	Chocolate Ladybugs	Ginger Snaps	Banana Chocolate Chip Mini Muffins	Green Edamame Dip	Popcorn with Brain Butter
Lunch	Homemade Chicken Penicillin Soup	Rainbow Quinoa Salad	Salmon and Swiss Cheese Crepes	The TLT Wrap	Veggie Sushi Hand Roll	No-Bake White Mac and Cheese	Grilled Cheese Stackers and Zucchini Sticks
P.M. Snack	Jersey-Fresh Bruschetta	Pesto-Stuffed Cherry Tomatoes	Chocolate Banana Crepes	Raspberry Crumble	EZ-Make Cookies	Pizza Potato Skins	Sweet Potato Crunchies
Dinner	Turkey Burgers with Sweet Oat Rolls	Sweet Potato Gnocchi with Basil Pesto	Moo Shu Chicken	Mike's Sicilian Stew	The Pizza Challenge! with Whole Wheat Pizza Dough	Veggie Pancakes with Creamy Broccoli Soup	Shabu-Shabu HealthBarn USA

Gluten-Free Menu

	Monday	Tuesday	Wednesday	Thursday	Friday	Saturday	Sunday
Breakfast	Rainbow Swirly Smoothie	Farm-Fresh Omelet	Maple Walnut Oatmeal	Sweet Berry Polenta	Crunchy Granola with Walnuts with yogurt	Mini Potato Leek Frittata	Berrilicious Risotto
A.M. Snack	The Barn Bar	Creamy Herb Dip with veggies for dipping	Homemade Chocolate Milk with fresh fruit	Chocolate Lady Bugs	White Bean Dip with veggies for dipping	Holy Green Guacamole with corn chips for dipping	Homemade Fruit Roll-Ups
Lunch	Spinach Pesto Pasta (sub quinoa pasta)	Veggie Sushi Hand Roll	Spinach Salad with Raspberry Vinaigrette	Rainbow Quinoa Salad	Pasta and Sweet Peas (sub quinoa pasta)	Veggie Chili	Citrus and Herb Shrimp Kebabs
P.M. Snack	HealthBarn USA Snack Mix	Popcorn with Brain Butter	Hydration Salad	Chickpea Delight with veggies for dipping	EZ-Make Cookies (sub gluten-free cereal)	Chocolate Pudding	Mango and Peach Salsa with corn chips for dipping
Dinner	Mike's Sicilian Stew	Steamed Salmon Pouches and Mixed Greens with Flaxseed Oil Dressing	Chicken Fiesta Fajitas with corn tortillas	Quinoa with Kale and Walnuts	Chinese Chicken Rice Bowls	Brown Rice Risotto with Shrimp	Shabu-Shabu HealthBarn USA

Vegetarian Menu

	Monday	Tuesday	Wednesday	Thursday	Friday	Saturday	Sunday
Breakfast	PB&J Muffins	Rainbow Swirly Smoothie	Carrot Cake Muffins	Whole-Grain Breakfast Cookie	Creamy Berry Crepes	Chocolate Zucchini Cupcakes	Sweet Potato Pancakes
A.M. Snack	The Barn Bar	Ginger Snaps	Creamy "Ranch" Dressing with veggies for dipping	Soft Pretzels	Banana Chocolate Chip Mini Muffins	Green Edamame Dip	Carrot Halwa Dip with veggies
Lunch	Spinach Pesto Pasta	Italian-Style Lentil Soup	Quinoa Falafel	Spinach Salad with Raspberry Vinaigrette	Veggie Sushi Hand Roll	Bulgur Tabbouleh with pita chips	Tomato Dumpling Soup
P.M. Snack	Spinach Artichoke Dip with pita chips	Pesto-Stuffed Cherry Tomatoes	HealthBarn USA Snack Mix	Caprese Salad on a Stick	EZ-Make Cookies	The Perfect Pop	Sweet Potato Crunchies
Dinner	Veggie Stir-Fry with Soba Noodles	Sweet Potato Gnocchi with Basil Pesto	Eggplant Parmesan Towers	Cheesy Lasagna Rolls	Quinoa-Stuffed Peppers	Yum! Yum! Dumplings and Mixed Greens with Flaxseed Oil Dressing	Indian Veggie Medley

Acknowledgments

Double thumbs up to Becky Cabaza for an amazing collaboration on writing *Appetite for Life* with me. She truly embraces the healthy way as a parent, and brilliantly synthesized seven years of HealthBarn USA into a user-friendly guide for families.

I'm grateful to Cynthia DiTiberio at HarperOne, who believed in the HealthBarn USA platform right from the beginning. And to both Cynthia and Jeanette Perez, who, inspired by their own seedlings, knew firsthand how to shape *Appetite for Life* to be a much-needed resource for parents.

A special thank you to my agent, Coleen O'Shea, who brought together a fantastic team to make *Appetite for Life* a great success while fearlessly guiding us through the first-time publishing process.

Recipe Leadership Team
Susan Deborah Goldsmith
Molly Fallon, RD

Test Kitchen
Kay Truckenmiller
Suzanne Celentano
Mary Opfer
Jessica Butler
Amethyst Scolnick

Recipe Credits
Curtis Aikens
Keiko Kimura
Gino Rizzo
Cynthia Schumo
Chelsea Zimmer
Wolfgang Puck & Team
Elizabeth Tretinik
Kaushik Ghosh
Donna Bilenchi
Juli Huddleston
Jessica Butler
Amethyst Scolnick
Jill Pettit
Tami J. Mackle, MS, RD
Elyse, Jack, and Aidan Ryan
Suzanne Nobile
Suzie Yu
Lauren Cianciotta
Atsuko Yokosawa
Dr. David Riley
The California Walnut Commission
Robyn Unrath